White Boy
A Memoir

White Boy

A Memoir

MARK D. NAISON

TEMPLE UNIVERSITY PRESS
Philadelphia

Temple University Press, Philadelphia 19122
Copyright © 2002 by Temple University
All rights reserved
Published 2002
Printed in the United States of America

⊗ The paper used in this publication meets the requirements of the American
National Standard for Information Sciences—Permanence of Paper for Printed
Library Materials, ANSI Z39.48-1984

Library of Congress Cataloging-in-Publication Data

Naison, Mark, 1946–
   White boy : a memoir / Mark D. Naison.
      p. cm.
   ISBN 1-56639-941-6 (alk. paper) — ISBN 1-56639-942-4 (pbk : alk. paper)
   1. Naison, Mark, 1946–   2. Naison, Mark, 1946—Relations with African Americans.
3. African Americans—Study and teaching (Higher)—New York (State)—New York—
History—20th century.   4. College teachers—New York (State)—New York—Biography.
5. White men—New York (State)—New York—Biography.   6. Jews—New York (State)—
New York—Biography.   7. Brooklyn (New York, N.Y.)—Race relations.   8. Brooklyn
(New York, N.Y.)—Biography.   9. New York (N.Y.)—Race relations.   10. New York
(N.Y.)—Biography.   I. Title.

E185.98.N35 A3 2002
974.7'23—dc21

                                                                    2001057450

To Sara and Eric,
who have been crossing boundaries all their lives

Contents

Preface

A WHITE PERSON who teaches African-American studies is sometimes the focus for startling questions. I decided to write this memoir after a particularly bizarre encounter at a small private tennis club in Brooklyn in the fall of 1996. After losing a long match in the semifinals of the club tournament, I was recovering in the clubhouse when a middle-aged white man sat down next to me and asked what I did for a living. "I'm a college professor," I said. "What do you teach?" he asked. "African-American studies," I replied. The man looked at me with complete astonishment. "You mean they let you do that?" he asked. When I assured him that I was secure in my job, and had been for twenty-five years, and that I was on good terms with my black students and colleagues, he looked skeptical and asked about Leonard Jeffries, the controversial former chair of the City College black studies program, whose eccentric theories of racial difference had made him a media celebrity.

Something in me snapped. This was at least the *hundredth* time that someone had brought up Leonard Jeffries when I mentioned what I taught. After patiently explaining that Professor Jeffries was not representative of my colleagues at Fordham University or the other black scholars I knew, I thought about the perceptions that prompted this man's questions. Like many whites I met in the late 1980s and early 1990s, he was convinced that black intellectuals had become so hostile to whites that I should have been driven out of my job. His image of the black community left no room for tolerance, empathy, and intellectual curiosity. The historical narrative he believed in made caricatures of the black people I had known for thirty years as students, colleagues, and friends while it erased some of the most important experiences of my adult life, along with much of what I had learned as a student of African-American and American history. Confronted once too often with a racial discourse that rendered me invisible, I needed to present my own point of view. The next morning I started this memoir, trying to explain how a Jewish boy from Crown Heights, whose childhood passions were sports and rock and roll, ended up as a professor of African-American studies, and how this odyssey reflected powerful, but often overlooked, themes in America's tangled racial history.

According to the dominant narrative of civil rights history, the black studies movement was one manifestation of a powerful nationalist impulse that swept through the black community in the late 1960s, smothering the romantic interracialism that had accompanied the civil rights movement and forcing whites to work for racial justice exclusively within white communities. From that point on, according to this narrative, racial separatism became the dominant ideology within the black community, leading to the de facto segregation of campuses and cultural organizations and nurturing a black political discourse that was inward looking and defensive. In reality, things are far more complicated, and my story illustrates some of the problems inherent in this oversimplified yet widely held view.

Racial polarization, white flight, and black-Jewish tensions did not suddenly appear with the onset of the Black Power movement. I encountered them all in my own Crown Heights neighborhood in the late fifties and early sixties, when the community began undergoing rapid racial change. Although I had black playmates as a child, and I was exposed to images of racial harmony through rock and roll and the Brooklyn Dodgers baseball team, my age of racial innocence was relatively brief. By the time I entered Columbia University in the fall of 1962, I was already a veteran of street-corner and locker-room fights, as well as bitter arguments with my parents about my participation in civil rights protests and the impact blacks were having on Brooklyn's Jewish neighborhoods.

These conflicts only escalated when I left for Columbia. While I immersed myself in civil rights work and began studying black history, my parents made their own racial statement by moving to an apartment in an all-white section of Queens. Our relationship approached the breaking point during my senior year in college, when I fell in love with a black woman. Ostracized by my parents, my girlfriend and I were enthusiastically accepted by her extended family of transplanted southerners, which proved far more open to interracial relationships than the lower-middle-class Jews I had grown up among.

The Black Power movement, which came to Columbia in the late sixties, added another layer of tension to our lives. As ideas of self-determination and black unity spread through the black intelligentsia, interracial organizations and relationships came under pressure. My girlfriend and I encountered opposition to our relationship from some black students, and during Columbia's 1968 student strike we occupied separate buildings. But the black community's traditions of tolerance and hospitality were not instantly erased by the spread of nationalist ideas. Even in the late sixties, my girlfriend and I, who were together for six years, had a vibrant multiracial social life with her extended family, with the black high school students we worked with in Columbia Upward Bound, and with black and white friends who stayed at our communal apartment on the Upper West Side.

The influence of the Black Power movement should not be underestimated. It produced a withering critique of American racism, inspired new standards of beauty and artistic expression, and ushered in much more assertive styles of leadership and personal comportment among African-Americans. But involvement in this movement did not preclude an openness to multiracial strategies and relationships. I forcefully encountered this duality when I joined Fordham University's black studies program in the fall of 1970. I was hired for this position by an all-black search committee, not only because of my research on black history but because the program's founders saw teaching whites about African-American history and culture as complementary to their mission of promoting black unity and empowerment.

Formed as a result of a student sit-in, Fordham's Afro-American Institute had a "movement" atmosphere. Its students and faculty were political activists, committed to increasing the power and influence of blacks on the Fordham campus and in the political life of New York City. But perhaps the most important and difficult of its tasks was to make learning about the black experience a focus of intellectual excitement and to push the Fordham curriculum to encompass non-Western cultures and civilizations. Here I found my calling. I became an evangelist for black studies among white and Latino students, telling them that they could not understand their own lives and history without understanding the black and African elements in their music, language, and material culture.

Some black students resented what I was doing. I had several "stare downs" with student nationalists in the program office during my first year of teaching. But as enrollment in my classes swelled, and I became friends with my faculty colleagues, the hostility dissipated and I found myself drawn into the strategy sessions, demonstrations, lectures, and parties that the Institute sponsored. The Institute's bruising, uphill struggle to win the respect of the Fordham faculty, who seemed to think that wisdom and knowledge derived exclusively from Europe, created a powerful bond among our faculty and students. By 1976, when my colleagues and I were finally granted departmental status, my race had ceased to be controversial and I could function, when needed, as spokesperson for an institution that was both black and multiracial.

For the last twenty-five years, I have taught black and urban history to thousands of students. I served as chair of black studies for seven of those years and as director of urban studies for most of them. The department I represent is the most multiracial institution on the Fordham campus, a place where students of many backgrounds explore black history and culture in an open, ecumenical atmosphere. If you are black or white, Asian or Latino, it is an excellent place to find a boundary-crossing experience. If this defies conventional wisdom about the politics of race in the United States, perhaps that wisdom needs to be revised.

A NOTE ON NAMES

The account that follows aims for historical accuracy in all respects but one—the names of participants. Although major historical figures always appear under their own names, I have tried to disguise the identities of individuals I have known or worked with who might be compromised by my portrait of them. Names the reader encounters in the text may or may not be pseudonyms; for the protection of the people I discuss, I offer no cues in the text as to which names are real.

Acknowledgments

THIS BOOK could not have been written without the help of a great many people. Foremost among these are my colleagues in African and African-American Studies at Fordham University, especially my friend of thirty years, Claude Mangum. Claude accompanied me through every step of the writing, helping me find archival material, correcting factual inaccuracies, and encouraging me to persevere when doors were being slammed in my face. Those who read this book will know why Claude is my hero. I also benefited from critical readings of the manuscript by Mark Chapman, Jerome Contee, Alvin Leonard, Leslie Massiah, and Quinton Wilkes, and from the steady encouragement of my department chair, Irma Watkins-Owens. Alfred Turnipseed, Jr., administrative assistant extraordinaire, helped me with numerous research tasks connected to the book. Key administrators at Fordham also deserve thanks, especially Rev. Jeffrey Von Arx, S.J., Dean of Fordham College, and Rev. Gerald Blaszczak, S.J., University Chaplain, whose commitment to African-American studies made work on this book much easier, and Don Gillespie, Director of Institutional Research, who gave me complete access to enrollment and admission files.

I also received tremendous support from family members, friends, and fellow scholars in African-American and radical history. My wife Liz had initial doubts about this project, but then became its strongest supporter, using her brilliant editorial skills to improve my prose, and keeping me from self-destructing during the many phases of rewriting. My friend John Ehrenberg helped steer this project through the minefields of the publishing industry, helping me refine my political message, introducing me to editors, and making sure I did not explode in the face of real and imagined insults. It was John who introduced me to Cecelia Cancellaro, the gifted freelance editor who refined the final version of the manuscript.

A large group of people who lived through the events in the book played an important role in refining the manuscript and helping me check facts. Steve Brown, Paul Buhle, Eric Foner, Bruce and Wendy Hazard, the late Robert Herzberg, James Kelly, Jay McGowan, John Mogulescu, Joe Muriana, Marge and Harry Phillips, and Ray Reece all read through portions of the manuscript they were familiar with and made numerous useful suggestions. In the case of Steve, Wendy, Bob and Ray, their contribution including editing. I also benefited from the encouragement of a politically diverse group of scholars and journalists who were intrigued by the book's subject matter, especially Trevor Coleman, Greg Donaldson, Randall Kennedy, David Levering Lewis, Marilyn Mobley McKenzie, Nell Irvin Painter, Roy Rosenzweig, Jim Sleeper, Donald Spivey, and Jeffrey Stewart. To my editor at Temple University Press, Janet Francendese, I am forever grateful for taking a chance on the manuscript when no one else would and for choosing as readers Robin Kelley and David Roediger, whose suggestions have made this a much better book. To Robin, who has supported this project for the last three years, and has taught me so much about hip hop and popular culture, a special "shout out" is due.

My students at Fordham have been an enormous source of inspiration. The enthusiastic response I got from my classes when I assigned drafts of the early chapters let me know this project had potential when no publisher seemed to think so, but I also benefited from the encouragement of individual students who regarded this book as an extension of their own lives and made sure that I saw it through to completion. Brian Purnell, Kelli Peoples, Kendra Newkirk, Amy Nicosia, Derrick Cooley, Randy Cohen, Nick Napolitano, Tiffany Raspberry, Deanna Singh, Annie Golden, Ray Gonzales, Simon Raffel, Katie Hallisey, Eileen Markey, Pat Butler, Julie Poll, and Aileen Leonard have all been involved with this book and have made valuable commentary on the manuscript. In addition, two Park Slope friends, Sandra Calamine and Lou Menashe, offered commentary on the first two chapters, which helped me capture some of the atmosphere of the Brooklyn streets we all grew up on.

Finally, I want to offer special thanks to my children, Sara Naison-Russell and Eric Naison-Phillips, and my son-in-law, Malik Russell. It is every author's dream to have their children interested in the book they are writing, but when your kids eagerly read every chapter, talk up the book to their friends, express interest in planning your book party, and put together a CD of songs from the book, you think you've died and gone to heaven. Sara, Eric and Malik, you're three good reasons why Brooklyn is truly the center of the universe.

1   Crown Heights in the 1950s

BORN IN 1946, I grew up in a red brick apartment building at
the intersection of Lefferts and Kingston Avenues in the Crown Heights
section of Brooklyn. Today Crown Heights is a national symbol of black-
Jewish tensions, with Afro-Caribbeans and Hasidic Jews living in
uneasy proximity. In the 1950s, it was a peaceful neighborhood popu-
lated largely by second- and third-generation Jews and Italians, with a
sprinkling of Irish and African-American families. The absence of racial
and religious conflict was not accidental. Cherishing the opportunity to
retreat into private life after years of war and economic hardship, Crown
Heights residents seemed determined to shield their children from the
weight of history. Anxious to have their children grow up American in
a society opening its doors to minorities, my parents' generation worked
hard to hide the scars that had been inflicted by the Depression, the
Holocaust, and the terrors of the Jim Crow South. Through a communal code of silence upheld by religious leaders and the mass media, the
people of Crown Heights tried to erase tragedy from their daily experience and give their children a feeling that the world was fundamen-
tally benign, a place of adventure and opportunity where no accomplishments were out of reach.

Nevertheless, the social geography of Crown Heights was influenced
by immigrant traditions and ethnic differences. Most of the Jews in the
area lived in six-story elevator apartment buildings put up in the 1920s;
there were four at the intersection of Lefferts and Kingston, one on each
corner, and ten more within a three-block radius. Most of the Italians
lived in a five-block-square area of wooden and brick one-family homes
that everybody called "Pigtown." Located one block south and west of
my corner, Pigtown had its own Italian-language parish, which ran
annual street festivals, and back yards that contained vegetable gardens
and chicken coops. Directly to the south of my apartment house there
were rows of three-story walkups in which Italians and Jews lived
together.

Other nearby neighborhood landmarks included PS 91, a huge, red brick public school with a concrete schoolyard that contained several basketball courts, and a vest-pocket park with a playground, handball courts, a full court basketball area, and a large softball and football field. Six blocks to the south was Kings County Hospital, the largest concentration of hospital buildings in New York City. Six blocks to the west stood Ebbets Field, the fabled home of the Brooklyn Dodgers.

Neighborhood life was highly ritualized, giving Crown Heights a village-like atmosphere. On weekdays men went off to work, some by car, some by subway, while women walked their children to school, conversed with one another from apartment windows, and dried their laundry on clotheslines that hung from or between apartments or stood in backyards. On weekends the men sat in folding chairs on street corners or stood outside the candy stores talking with the local bookie, while the women sat on benches by the park, the grandmothers in one section, the women with baby carriages in another. There were still street peddlers, a roving knife sharpener, a rag picker in a horse-drawn wagon who yelled "any old clothes," and numerous vacant lots, where children could chase one another, play ball, and even roast potatoes and marshmallows over a fire. Several small stores within a block of our apartment met most family needs. We had a grocery store, a dry cleaner, two candy stores, a hair salon called "Blonds and Dolls," and a Jewish delicatessen that sold pickles, nuts, smoked fish, and a middle-eastern delicacy called halvah.

Although the neighborhood contained a sizable number of elderly people who spoke only Yiddish or Italian, the largest group in the community were American-born married couples who were educated through high school and spoke English at home and at work. Crown Heights in the fifties was filled with young children, most of whom had been born during World War II or immediately after. Most of the men and women in these families had been poor during the Depression and cherished the modest prosperity they were experiencing. Although no one had more than two bedrooms, this seemed spacious, if not luxurious, to people who had been doubling up with relatives for most of their adult lives. Cars and television sets, once rare in this neighborhood, but virtually universal possessions by the mid fifties, had become important features of family life. People gathered in groups on weekday evenings to watch their favorite shows and took excursions throughout the city on weekends to visit their relatives.

Despite new technologies, the vitality of street life remained the neighborhood's defining characteristic. While adults sat or stood in groups to gossip, gamble, or talk politics, kids used every available piece of space for games and contests. The lives of children, like those of adults, were rigidly divided by gender. Boys played cowboys and Indians in the alleys, used sidewalks for boxball and box baseball, and played stickball, football, and punchball in the street. Meanwhile girls played with dolls in their apartments and jumped rope and played hop- scotch on sidewalks under the watchful eye of their mothers. If you were a boy, every nook and cranny of the neighborhood was a zone of adventure and competition, a place where kids fought, tested each other, and made friends and enemies; but girls were prohibited from activi- ties that involved physical aggressiveness or the risk of getting dirty. In all my years in Crown Heights, I never saw a girl play basketball or stickball, throw a football or hit a baseball, roast potatoes in a vacant lot, or join in games of ring-a-levio and johnny on a pony.

Racial boundaries in Crown Heights, at least on the surface, were far less obvious. In the 1950s, only a sprinkling of black families lived in the fifteen blocks between Eastern Parkway and Kings County Hospi- tal, and most of them seemed solidly working class. None of my neigh- bors appeared to fear the black people in our midst or worry about their children's behavior. The poor and troubled families in the neighbor- hood, the ones everyone kept away from or felt sorry for, were all white. Whereas Crown Heights today is a community where black-Jewish divi- sions permeate every aspect of life, from schooling to shopping to pat- terns of sociability, in the early fifties, working-class and lower-middle- class Jews seemed to express little overt hostility toward the neighborhood's small black population. The Jews whom I grew up among were secular, politically liberal, and—at least until large num- bers of blacks started entering their neighborhood in the early 1960s— reluctant to express racial hostility in front of their children. In my child- hood, I never heard a neighbor or a member of my family use the word "nigger." Feelings about blacks, whether positive or negative, were masked behind the very ambiguous term *schvartze* (Yiddish for black), which could be either a term of description or a racial epithet. As a child, I found it difficult to know which meaning was being employed because adults invariably reverted to Yiddish when talking about African-Americans. Their racial prejudices, whether subliminal or explicit, were not something proudly passed on from parents to children. Adults seemed embarrassed, even ashamed to talk about racial issues.

The children in my neighborhood were even less prone to make race a public issue. There were two black kids in the pack of thirty-odd boys I hung out with, Franny and Franklin, and they were included in every one of our activities, from running in the alleys to playing handball and basketball and football. I never heard anybody insult them with a racial slur or exclude them from an activity because of their racial background. The biggest division in our neighborhood was between Italians and Jews, and even this was not marked with great hostility. Jewish kids from "Lequerville" (the term we used to describe our section of Crown Heights) played with Italian kids from "Pigtown" as much as we fought with them.

The neighborhood also had little, if any, violent crime. Until I was ten or eleven years old, the only policemen I saw were traffic cops. Organized crime was a muted presence—my friend Barry's father was the local bookie—but there were almost no burglaries, muggings, car thefts, or assaults, much less rapes or murders. Because Crown Heights was filled with extended families and people (mostly women) who were not in the paid labor force, there was no need for volunteer security patrols or a heavy police presence. These informal block watchers made the neighborhood safe and secure at all times of the day and night, a feature that my parents, who had grown up in much poorer and more dangerous areas, appreciated greatly.

In the mid-1950s Crown Heights had few very poor people and only a handful of rich ones, making for a rough equality that undoubtedly fostered social harmony. However, there was one striking social disparity—the widespread employment of African-American and Afro-Caribbean women as domestic workers. Almost every Jewish family in our neighborhood, even those where wives were not employed, had African-American women come in to clean their apartments or help care for children. Jewish women referred to these workers as their "girls," even though the women they employed were often older than they were. Every morning they arrived in a group on the Kingston Avenue bus from Bedford-Stuyvesant, and they left by the same route early in the evening. Their educational and cultural attainments varied greatly, as did those of the people who employed them. The woman my mother employed, "Adler," had no trace of servility or deference. A well-spoken woman with a light-brown complexion and straight hair, Adler carried herself more like a schoolteacher than a maid, and she sat down with my mother for coffee like a family friend. My mother, an ardent trade unionist who had worked at numerous blue-collar and clerical jobs before becoming a teacher, insisted that I treat Adler with politeness and respect. But Adler's presence raised disturbing questions. Why was someone so capable and intelligent cleaning our house? Why wasn't she doing what my mother was doing? Racial barriers in New York, which kept African-Americans from getting jobs as secretaries, sales clerks, and bank tellers, had created a pool of black women workers with few alternatives to domestic labor. By drawing upon this labor force, lower-middle-class Jewish families simultaneously improved their own standard of living and acquired a morally damaging complicity with racial discrimination.

CHILDHOOD IDIOSYNCRASIES

The racial issues in my neighborhood, overt and covert, had little impact on my early childhood. The biggest problem I faced was a dissonance between the values of my parents and those of most other families in my neighborhood. My parents were schoolteachers, Jewish intellectuals who revered education and wanted me to become a professor or scientist. They took me to zoos and museums and concerts, gave me piano lessons, provided me with electric trains, chemistry sets, and books on dinosaurs, animals, and outer space. For their own enjoyment, they stocked our apartment with books, records, and musical instruments, and filled our walls with inexpensive reproductions of paintings they saw in museums. My parents regarded themselves as members of an intellectual elite whose job was to bring culture and civilization to unappreciative New York public school students. My achievements were to provide proof that their talents had not gone to waste.

This way of life made us very different from most of the Jews in our Crown Heights neighborhood. Most of our neighbors were tough, earthy people who were more influenced by American popular culture than by Jewish intellectual and cultural traditions. Although their occupations varied—they were skilled factory workers, small businesses owners, taxi drivers, clerical workers—they had the cynical air of people who had to fight their way out of poverty by means both fair and foul. They spent much more time watching television than reading, and were more inclined to go to the racetrack than a museum. Gambling and card playing were omnipresent. Women played mah-jongg and canasta, while the men played pinochle, casino, and gin rummy and bet on ball games and the horses. Little attention was given to religion. Most people went to synagogue only on the high holy days, and they sent their kids to Hebrew school so they could go through the ritual of a bar mitzvah, not so they could become religious Jews. Childrearing was approached rather casually. Children were expected to do well in school but also to be well-rounded individuals who could dance, play cards, compete in sports, and, if they were girls, dress up and look pretty. People were judged by their physical appearance, the clothes they wore, the cars they drove, and the food they served at weddings, bar mitzvahs, and family parties.

Eating seemed to be the neighborhood's favorite pastime, the activity where social ties were cemented and the burdens of any painful history could be set aside. Wherever they went, children my age were deluged with food: homemade potato latkes and matzoh ball soup prepared by grandparents; chow mein and egg foo yong ordered at Chinese restaurants; deli sandwiches of roast beef, corned beef, tongue, and chopped liver; Sunday breakfasts combining bagels, cream cheese, and platters of smoked fish with onion and salami omelets. Among the secular Jews of Crown Heights, the size and health of their children was more important than their aptitude for learning or their knowledge of Jewish tradition. Most of the children and adolescents in the neighborhood were big and strong, reaching their parents' height and weight by the time they were twelve or thirteen years old, and they possessed a physical self-confidence rarely seen in the shtetels of Eastern Europe or the crowded immigrant slums in which their grandparents had once lived.

Unfortunately for me, my parents were determined to uphold the tradition of Jewish intellectualism in this earthy, materialistic community no matter how much it isolated us. Although their combined income as schoolteachers was no more than that of our neighbors, they regarded themselves as intellectual royalty in a world of philistines, and they decided to use me, their only child, as the vehicle to display their superiority. I was taught to read by the time I was three, forced to perform at piano recitals and enter science fairs, and paraded in front of neighbors and relatives to show off my knowledge of science, politics, and current events. While exposure to books and museums awakened my intellectual curiosity, being shown off as the product of exemplary childrearing exposed me to incessant teasing and considerable hostility. My peers mocked me for having early curfews, for having to go to lessons and recitals, for getting high scores on standardized tests, and for being praised by teachers for winning science fairs and spelling bees.

Two things saved me from complete social ostracism. First, my parents both worked full-time and lacked the time and energy to supervise my weekday afternoons and weekend mornings. During those times, I could run relatively unsupervised with the pack of neighborhood boys. Second, I was strong and reasonably athletic, and I had been given valuable fighting skills by my father, who had been victimized as a child on the streets of Brownsville, Brooklyn's toughest and poorest Jewish neighborhood. Only five feet, four and a half inches tall, with a receding hairline, glasses, and shoulders slightly hunched from adolescent rickets, my father taught me three wrestling holds—a hammerlock, a headlock, and a full nelson—and he bought me my first pair of boxing gloves when I was three. He also stocked the house with sports equipment and played catch with me whenever he could, even though he was horribly uncoordinated. By the time I was eight, I had become competent in most ball sports and could use my wrestling holds to fling tormenters to the ground and sit on them until they "gave up."

The tension between my parents' standards and neighborhood mores made my quest for social acceptance a daily struggle. Every once in a while, my parents seemed to let their ambitions and fears transcend the bounds of common sense. It was bad enough that I was not allowed to drink out of other kids' soda bottles, share their candy, or go with them to the movies and the bowling alley. But then, while I was still in elementary school, I was also saddled with the burden of skipping a grade. While I was in third grade at PS 91, my parents became so excited at my score on a citywide reading test that they marched me into the principal's office and insisted I be accelerated on the spot. The next day, the principal placed me in a fourth-grade class, where the other students looked at me as though I were a quiz-show geek suddenly dropped into their presence. Very quickly, they assigned me the nickname "Eggy" (for Egghead) and warned me not to raise my hand too often when the teacher asked a question.

Shortly after, two tough Italian boys in my new class, Anthony and Charley, approached me and asked me to pay them five cents a week in protection money. If I gave them this money, they would make sure that nobody in the school would beat me up. If I did not, *they* would beat me up. Intimidated by my new surroundings, I went along with their scheme and discovered it had a surprising wrinkle. At the end of each month, Anthony and Charley would take the five or six kids under their protection to a luncheonette in Pigtown, where they would buy each of us a "mush," a local delicacy that consisted of sauerkraut and mustard on Italian bread. Someone, probably the Mafiosi they had observed in Pigtown, had taught them that a good criminal displays benevolence and community spirit. In an era when organized-crime families controlled much of New York's waterfront, trucking industry, restaurant business, and construction trades, Charley and Anthony were being given valuable training.

Several months and many nickels later, I decided to rebel. When Anthony asked me for his weekly stipend, I solemnly told him I no longer needed protection. Determined to teach me a lesson, Anthony started raining punches on my head and discovered, at about the same time I did, that I had an extremely high pain tolerance. When his barrage ended, I shook my head, grabbed him in a headlock, and squeezed him until he said "I give up." As he got up, I worried that I might have to fight every Italian kid at PS 91, but Anthony had a more creative way of saving face. He put his arm around me, congratulated me on my victory, and invited me to play on a neighborhood football team his father was coaching.

Being part of the Pigtown junior football team was a gratifying experience. Anthony's father was a good-natured man who loved to watch boys tackle each other and made extremely creative use of the word "fuck," employing it as a noun, a verb, and an adjective. There were no uniforms and no opponents; practices consisted of brutal intersquad scrimmages in which, in our coach's words, we would try to "run the fuckin' ball down their fuckin' throats." In the clash of bodies and the dirt-encrusted pileups that ensued with every exchange of the football, I found a blessed anonymity. To Anthony's father, I wasn't a future scientist, scholar, or inventor; I was just a thick-bodied kid who enjoyed hitting anything that moved and never complained when he got cut or got dirty.

Unfortunately, my parents took a very dim view of this experience. To protect me from injury, and from the implied threat to my upward mobility, they forbade me to play tackle football. I decided to disobey them. Pretending to play punchball or hide-and-seek in the alleys, I would sneak off to join the football games, hoping to disappear in the pileups. However, my parents, who had a view of every field and schoolyard from their bedroom window, and who enlisted my grandmother to watch me with binoculars whenever they weren't around, quickly found me out. One rainy Sunday morning, as I was smashing through the line to make a tackle, I looked up and saw an extraordinary sight—my father, all five feet, four inches of him, running in my direction in his teaching uniform: a sports jacket, slacks, and a bow tie. When he reached me, he slapped my face, grabbed me by the back of my shirt, and dragged me off the field in front of the thirty-odd players and spectators, all the while screaming, "You brat, you ingrate, how can you do this to us!" Anthony's father, a heavyset longshoreman who ran practices wearing workshirts and boots, looked on in stunned silence and evident sympathy. By the next day, every kid in my class had heard about what happened, but my father's action were so bizarre that no one had the heart to tease me about it.

But this incident took its toll. No words could convey the rage I felt at my parents for humiliating me in front of the entire neighborhood. In moments of vulnerability, I now felt a white-hot anger that quickly turned to physical aggression. Throughout the rest of my elementary school years, my relations with my parents became volatile, marked on my side by screaming tantrums, slammed doors, and thrown objects, and on theirs by punishments that included withholding television privileges, slapping my face, and washing my mouth out with soap. Even my friends became wary of provoking me, fearful that a good-natured comment about my piano lessons or science-fair projects might draw a barrage of punches.

A CHILD OF POPULAR CULTURE

Gradually I was able to find more constructive outlets for my anger. Prohibiting me from playing tackle football did not transform me into a concert pianist or inventor; rather, it drove me to channel my energy into baseball, stickball, basketball, and punchball, and to devote huge amounts of time to watching and reading about college and professional sports. Increasingly, I shut my parents out and retreated into my own world, one ruled by the symbols of an American popular culture that they held in contempt. Sports became the hallmark of my personal identity, the one thing I did well that my parents could not claim credit for. On weekday evenings, I would go to the night center at PS 91 and play basketball, nok hockey, or ping pong. Every weekend morning, I would get up at 7:00 A.M. to shoot baskets in the schoolyard, pitch tennis balls at a rectangular box drawn on an apartment building, or throw a Spalding rubber ball (spaldeen) against a handball court and catch it with my glove. The endless repetition of solitary practice gave me valuable moments of calmness, an escape from the tension I experienced trying to cope with my parents rules and expectations. Standing alone in the schoolyard while everyone else slept, shooting hundreds of layups, hook shots, and one-handers, feeling my heart pounding and the sweat running down my back, I found an order and predictability that escaped me in personal relationships.

I also became fanatically absorbed in the activities of New York's professional sports teams, which in Crown Heights aroused the kind of passion that religion and politics had once inspired in immigrant Jewish neighborhoods like Brownsville, Williamsburg, and the Lower East Side. In my entire childhood, I never saw anyone hold a street rally, pass out a leaflet, or recruit people for a demonstration, but I overheard hundreds, if not thousands, of conversations about baseball, basketball, football, and the horses. The men on my block, most of whom were union members and some of whom had once been socialists, were at their most animated when talking about sports, and they eagerly transmitted these enthusiasms to their male children. In my neighborhood, located less than a mile from Ebbets Field, knowing Jackie Robinson's batting average, Duke Snider's home run total, and Willie Mays's latest box score allowed me to enter the informal fraternity of male street life. Becoming fluent in this discourse became my personal mission. I studied the daily sports pages, memorized the box scores of local teams, and watched every baseball, basketball, and football game that was shown on television. I could sing the jingles of the beer companies and razor-blade manufacturers who sponsored these events, imitate the announcers, and reel off the final scores of every game I watched.

I had an important ally in this mission of subversion, my Uncle Mac, who lived directly below us with his wife and two sons. Mac, my mother's young brother, knew my parents disapproved of his values and lifestyle. A tall, handsome man who worked as a dispatcher for a coal distributor, Mac was a knowledgeable sports fan and an inveterate gambler. Offended by my parents' condescension toward him, he extended a permanent invitation for me to join him for evening and weekend television viewing in his apartment, knowing full well that my parents much preferred that I spend my time reading or practicing the piano. Mac made this space a zone of male camaraderie. With the television tuned to baseball, basketball, and football games, Mac would hold forth on the strategy of the games and the characteristics of the players, periodically punctuating his comments with cries of "Esther, bring me a soda," directed at my long-suffering aunt. I worshiped his two sons, Harvey and Stephen, who were among the best athletes in the neighborhood, and I loved being able to sit back and enjoy the action without feeling any pressure to display my intellect.

Ironically, in Mac's apartment, I encountered an environment where women were treated like servants but race was regarded as irrelevant, as least in the artificial world of professional sports. In the mid 1950s, African-American athletes were beginning to appear in every major venue of televised sports, from Friday night fights to high school basketball and football, but the media rarely employed a language of racial difference. Announcers and sports writers did not refer to the race of players and almost never discussed the problems black athletes encountered with teammates, opponents, coaches, fans, and hotels and restaurants. My Uncle Mac and his friends seemed comfortable with this "color-blind' approach. In my hundreds of hours of watching television with my Uncle Mac or listening to him talk sports on the corner, I never heard him, or anyone else, speak disparagingly about the race of a player, or indeed comment on it at all. Whether this was a particularly Jewish phenomenon, or characteristic of all Brooklyn ethnic groups in the fifties, is difficult to say. As a group, Jews of my parents' generation did not see the emergence of black athletes in professional sports as a threat, and indeed may have viewed it as something that would benefit Jews and other minorities. They were an important part of the cohort of Brooklyn fans who had embraced Jackie Robinson when he broke into the Major Leagues in 1947. At least in my neighborhood, they did not try to undermine the media's depiction of sports as a place where fair play and ability ruled and race and religion were irrelevant.

Because of this confluence of media images and neighborhood attitudes, my friends and I grew up viewing black and white athletes playing ball together as natural and normal. We were passionately involved with the careers of star black athletes, especially baseball and basketball players. We practiced stealing home like Jackie Robinson. We made basket catches like Willie Mays. We took hook shots like Ray Felix, the tall (and not particularly outstanding) center of the New York Knicks. But we did the same for white players we admired, and we didn't see a player's color as a factor in our endless comparisons and evaluations. In arguments about who was the better center fielder, Duke Snider of the Dodgers, Mickey Mantle of the Yankees, or Willie Mays of the Giants, I heard kids refer to the players' batting stance, power, running ability, grace, fielding prowess, and ability to perform under pressure, but never to a player's color. We had no sense that the black athletes we saw on television were pioneers, that they were challenging a centuries-old legacy of exclusion and contempt. Rather we saw them as individual ballplayers with distinctive ways of performing the techniques their sport required, people we admired or despised for "nonracial" reasons.

We had black athletic heroes without seeing their blackness as socially significant. Yet our attachment to black athletes, even in this "color blind" form, had important social consequences. The activities we loved the most, that touched the deepest chord in our emotions, evoked visual images of blacks and whites working together. When race relations became polarized in the 1960s, these images may have conditioned us to respond more positively than our parents to African-American activism and changes in the racial composition of our schools and neighborhoods.

The same mixture of openness and tunnel vision marked our response to another racially hybrid cultural phenomenon that entered our lives in the 1950s, rock and roll. In the spring of 1956, when I was in fifth grade, the "rock and roll craze" swept through my peer group, awakening our preadolescent sexuality and turning us into passionate consumers of popular music. The eleven- and twelve-year-old boys I spent time with suddenly began to listen to music radio, buy cheap phonographs with plastic converters suitable for playing 45 rpm records, and invite female classmates to parties to dance to the latest hits and retreat to the closet for kissing games. This change was sparked by a shift in format among the mass-market radio stations. After years of anesthetizing the public with songs like "How Much Is That Doggy in the Window," disk jockeys began to promote records that had hard-driving rhythms and seductive harmonies, many of them featuring African-American artists, and to market them to adolescents as a sign of generational rebellion. Recording companies shrewdly promoted the music with images of young people—most of them white—screaming in the aisles at rock and roll shows, doing flamboyant and acrobatic dance steps, and singing on street corners while snapping their fingers to the beat. My friends and I responded to these images by trying to learn the latest dance steps, by playing the music at dances and parties, and by spending our money on records, phonographs, and transistor radios. The music also brought us together with girls in our neighborhood, whom we had treated as members of a different species prior to this time.

Because rock and roll crossed gender lines, its role in exposing white kids to African-American cultural influences may have been even greater than that of sports. Through clever marketing, a group of Jewish kids in Crown Heights were persuaded to adopt African-American music as the centerpiece of their generational identity, something that sharply distinguished them from their parents and teachers. I vividly remember the first rock and roll record that was played at our parties. It featured Frankie Lymon and The Teenagers singing "Why Do Fools Fall in Love," a masterpiece of harmonic singing with an irresistible opening passage. We were fascinated by this record, which was representative of a genre—rhythm and blues—that had been popular in black urban neighborhoods for years. We not only danced to it, we sang along with it over and over until we had mastered its central elements—a bass line establishing rhythm, choruses in three-part harmony, and lead singing that used falsetto to reach higher octaves. But we never thought of ourselves as "white" people imitating "black" music. "Why Do Fools Fall in Love" was not promoted as the product of an African-American musical tradition but as part of a *nonracial* phenomenon that brought black and white performers together and appealed to people on the basis of their age. The rock and roll show, whether on the airwaves or live, was an exercise in musical eclecticism, throwing together the country harmonies of the Everly Brothers, the barrelhouse piano of Fats Domino, the rockabilly and blues of Elvis Presley, the gospel-influenced shouting of Little Richard, the electrifying guitar riffs of Chuck Berry, and the rhythm and blues sounds of artists like the Platters and the Drifters. Like the sports teams we followed religiously, rock and roll drew us away from our immigrant past and made America seem like a magical and inviting place, open to people of every background who possessed the requisite talent. For our generation, part of becoming American was becoming culturally "black."

While my parents kept driving me toward academic excellence, by the time I entered junior high school, in the fall of 1957, I had seized upon sports and rock and roll as vehicles for social acceptance among my peers. At Winthrop Junior High School, a five-story, white brick building about a mile from my home, I found myself, along with about a hundred classmates, in an accelerated track that completed three years of school in two. Knowing that I was going to enter high school at age thirteen, I put ferocious effort into making myself as inconspicuous as possible in the world outside the classroom. I studied sports figures and rock and roll stars with the same passion that my parents had approached science and history, determined to win acceptance from older, more confident youngsters who appeared to float through life without the academic pressures I encountered.

Winthrop Junior High proved to be a comfortable place for me, an all-Jewish enclave in a neighborhood about to undergo rapid racial change. Located on Remsen Avenue and Winthrop Street on the border of East Flatbush, in a neighborhood that is now predominantly Afro-Caribbean, it had about a thousand students, no more than twenty of whom were black. Most were lower-middle-class Jews. Drawing on a larger and more prosperous neighborhood than PS 91, the school had only a handful of really tough kids, most of whom hung out by a nearby luncheonette showing off their black leather jackets. The majority of students at Winthrop were clean cut, ambitious, and academically serious; getting good grades there did not subject you to ridicule. Sports at Winthrop were omnipresent and highly respected. The morning began with handball or stickball games played against the concrete wall of the schoolyard. Then came games of johnny on a pony, often involving fifty boys at a time. After school started, the most popular game was basketball, which the boys played in a highly competitive way. The baskets in the boys' gym classes were organized by ability, and the goal of each player was to be acknowledged by the local superstars, who selected the kids who played on the top court. To make myself valuable to them, I spent hours alone in the schoolyard practicing, trying to compensate for my lack of foot speed with shooting skill and strength.

My efforts to gain popularity with girls were equally energetic, though far more confused. Because I had no sisters or female cousins, and because the culture of my neighborhood was rigidly sex segregated, I found it difficult to relate to the girls I was interested in romantically. The things I cared about most—why the Dodgers had left Brooklyn and whether Mickey Mantle was better than Willie Mays—were not things I could talk about to most girls I knew. In this setting, rock and roll became the outlet for my romantic longings and the antidote to my social awkwardness. I learned the words of every new rock and roll song and practiced singing the bass lines and lead voices in the hope that I would be invited to join a singing group, thereby making me popular even if I was tongue-tied in conversation. I also learned the three dances that were in vogue in the late fifties—the lindy hop, the fox trot, and the cha cha—and took advantage of my one opportunity to practice them in mixed company, the bar mitzvah circuit. There, amid trays of caviar and coldcuts, chopped liver sculptures, and dinners that began with Jewish appetizers and ended with baked Alaska, teenagers joined in wild celebrations of Jewish American materialism that often ended with drunken men dancing on tables and women in low-cut dresses performing burlesque routines. The bands played rock and roll for the younger crowd in between Frank Sinatra songs and Jewish staples like "Hava Nagilah." With the help of screwdrivers and manhattans stolen from the bar, I found the courage to ask girls to dance. The louder and faster the music was, the happier I felt. I was much more comfortable moving to the beat than talking.

By the time I graduated from junior high school in 1959, I had started to feel optimistic about the future. With a lot of hard work, I had learned to insulate myself from my parents' demands and construct an alternative identity, drawn from popular culture and the folkways of my Brooklyn neighborhood, that was serving me well. Like most people in Winthrop, I looked forward to high school. Through years of practice, I had made myself a strong, all-around athlete and anticipated playing on a high school team. I had become skilled in tennis during summer vacations and felt confident I could compete on the varsity level. The prospect of success and acceptance in the things America valued beckoned to me, unimpeded by the doubts and insecurities that plagued my parents' generation and the financial pressures they faced. To me, high school evoked images of ball games and dances, of athletes in letter sweaters flanked by cute-looking cheerleaders, of academic triumphs and a vibrant social life. I never dreamed it would bring violence, class conflict, and racial tension.

But the age of innocence was ending in Crown Heights. The opening of a new high school in our neighborhood, George W. Wingate, in 1956, coupled with a rapid southward expansion of Brooklyn's black population, was bringing a rapid end to the color-blind era in our community's history. The Wingate student body included several hundred African-Americans who took the bus in from Bedford-Stuyvesant, and their arrival triggered waves of anxiety among Jews and Italians who had previously lived in harmony with their small number of black neighbors. For residents of Crown Heights, young and old alike, race would become a central preoccupation, something they talked about, and acted on, in a highly conscious way. Dimly aware, from television, of the Montgomery bus boycott and the Little Rock school integration dispute, I had never thought of these issues as having relevance to my life. My insular, homogeneous world, was about to open up.

2   Race Conscious

THE ARRIVAL of black students at Wingate High School dramatized population shifts that were rapidly changing the social geography
of Brooklyn and other northeastern urban centers. Driven by collapsing agricultural economies and drawn by the hope of a better life, people of African descent, some from the South, some from the Caribbean,
were arriving in Brooklyn by the tens of thousands in the 1950s. Most
initially settled in Bedford-Stuyvesant, a predominantly African-American community in north central Brooklyn bordered on the north by the
Brooklyn Navy Yard and on the south by Atlantic Avenue, Brooklyn's
largest and busiest east-west thoroughfare. But as Bedford-Stuyvesant
started to experience overcrowding and decay, many of its residents
sought housing in adjoining neighborhoods. Barred by discrimination
from moving to the southern portions of the borough, where new housing was being constructed at breakneck speed, they pushed southward
into Crown Heights, and eastward into Brownsville, predominantly
Jewish neighborhoods where small numbers of black residents already
lived. Their arrival created panic in communities that had seemed to be
traditional bastions of liberalism. Egged on by real estate brokers who
sought to profit from panicked selling, Jewish families fled to Queens,
Long Island, and the southern part of Brooklyn, vacating homes and
apartments by the thousands under the press of the black advance.
When I arrived at Wingate in the fall of 1959, the line of black settlement
was about a mile and a half north of us and about two miles east of us,
and it was moving steadily in our direction.

Although people of my parents' generation seemed very worried
about Brooklyn's changing racial composition, my friends and I felt no
personal threat. We had heard rumors about African-American gangs
like the Chaplains and the Bishops, but we made no distinction between
them and white gangs like the Fordham Baldies, which had created
such a panic in Brooklyn that school once had to be canceled for half a
day when I was in sixth grade. Moreover, none of us had ever been
harassed or attacked by black kids, either in our junior high school,

which was 97 percent white, or in our travels around Crown Heights, which took us to movie theaters, bowling alleys, restaurants, and the gymnasiums of Jewish centers, some of which were more than a mile from our homes. Our interracial contacts, limited though they were, tended to be positive. Our weekend full-court basketball games in the local park included several black players, some from our neighborhood; but at least one was a kid our age from Brownsville who suddenly showed up one day and joined our game. Chucky was a great player as well as an evangelist for an exciting style of basketball we had seen on television but had never witnessed firsthand. Most of the players in our schoolyard, including the black kids, played the game in a linear way, moving up the court in straight lines, driving directly to the basket, and either putting up a shot or passing it out. Chucky moved sideways, as well as forward, when he had the ball. He dribbled in zigzag motions, moving his head and shoulders in rhythm with his dribble, making it impossible for a defender to figure out where he was going. When he drove to the basket, he jumped high in the air and hung there with his knees bent while the defender tried to block his shot, moving the ball to evade the defender's hand and putting the ball in for an easy layup or giving one of his teammates a perfect pass. Chucky effortlessly dominated our full-court games, despite the fact that he was two inches shorter than the other players. He tried to teach us some of his favorite moves and served as unofficial team captain when we played games against older kids or players from adjoining neighborhoods. Nobody knew where he lived, or where he went to school, but he brought moments of grace and artistry into our lives, expanding the horizons of both our game and our imaginations.

When we arrived at Wingate, my friends and I were more intrigued than intimidated by the presence of a large group of black students. Constructed in the mid-1950s, Wingate resembled a suburban high school more than the fortresslike, five-story structures that housed most of New York City's students. Located between Kings County Hospital and the border of the Italian section of Crown Heights, it featured a streamlined white brick exterior and airy classrooms, a huge gymnasium and modern auditorium, and a large outdoor sports complex. Wingate looked like an inviting place to go to school, but it proved to be the site of an uneasy experiment in racial diversity complicated by class and cultural differences. About 70 percent of its students were working- and lower-middle-class Jews who were academically motivated and optimistic about their futures. Many were in honors classes that prepared students for college. Another 10 percent were Italian kids from the immediate area, most of them poorer and tougher than their Jewish classmates. Another 20 percent were African-American, almost all of whom came from Bedford-Stuyvesant via the Kingston Avenue bus. To get to Wingate, they had to walk five blocks from the bus stop on Empire Boulevard, forcing them to pass directly through an Italian neighborhood whose residents were openly hostile to their presence. When the school first opened, a black student had been shot by a group of young Italians, and ever since police had been stationed outside the building at arrival and dismissal hours to prevent any more such incidents.

At Wingate the black students from Bedford-Stuyvesant carried themselves very differently from the black kids I grew up with, who had displayed no distinctive cultural attributes (or at least none we noticed). First of all, they walked together in large groups, congregated together outside the school, and ate together in the cafeteria. Their cohesiveness was striking and more than a little unsettling, especially since it was reinforced by colorful patterns of speech. Many of the Bedford-Stuyvesant students spoke to each other in a 1950s version of street slang that was completely unfamiliar to me and my cohort. It was filled with distinctive greetings like "hey, baby" and "hey, man" and inventive references to body parts and sexual acts, and accentuated by the frequent use of the term "motherfucker." Though four-letter words were commonplace in white ethnic Brooklyn, the use of "mother" to embellish the most common Anglo-Saxon curse word was something we had never heard before. Then the Bedford-Stuyvesant students dressed far more stylishly than any other group of students at Wingate. In our section of Crown Heights, even the wealthier kids (and the black kids) wore department-store clothes bought for them by their parents, and they rarely cared about the brand, color, and condition of what they had on. The Bedford-Stuyvesant crew, by contrast, often wore clothes that were pressed, ironed, and color coordinated, and sometimes topped by hats worn at a rakish angle. They even *walked* differently than the white or black kids from Crown Heights. Many of the black male students walked with a bouncing, rolling step that was almost dancelike, especially when they were moving in a group. The black girls walked with a slightly less noticeable strut. These girls were also far more physically and verbally aggressive than most of the white girls at the school. On several occasions, black girls got into altercations with one another in the streets outside the school, complete with punching, hair pulling, and loud, almost theatrical cursing. My friends and I had never before seen girls square off in public, much less curse one another at the top of their lungs.

School officials seemed to deal with these cultural differences by encouraging, or at least tolerating, almost complete racial separation. There were never more than one or two black students in my classes. Virtually all of the Jewish kids were in regents or honors classes, while most of the black kids were in the commercial or general track. The cafeteria was also rigidly segregated. The only racially mixed table consisted of players on the school's championship basketball team, seemingly the only institution in the school that crossed racial lines. The tension was so palpable that a few students who came from left-wing families decided to organize a Human Relations Club to foster more positive interactions between the races. I joined the group but noticed that its few black members were from the academic track and seemed to have little in common with the majority of black students at the school.

Despite these divisions, I was very excited to be at Wingate. Many of my best friends from Winthrop were in my classes, and the school had an excellent tennis team, a sport at which I now excelled. The group of players that I joined that fall was bright, disciplined, and extremely competitive. All were either Jewish or black, children of small businessmen and civil servants who approached tennis with the single-minded dedication of people determined to achieve higher social status than their parents.

But in November of my sophomore year (junior high in New York went through the ninth grade), an altercation in the locker room after a gym class, one with powerful if ambiguous racial overtones, brought an end to my career at Wingate. After making the varsity tennis team, I had been placed in a physical education class that included a sizable number of black students from the school's track team. I got along well with the group I played basketball with, but started to have trouble with some black students who dressed next to me in the locker room. As a physically immature thirteen-year-old, with a blond crew cut and glasses, no more than five feet, six inches in height, I appeared to be a typical Wingate honors student and therefore presented a tempting target for teasing to the group of bigger, older kids who congregated in the adjacent row of lockers. They started off with a subject I was extremely insecure about—sex. One day the black kid dressing next to me, a lanky six footer, asked me, "Have you ever gotten any pussy?" I was very confused by his question. Only much later did I discover that he was asking whether I had ever had sex with a girl. I thought he meant "have you ever touched a girl's private parts?" which was something I thought a sexually experienced boy my age *should* have done, so I said "Yes, I think so." My neighbor shook his head in disbelief at this pathetic comment, and, for the moment, decided to leave me alone.

Two weeks later, he started in on another subject. As we were getting dressed to play ball, he said to me in a threatening voice, "You stole my sweat socks!" I looked at him as if he were crazy, said, "No, I didn't" and ran out to play basketball. As I joined my regular game of three on three in the Wingate schoolyard, I was trembling with fear. The person who had confronted me was at least six inches taller than I was and had a cool self-confidence that seemed truly ominous. But the thought of telling a teacher about my problem never crossed my mind. Despite my studious appearance, I was so determined not to let anyone push me around that backing down in the face of physical danger was far more frightening to me than getting beaten up. When my basketball game broke up, I walked back to the gym slowly and sadly, forcing my feet to move with fatalistic air of someone going to his own execution.

When I reached my locker, my neighbor had gathered a group of five or six of his friends, who formed a circle around us so no one could see what was going on. As soon as I sat down to get dressed, he proclaimed to his friends, with loud indignation, "This motherfucker stole my sweat socks!" As frightened as I had ever been in my life, I replied, in a shaking voice, "What are you talking about? I didn't steal anything." My Jewish honor-class friends were nowhere in sight, and by this time my hope of leaving the situation unscathed had disappeared. Surrounded by six older, bigger students who appeared to enjoy my discomfort, I continued to get dressed, determined to show that I could not be intimidated. As I prepared to leave, my accuser ordered, with unconcealed contempt, "Tie my shoelace." At this point, my fears were swept aside by a surge of pure rage and hatred. I stood up, looked him in the eye, and said, "Fuck you!" Stunned by my response, he reached back and punched me hard in the face. I do not remember what happened next; I must have passed out, either from fear or from the force of the punch. When I woke up, my white friends had returned and took me to my homeroom class, where I promptly threw up all over my desk. Since this was the last class of the day on a Friday, I went home worrying about how I would deal with the situation come Monday. I was determined, however, to go right back to my place in the locker room as though nothing had happened.

My parents had a different idea. When they heard what had happened, they refused to let me return to Wingate. Using their Board of Education connections, they had me transferred into Erasmus Hall, an old and famous high school in the Flatbush section of Brooklyn. It had a national reputation for academic excellence and very few black students. On Tuesday of the following week, I was sitting in the office of that school's assistant principal and getting my schedule, which consisted of five honors classes along with homeroom and gym, and my bus pass. The next day, after two fifteen-minute bus rides, I was attending classes in a totally different physical and social environment. Erasmus Hall, a huge Gothic structure complete with towers and gargoyles, took up half a city block at the intersection of Flatbush and Church Avenues. The school had a courtyard that contained trees, lawns, flowers, and a wooden building dating back to 1754 that had been the original academy for which the school was named. Tradition was very important at Erasmus. School assemblies called "chapel" were held in an auditorium with wooden pews and stained-glass windows. The principal, who had a doctoral degree, told students they were privileged to attend such a venerable institution. But the school was bursting at the seams. It had enrolled 8,200 students, making it the largest high school in the United States. About half of them were Jewish; the other half was Italian, Irish, German, Scandinavian, and African-American, with blacks composing perhaps 5 percent of the school population. I didn't know a single student there.

My adjustment to Erasmus began with another episode of physical intimidation. My homeroom contained two small, tough-looking Irish kids who seemed to delight in torturing one student who looked like a walking stereotype of a Jewish bookworm—small, scrawny, disheveled, with dark-rimmed, poorly fitting glasses. They would poke him and punch him when the teacher wasn't looking and shove him in the halls. One day, thinking I was cut from the same cloth, they started jostling me and called me a "Jew bastard." I was terribly frightened, so much so I urinated in my pants, but I turned on them with a ferocity that took even me by surprise, grabbing the larger kid by the shoulders and slamming him against the wall so hard that he crumpled to the floor. Then I turned toward his friend and charged him, but he was already running down the hall to escape my wrath. My violent outburst seemed to earn me freedom from harassment, as these two aspiring Jew baiters never said another word to me the rest of the year. Compared to what I had experienced at Wingate, this was light stuff.

My academic experience at Erasmus Hall was very positive. The students in my honors classes were more articulate and sophisticated than their counterparts at Wingate. Many came from families where both parents were college educated and some had backgrounds in politics and the arts. For the first time, I was among aspiring professors, musicians, and writers as well as future doctors, lawyers, and businesspeople. In addition, Erasmus had a small but conspicuous number of students who were children of left-wing activists, and they were openly critical of American society and American foreign policy. Bettina Aptheker, whose father, Herbert Aptheker, was the Communist Party's leading scholar on African-American history, was the best-known member of a group of student iconoclasts who helped make classes exciting and kept the school administration on its toes. My classes in English and history produced passionate debates over nuclear testing, arms control, and the containment of communism, with teachers arguing for maximum deterrence and students arguing—well before it was fashionable—for disarmament and détente. In addition, some students openly protested the air-raid drills that were a regular feature of public-school life in the fifties. For as long as I could remember, every student had to participate in what, in retrospect, seems to be one of the more bizarre public rituals ever practiced in New York City. Twice a month, a loud siren would go off, all classwork would stop, and teachers would instruct their students to crawl under their desks and put their hands over their heads, or go to the basement and stand against the wall. According to our teachers, all this was preparation for the possibility of a Soviet nuclear attack. Until I got to Erasmus, everyone sheepishly cooperated in this charade, never articulating their strong suspicion that if the Russians ever hit New York, *nothing* would save us. But here, students actually refused to put their hands over their heads, and they attacked the government and the school system for disguising the horrors of nuclear war and encouraging students to accept an arms race that had the potential to destroy the planet. Sometimes they were sent to the principal's office; sometimes teachers ignored them and let them have their say. But these students definitely raised my awareness about policies I had taken for granted. They also made me interested in attending meetings of protest organizations at the school, the largest of which was Students for a SANE Nuclear Policy.

This contentious, politically charged atmosphere made me feel right at home at Erasmus. I loved to talk, and I now had an opportunity to create a new public persona among people who knew nothing about me. Traits that made me unusual in my neighborhood were unremarkable here. Virtually all Erasmus honors students had skipped a year, and many had parents who took them to concerts, zoos, and museums. Some had higher scores than I did on reading and IQ tests. Although Erasmus allowed me to become more comfortable with my intellectual side, sports remained the emotional center of my life. I tried out for and made the Erasmus tennis team, played basketball whenever I could, and attended every single game of Erasmus's excellent varsity basketball team. Basketball served as a powerful bridge between my life in Crown Heights and my activities at my new school. Both Wingate and Erasmus were part of a basketball division that was the most competitive in New York City. It contained three of the best players in the United States: Roger Brown from Wingate, Connie Hawkins from Boys High, and Billy Cunningham from Erasmus. The atmosphere at the games was electric as they showcased the growing African-American presence in the sports culture of Brooklyn.

Through basketball I strengthened a friendship with Myron Druxerman, a childhood pal who still attended Wingate. Myron loved the game even more than I did. An average athlete for most of his childhood, he had grown to six feet, two inches by his fourteenth birthday. He made the junior varsity basketball team at Wingate during his sophomore year. He wanted to practice during every spare moment and recruited me as his sparring partner. We worked out together in the schoolyard every weekend and played together on a Jewish Center team organized by Jamie Moskowitz, the head varsity coach at Madison High School and a Brooklyn basketball legend. Myron loved being around the game, and in particular he enjoyed being part of the multiracial community of players at Wingate. He spoke very enthusiastically to me of his black teammates and invited several of them to play with us in pickup games.

The basketball culture Myron drew me into provided an experience of racial harmony that helped to counter my parents' increasingly bitter feelings. For them, the fight in the Wingate locker room symbolized the dangers "the schvartzes" posed to the Jews of North Brooklyn. Under the press of black migration, their color blindness dissolved into bitterness and fear. Increasingly their comments to me made explicit reference to race. I should watch where I walked and avoid black teenagers who congregated in large groups. Social relationships with African-Americans were difficult, they advised me, because even those from middle-class families "have different moral standards than we do." With friends and neighbors they traded stories of robberies, muggings, and rude and boisterous behavior by black teenagers, and they talked about moving into all-white neighborhoods in the southern part of Brooklyn or leaving the borough entirely. There was no empathy in their comments, no sense that African-Americans had anything to contribute to the cultural life of the communities they moved into.

My mother's comments were particularly upsetting because she had always been kind and considerate to the black people in our immediate neighborhood—especially Adler, our housekeeper, and our superintendent, Mr. Stokes. She often hugged her own black students when she met them on the subway or in department stores. But her deeply emotional racial diatribes blended historic memories of Jewish vulnerability with the fear that close proximity to blacks could threaten our family's ascent into the middle class. The very real clash of cultures in the streets of Brooklyn between lower-middle-class Americanized Jews and working-class black Southern migrants became, in my mother's fervid imagination, the harbinger of some new tragedy about to befall the Jewish people. Like many of her friends and neighbors, she seemed terrified that neighborhood integration meant the massive influx of uneducated rural people bringing high levels of noise, boisterous behavior, overcrowding, and violence. The stigma of dark skin magnified the danger. Although Brooklyn had its share of black professionals and civil servants, many of the new migrants, especially those arriving from the American South, were products of rural areas and small towns who possessed little formal education, few marketable skills, and a culture that prized expressive language and emotionalism as antidotes to poverty and racial persecution. Confined to crowded, decaying neighborhoods with inferior schools and public services, and blocked from decent jobs by employer and union discrimination, many found Brooklyn a place of disappointment and dashed dreams. Jews of my mother's generation, who believed their own ascent to the middle class had come through rigorous self-denial, saw black poverty and anger as evidence of moral and cultural deficits, not as responses to the discrimination that cramped their lives at every turn.

My parents' racial outbursts, increasingly common during my high school years, deeply offended me. Brought up in relative comfort and security, I did not view African-Americans as threats to our family's hard-won respectability and middle-class status. Indeed, I *identified* with them as common objects of my parents' hysterical attacks. The puritanical standards by which they condemned African-American culture were the same ones they used in banning me from tackle football and from seeing movies with my friends, and in saddling me with impossible academic expectations. Expressive elements in African-American folk culture intrigued me more than they repelled me. Having grown up with black heroes in sports and music, and having embraced integrated cultural forms as building blocks of personal identity, I experienced my parents' attacks on black people as attacks on my own quest for happiness and independence.

Apart from the Wingate locker room incident, my own contacts with Brooklyn's black community were overwhelmingly positive. The schoolyards where I went to hone my basketball skills all had racially mixed games. The public tennis courts where I played three days a week attracted a sizable number of black players; and nearly a quarter of my regular hitting partners, who were the best high school players in Brooklyn, came from Afro-Caribbean and African-American families. I traveled to and from Erasmus with a black girl, Daphne Dyce, who was the only other student in my classes who took the Kingston Avenue bus to school. A dark-skinned girl who wore glasses, Daphne was an honor student and track star whose Jamaican immigrant parents had made her take German to get into Erasmus. She was smart, cynical, and easier to talk to than most other girls in my classes because of her knowledge of sports. She was a valuable companion in my long ride to school.

Throughout my high school years, racial issues would be a powerful source of division within my family, my neighborhood, and within the white population of Crown Heights generally. Much of this division was generational. By the early 1960s many adult Jews in Crown Heights were describing Brooklyn's growing African-American population as a threat to their safety and security. My parents and their friends, who supported nonviolent civil rights demonstrations in the South, thought that living in integrated neighborhoods would expose them to crime, violence, and disorder. They planned to leave Crown Heights if the black population got too large. My contemporaries, largely Jewish athletes and honor students, seemed more willing to accommodate to an integrated environment. Some were fearful, some were indifferent, but many found it exciting to live in changing times and were fascinated by African-American culture. In my circles, contact with African-American athletes, and knowledge of African-American music, conferred prestige. My cousin Stephen, an outstanding basketball player who was one of my childhood heroes, was transformed by Columbia into a passionate jazz fan. He made it his business to expose his younger brother Harvey and me to the sounds of Dave Brubeck, the Modern Jazz Quartet, and other musicians he loved. I even knew a small number of Jewish kids whose language, posture, and dress were shaped by an African-American street ethos, and who marked their "hipness" by trips to the Apollo Theater and familiarity with the disk jockeys on WWRL, New York's black radio station.

Not everyone of my parents' generation shared their views. A small community in Brooklyn supported civil rights on moral and political grounds, and involved themselves in racial issues through political activism as well as cultural identification. This group consisted of people who had been in, or close to, the Communist Party in the 1930s and 1940s, before the Red Scare had made such affiliations dangerous. Although no one like this lived in my immediate neighborhood, several had sons and daughters at Erasmus. Their guiding political principle was that unity between blacks and whites was essential to all social progress in the United States. They saw the race problem in the United States not just as a matter of unjust laws in the South but of a deeply rooted, crippling prejudice that affected white people all over the country, including in ostensibly "liberal" Brooklyn.

I found such viewpoints intriguing, but I was not yet ready to become "political." At heart I was still a child of popular culture whose fantasy life centered around sports and music, and who found in these activities a refuge from my parents' unrelenting demands. My parents, enraged that I spent so much time on "frivolities," no longer knew how to control me. By the time I was fifteen years old, I was six feet tall and weighed 180 pounds, and I was not easy to discipline by conventional methods.

The war between us continually erupted over academics and racial issues. It infuriated my parents that I was not one of the top five students in my class at Erasmus, which numbered sixteen hundred at the time I graduated. When they saw me getting 95s with moderate amounts of work, they would denounce me as an "underachiever." "If you worked as hard as other kids in the school," they would scream, "you'd get 99s and 100s." But I refused to let their criticism undermine my self-confidence. I would stoically bear their insults or retreat into my room and read. To insulate myself from their attacks, I got in the habit of reading nineteenth-century novels and immersing myself in a fantasy world where conflicts occurred over love and ideas rather than petty ambitions and rules. I read *Anna Karenina, The Brothers Karamazov, Tom Jones,* and *Les Misérables* in the privacy of my bedroom, where I was getting a better education than in my high school English classes.

Our conflicts over race, and specifically civil rights work, were more intermittent. During the spring of 1960, a group of Erasmus students organized a chapter of the Congress of Racial Equality (CORE) in response to the sit-in movement that black college students were organizing throughout the South. The group's first big project was to picket Woolworth's in Brooklyn, as a way of pressuring the company to desegregate its stores in the South. Later, Erasmus CORE turned its attention to a boycott of Ebinger's Bakery to force it to hire African-American delivery and sales people. Ebinger's, which sold high-quality baked goods in stores throughout Brooklyn, had an all-white sales staff that no longer matched its clientele. The campaign was coordinated by the large and militant Brooklyn chapter of CORE, located in Bedford-Stuyvesant, which saw it as an excellent opportunity to tackle discrimination in its own community.

At the beginning of my senior year at Erasmus, I decided to participate in this campaign. Telling my parents of my intentions set off a ferocious argument about blacks, Jews, and civil rights.

"Why are you trying to help the *schvartzes?*" my mother asked me. "They certainly wouldn't do anything to help you. If you are going to help someone, why don't you help the Jews?"

"I wasn't aware that Jews needed help," I replied. "Jews in America aren't beaten up for trying to vote or buy a hamburger. They aren't facing discrimination all over the country. What do you want me to do? Go to Israel and join a kibbutz?"

"Don't be so smart," my father said. "You can throw away your whole future by signing a petition or marching on a picket line. Let the *schvartzes* fight their own battles. Don't be like the teachers we knew who joined the Communist Party and ended up losing their jobs. Jews always get in trouble when they try to help other people."

This dialogue revealed the powerful anxieties my parents had kept hidden during my formative years. Although they had always expressed pride in their Jewish ancestry and boasted of Jewish accomplishments in science and the arts, they did not instill in me strong religious convictions or an acute sense of Jewish vulnerability. Like many other parents in postwar Crown Heights, they said very little about anti-Semitism and never talked about Hitler and the Holocaust. They sent me to Hebrew school to acquire Jewish consciousness, but my teachers there described Jewish history as a triumphal march of the Jewish people against tyrants and enemies, not a tragedy. The founding of the state of Israel was the culmination of this heroic story. I was taught much more about Pharaoh and Haman than I was about the Nazis and was trained to see Jews as a fighting people who usually vanquished their opponents. Given this perspective, it was hard for me to accept my parents' equation of black and Jewish suffering, or view Jews as a people that needed help. For nearly two years, I had been bombarded with television images of African-Americans being beaten, jailed, and even killed trying to eat at public lunch counters, use bus terminal waiting rooms, and register to vote—rights that American Jews could exercise freely. Even in Brooklyn, Jews seemed a much more advantaged group than blacks. Many Jewish families had black maids and housekeepers, but I saw very few African-Americans in business and the professions. I had also experienced so little anti-Semitism that to equate it with racism seemed ludicrous. In all my schools, the Jewish kids were the best students, the best athletes, and the most popular and confident people. Describing Jews as "victims" seemed to be dishonest and self-serving.

My parents' perspective was profoundly different. In response to my gravitation to civil rights activism, they began talking more explicitly about their experiences with anti-Semitism, which had dominated their lives

from the time they were children. They encountered it on the streets of
New York, where they had been chased and harassed by Irish teenagers.
It came up when they searched for jobs or looked for a place to stay while
on vacation, and it colored their treatment by colleagues and administrators in the New York City public schools during the Depression. My father
had changed his name from Nosofsky to Naison to make his life as a
teacher easier. For them the Holocaust was not something remote. Both
had lost relatives to the Nazis and had suffered the additional horror of
knowing that a good many Americans supported Hitler's policies, at least
in the beginning. During the late 1930s, they had heard Father Coughlin
praise Nazi Germany on national radio broadcasts and had watched nerv-
ously while the German-American Bund and the Christian Front held pro-
Nazi demonstrations in New York City. They harbored deep fears that
another wave of anti-Semitism might erupt. To them, African-Americans
were not a people with a tragic history; they were another group of *goyim*
ready to turn against the Jews when it was convenient to do so. The line
of African-American settlement was now less than a mile from our apartment in Crown Heights, and my parents felt threatened by people whose
poverty they feared and whose values and culture they held in contempt.
When I accused them of prejudice, they replied that any group of uneducated people was a threat to the Jews. "The shanty Irish are worse than
the Negroes," they would proclaim triumphantly.

My parents' entire response to civil rights could be summed up by
the phrase, "Is it good for the Jews?" They supported sit-ins to desegregate southern business establishments and admired Martin Luther
King's crusade for citizenship rights, but were suspicious of northern
protests against discrimination in housing and employment, which
might make Jewish landlords and storeowners a target of popular anger.
They also worried that participation in demonstrations might jeopard-
ize my future. They had seen friends lose jobs during the McCarthy era
because of their youthful involvements, and they did not want the same
thing to happen to me. They laid down the law for the Ebinger's campaign: I could go to meetings and rallies but could not sign any petitions or march on any picket lines. I pretended to agree to their conditions and then did exactly the opposite.

The Ebinger's campaign, as my parents suspected, brought me
squarely into the company of students whose parents had been in or
close to the Communist Party. Several meetings took place at the East-

ern Parkway apartment of Eleanor Stein, a junior at Erasmus, whose mother, Annie Stein, had been the leader of a large and successful campaign in the early 1950s to desegregate restaurants and theaters in downtown Washington. She had turned her attention to housing and employment issues since moving to Brooklyn and had developed ties with many community activists in Bedford-Stuyvesant. On one occasion, she took us to the Fulton Street office of the African-American attorney Thomas Russell Jones, where our all-white and mostly Jewish group of twenty-odd students was given a warm welcome and put to work making signs for the boycott. Jones had been a young leader of the National Negro Congress, a left-wing civil rights group founded in the late thirties, and he was equally comfortable working as a legal advocate for African-Americans or as a strategist for protests that spanned diverse neighborhoods and constituencies. Under his leadership, the Ebingers campaign put enough pressure on the company to force it to change its hiring policies. Jones built on this and other protest efforts to become one of the founders of the Bedford-Stuyvesant Restoration Corporation and a judge in the New York State Supreme Court.

One of the most intriguing aspects of the Ebinger's campaign was the exposure it gave me to the culture of the children of the Old Left. Most members of Erasmus CORE had grown up going to left-wing summer camps, and they were fans of African-American musicians who had been blacklisted for their beliefs. With loving hands, they put on records by the African-American blues singer Hudie Ledbetter (Leadbelly) and the folksinger, actor, and human rights activist Paul Robeson. To a person whose musical tastes had been shaped by rock and roll, their spare and haunting voices, redolent of prisons, work gangs, and endurance in the face of hardship, had an unsettling quality. Like many of my neighborhood friends, I associated black music with good times rather than tragedy, but Robeson and Leadbelly evoked the brutality of a Jim Crow society with such power and simplicity that it sent chills through me.

While moved by this message, I was not ready to relinquish my dreams of popularity and athletic success. I could not see myself giving up basketball games, parties, and tennis matches for the life of a full-time protester. But no matter how optimistic I was about my personal prospects, I could not rid myself of the sense that there was a serious and morally compelling racial problem in America. The horrors of southern segregation had begun to enter my consciousness, largely through televised images showing nonviolent protesters being beaten during the 1960 student sit-ins and the 1961 Freedom Rides, a CORE-sponsored protest designed to desegregate bus terminals in the deep South that were used in interstate travel. But I was more disturbed by the racial fears and prejudices I saw emerging in my neighborhood and family. My apartment was a hornet's nest of tension, and Crown Heights was rapidly being abandoned by English-speaking Jews, to be repopulated by blacks and Jewish immigrants from Eastern Europe who belonged to unfamiliar religious sect. My friends and I started to notice Hasidic Jews on the streets of Crown Heights, strange-looking men wearing long black coats and fur hats even in warm weather, women with ankle-length dresses, and yarmulke-clad male children with long curls *(pais)* and white strings hanging down from their vests (tzitzis). When we saw these kids at the local schoolyard playing on the monkey bars and the swings, we called them "the yarmulke bops," but we were more confused than angered by their presence. The comfortable insular world we had grown up in was changing, and we sensed that our future lay outside of Crown Heights.

When I graduated from Erasmus in the spring of 1962 and prepared to attend Columbia University, I was glad to be leaving my neighborhood. Columbia represented romance and opportunity, the school where Allen Ginsberg and Jack Kerouac launched the Beat Generation, C. Wright Mills denounced conformity and bureaucracy, and my cousin Stephen learned to love jazz. For the first time in my life, I would be living away from home and would have a chance to find activities I valued and enjoyed without my parents' smothering oversight. But the world of Brooklyn streets and schoolyards would always remain inside me, filling me with rage and paranoia but also giving me an energy, irreverence, and appreciation of cultural difference that no amount of Ivy League training could ever root out. Despite my provincial upbringing (I had never been west of Philadelphia or south of Virginia), I had had more diverse experiences with America's race problem than most of my future classmates, and that experience would serve me well as I tried to develop a new identity on Manhattan's Upper West Side.

3   Looking Down on Harlem

FROM MY first day on the Columbia campus, I realized I had underestimated the university's traditionalism and exaggerated its avant-garde spirit. In the early 1960s, Columbia described itself, without irony or humor, as a temple of Western culture, the "Acropolis on Morningside Heights." Located on a cliff overlooking Harlem on Manhattan's Upper West Side, it was built around a huge open plaza, where concrete steps and manicured lawns were surrounded by buildings with Roman columns and elegant domes, and where the names of philosophers, poets, and theologians were inscribed in stone. The buildings' equally grand interiors were embellished with rich wood paneling, original portraits of Columbia's past presidents, stained-glass windows, and chairs with plush upholstery. In Butler Library, the main repository of the university's printed holdings, the main reading room was at least a hundred feet long and fifty feet wide; its sixty-foot ceiling was adorned with art. The dormitories and classroom buildings had been named in honor of famous scholars, statesman, and captains of industry, great figures from the Anglo-Saxon elite who had ruled the nation since its inception. As a lower-middle-class Jewish student from Brooklyn, I felt as though I had been admitted to a private club that my parents and neighbors could never join. Awed, I wondered if I could make any impression on an institution so powerful and imposing.

The school's all-male student body included many Jews and Catholics, some from backgrounds similar to mine, but its faculty and administrators, in their dress and language, promoted Anglophilia and a prep-school ambiance. My writing and humanities instructors, the first Italian and the second Jewish, wore tweed suits and spoke with British accents perfected through years of practice. Administrators, who sported pipes and jackets with leather elbow patches, spoke with crafted elegance, often punctuating their remarks with quotes from famous authors. The students who had come to Columbia from prep schools and private day schools, who constituted about half of the student body, felt comfortable in this atmosphere. However, those of us with work-ing-class backgrounds, or who came from New York's ethnic neigh-borhoods, felt as if we had landed on a different planet. The language of the city's streets, with its inflections, hand gestures, shouts and curses, and its colorful imagery was rendered all but silent in the public life of the institution. The school's atmosphere was assimilationist and dem-ocratic. The Columbia man, whatever his background, was expected to learn the poise and emotional control of an upper-class Anglo-Saxon.

An undercurrent of racial arrogance also pervaded Columbia's atmos-phere, despite the liberal political outlook of much of its faculty. During the 1950s, Columbia had participated in a Robert Moses–sponsored urban renewal program that had removed nearly ten thousand low-income res-idents from Morningside Heights. Representatives of Columbia College showed little embarrassment about the university's efforts to clean up and "whiten" its surrounding neighborhood. From the very first session of freshman orientation, I heard administrators and student leaders refer to Harlem as a place to be avoided, a poor and troubled community that could be dangerous to Columbia students. "Make sure you get off at the 116th stop on Broadway, not the one on Lenox Avenue," they warned us with a nervous laugh. The school's admissions policies and curriculum did little to counteract such sentiments. Only 6 African-American stu-dents joined my freshman class of 660, all from prep schools or elite pub-lic high schools like Boston Latin or Bronx Science, and only one African-American taught on the college faculty, an anthropologist named Elliot Skinner. Courses on African-American history and literature did not yet exist. Columbia defined its mission—the dissemination of the tenets of Western civilization—in a manner that rendered African-Americans invis-ible. In my first two years at the school, I never heard anyone on its fac-ulty or staff refer to Harlem, a community with a rich and varied history, as a cultural resource or a place where the ideas and values of a great uni-versity should be tested and applied. The university had no community service program (it would create one three years later at the height of the civil rights movement) and did nothing to encourage students to work as tutors, youth leaders, or community organizers in poor and working-class Manhattan neighborhoods.

I also found the academic atmosphere of the university intimidating. After receiving my first C on a freshman English paper, I realized that my writing skills were far more limited than those of my classmates who had gone to prep school. Even though I enjoyed the course assignments, I had to write multiple drafts of my papers to get grades in the B range. Math was an even more humiliating experience. I foolishly enrolled in theoretical calculus and found myself in a class filled with math whizzes from New York's Stuyvesant and Bronx Science high schools. Our bearded professor wore big leather boots and made up the course as he went along. I had no idea what he was talking about and had to learn the entire course from the textbook, which was hardly a model of clarity.

Sports was the one dimension of college life where I achieved some measure of success. At Columbia, athletics was one of the few domains in which students from working-class backgrounds and public high schools set the tone. Catholic students from Western Pennsylvania, New Jersey, and Massachusetts dominated the football and baseball teams, while Jewish athletes from New York City's public high schools led tennis, fencing, and basketball. When I tried out for the tennis and basketball teams (I made the first), I found myself among kindred spirits: people who were tough, competitive, and utterly lacking in upper-class mannerisms or the accoutrements of wealth. Drawn together by pride in their physical prowess and insecurity about their class backgrounds, Columbia's athletes bonded together into a distinctive "jock" subculture which, beneath a façade of sexual bravado, displayed considerable openness and generosity of spirit. Aware that they needed to make friends quickly to survive in an alien environment, athletes held all-night bull sessions where they talked about parents, girlfriends, religion, politics, their dreams, their insecurities, their plans for the future.

I met my best friend from those days in freshman basketball tryouts. A lightweight football player from the Bronx, Louis Rappaport came from a background similar to my own and he shared my political values. Louis had an odd and striking appearance. About five feet, ten inches tall and weighing 150 pounds, he looked like anything but a competitive athlete. He had a narrow shoulders, a receding chin, and arms that flapped when he ran. But he was fast, wiry, and clever, and an excellent schoolyard basketball player. A graduate of Bronx Science, perhaps the city's most academically rigorous public high school, Louis had grown up with little money, an appreciation for ethnic differences, a visceral hatred of authority, and a passion for basketball. After being cut from the freshman basketball team, the two of us began playing basketball together three or four nights a week, and we developed a relationship that mingled deep affection and sharp competition. We also established ourselves as left-wing gadflies and ambassadors for New York street culture in our circle of freshman athletes. On one occasion, we mesmerized a group of Southerners and Midwesterners in the lounge of our dormitory by insulting one another's mothers for fifteen straight minutes, an exercise in verbal gymnastics that, we later discovered, was a variation on an African-American word game called "the dozens," which had somehow found its way into the culture of outer borough Jews and Italians.

We also tried to challenge the racial attitudes of our more conservative classmates, which must have been deeply disturbing to Columbia's small number of black students. Two African-American students lived in our dorm: Robert Stone, a junior basketball player whose father was the president of a traditionally black college in Texas; and Linton Johnson, a sophomore football player from an exclusive prep school in Connecticut. If they overheard the kinds of comments Louis and I were exposed to, they must have questioned why they ever came to Columbia. Some of Columbia's football players were vocal, unrepentant racists. Members of one of the largest football fraternities, Alpha Chi Rho, were notorious for attacking African students at the West End Bar if they were found sitting at tables with white women. One white freshman defensive back from South Africa bragged that he had "killed six niggers" while working as a mercenary in Rhodesia. Mild-mannered Southern athletes sometimes turned out to be unabashed defenders of segregation, people who saw blacks as primitive sexual predators who would destroy white civilization if they were not kept confined and controlled. Arguing with them was very different from arguing with working-class Jews who supported civil rights in principle but feared that an influx of blacks might destabilize their neighborhoods. When I tried to talk about race with Rick Roberts, a normally easygoing wrestler from Texas, he went into a tirade against integration that ended with the question that was meant to end all debate: "Would you want your daughter to marry a nigger?"

The undercurrent of rage and hysteria in Rick's voice frightened me. I wondered what it was like for Robert to know that some of his classmates viewed blacks with such contempt. Although everyone on our floor treated Robert with respect, he must have overheard some of the arguments about civil rights and the whispered comments about "niggers." While the university made every attempt to make race issues invisible, they were an obvious source of division on its campus, just as they were in my own neighborhood and the country at large. I spent a good deal of time thinking about this problem that seemed to be tearing America apart.

Adjusting to Columbia both socially and academically was so difficult for me, however, that my emerging political passions took a backseat to my individual problems. Accustomed to getting 95s in high school with little effort, I now had to study four or five hours a night just to get a B. Social life was complicated too. There were no girls in my classes or in any of my extracurricular activities. To meet them I had to go to mixers or fraternity parties, which led me to pledge a fraternity, a process that occupied a good deal of the little free time I had.

But by the end of my freshman year, in the spring of 1963, events in the national civil rights movement had started to gnaw at my conscience. As I watched Bull Connor use police dogs and fire hoses against schoolchildren in the Birmingham desegregation battle, I started to feel that I had to do more than offer verbal support for integration. I was also profoundly influenced by a novel I read after my spring final exams, James Baldwin's *Another Country*. This was the first black-authored book that I had ever read, and the experience of penetrating the emotional life of black characters and vicariously experiencing the effects of racism was eye-opening.

Before *Another Country*, I had never been exposed to a discourse that allowed me to understand that a black person living in the North might see the world differently than I did. So powerfully did the ethic of color blindness shape public discussions of race—in news reporting, music, sports, and Hollywood film—that none of my black teammates or acquaintances had ever talked to me honestly about how racial discrimination affected them, or how it felt to be black in a white-dominated society. My black friends acted as though their race was irrelevant, never letting their white friends know when they felt devalued or insulted. *Another Country* shattered this façade. Baldwin's portrayal of characters fatally damaged by America's racial divide forced me to imagine what it was like to live with persistent assaults on one's character and a crippling self-doubt.

That summer I took a job as a tennis counselor at a camp in the Delaware Valley run by the Erasmus High School basketball coach. In this all-white rural enclave, I had no outlet for my recently ignited political passions or my incipient intellectual engagement with the problem of race. Teaching tennis eight hours a day to wealthy Jewish kids from the suburbs of New York and Philadelphia bored and frustrated me. A few other counselors at the camp turned out to be kindred spirits. A drama counselor from Queens College, Andy Goodman, was inspired by the civil rights movement and intrigued by the Beat generation. On our days off, Andy, a few adventurous basketball counselors, and I would hitchhike around the Delaware Valley, sleeping in YMCAs and college dormitories, trying to meet women in bars, and occasionally getting harassed and chased by local teenagers who resented the college kids who invaded their area during the summer. Our adventures earned us a reputation as camp rebels, and we carried this identity back with us to our respective schools. Upon returning to Columbia, I decided to remake myself as a hipster. I got rid of my crew cut, grew a goatee, and started frequenting coffee shops and jazz clubs. I also went to my first meeting of the Columbia CORE chapter and volunteered to do tutoring and tenant organizing in East Harlem. Andy Goodman, at Queens College, underwent a similar odyssey, only his ended up tragically a year later in Mississippi.

The atmosphere of Columbia CORE dramatized the growing appeal of civil rights issues to white Columbia and Barnard students and the profound isolation of the University from African-American life. CORE was quickly becoming the university's largest political-action group, and I found a growing number of students poised to join the ongoing civil rights struggle. The first meeting I attended attracted nearly a hundred people. They were equally divided between men and women, and almost all were white. The participants had a distinctly bohemian appearance. Several women had hair down to their shoulders, and they wore long, flowing dresses with colorful beads and earrings. Many of the men had beards and mustaches; some wore cowboy boots and leather vests to complement jeans and workshirts. The group's leaders had a swashbuckling quality, projecting a sense that the hippest people on campus congregated at Columbia CORE. Men and women interacted with an ease and mutual respect that I had never seen at Columbia (or anywhere else!). The projects the group sponsored demonstrated that the civil rights movement was now seriously focusing on northern targets. CORE enrolled students to help uncover discrimination in housing, to participate in demonstrations against corporations that excluded blacks from skilled positions, to work with local tenants' organizations to resist displacement of low-income people, and to do fundraising for voter registration projects in the South. Although most CORE chapters in New York were multiracial or predominately black, Columbia CORE was an all-white organization whose culture was shaped more by the bohemianism of white liberal private schools than by African-American influences. Looking for a cross-cultural experience and an encounter with a low-income community, I passed over CORE's campus projects and signed up for one of the community programs in East Harlem.

One sunny day in October, I put on a suit and tie and walked across 110th Street from Broadway to Fifth Avenue, and then proceeded one block east and one block north to 111th and Park Avenue, where the American Friends Service Committee had an office. In this journey of less than a mile, which I would take scores of times over the next two years, I saw vast contrasts of culture and social condition. Leaving Columbia's West Side enclave, I walked down 110th Street from Broadway to Central Park West. The neighborhood became Puerto Rican, and my senses were bombarded by the smell of Caribbean cooking, the noise of children playing, and the sounds of Caribbean music coming from apartments, bars, and restaurants. When I reached Central Park and began walking toward Fifth Avenue, the neighborhood became African-American. Many of the residents of this part of Harlem were elderly, and the streets were quiet. When I crossed Fifth Avenue and headed north and then right on 111th Street, the noise level suddenly escalated and I was in the midst of hundreds of people talking, running, skipping rope, playing ball, dancing, and arguing. The language I heard most was Spanish. The smells were of food, car fumes, rotting garbage. In this neighborhood the buildings were five stories high. They had fire escapes in front, and their exteriors were gray and dark brown; their stonework and brick was cracked and smeared with pigeon droppings, their entrances crowded with people of all ages and a variety of colors ranging from beige to tan to dark brown. Columbia University seemed much farther away than a twenty-minute walk.

My first assignment was as a tutor in a local junior high school. My charges were two attractive, physically mature Puerto Rican girls of about fourteen years of age, whom I was told needed help with reading and social studies. Sensing the physical attraction and discomfort their presence evoked in me, they poked me, flirted with me, and sat on my lap when I tried to help them with their homework. Finally, when it was time to leave, they pulled me into a closet and tried to kiss me. Shaken by the experience, I told the school I would not return, and instead I volunteered for a tenant-organizing project run by the local office of the American Friends Service Committee. The program began with a two-week training session that taught us how to introduce ourselves to tenants, locate individuals with leadership ability who would agree to hold meetings at their apartments, and fill out forms for the city buildings department that would facilitate official inspections to identify violations of the city's housing codes. If we could document serious violations, the AFSC would put us in touch with lawyers who would represent the tenants in landlord-tenant court on a pro-bono basis.

Once my training ended, I was assigned the task of trying to organize the tenants of 87 East 111th Street, a grim-looking, five-story walkup directly across the street from the AFSC office. What I saw and experienced in that building would change my life. Its front door was unlocked, and the poorly lit main hallway smelled of urine. The hallway walls were riddled with gaping holes where rats had chewed through the wood and plaster. Plaster was falling from the hallway ceiling, and the staircase to the second-floor apartments was bent and buckled. Some of the apartments were no more inviting. One of the first tenants to invite me in was a heavyset black woman in her late teens or early twenties who seemed overwhelmed by the circumstances of her life. Her sink was filled with dirty dishes, clothes were strewn about her apartment, and her three-year-old ran around naked while she held a screaming baby. But most of the apartments I entered seemed like oases of order and pride in the midst of chaos. An elderly black couple invited me to share tea with them in a spotless apartment with dark-painted walls that sported new plaster patches where rat holes had been filled in. A Puerto Rican family with three children welcomed me to an equally clean apartment filled with brightly colored furniture, plants, prints on the walls, and a brand new television and hi fi. The values and goals of these families seemed strikingly similar to those of the upwardly mobile immigrant families I grew up among. But the problems they described to me—water damage from a leaking roof, intermittent heat and hot water, a broken front door, and huge rats that terrorized them and their children—had no analog in my experience. Whatever ideas I had acquired concerning the irresponsibility of slum dwellers shattered before my eyes. Here were admirable people trapped in intolerable conditions, and I was determined to try to help them.

Two nights a week, I would walk down from Columbia after dinner, speak to tenants about their problems, have them fill out official city forms, and try to identify a critical mass of tenants who were willing to form an organized council to negotiate with their landlord. It would often be close to midnight when I returned to campus. These encounters became as much a part of my college routine as attending class or going to tennis practice. I started to feel at home on the streets of East Harlem, enjoying the smell of Latin cooking, the pounding rhythms of Latin music, and, above all, the exhilarating feeling of defying fear and prejudice.

Little by little, the tenants' group at 87 East 111th Street made progress; building inspectors came and recorded violations, and the landlord started to make some minor repairs. But the tenants were soon emboldened by a rent-strike movement being organized in some black sections of Harlem by a charismatic neighborhood activist named Jesse Gray. A superb public relations specialist as well as a dedicated organizer, Gray had convinced the local press that thousands of Harlem tenants were prepared to withhold rent and demand an infusion of city money to help landlords make repairs and kill vermin. He also convinced the city council to consider legislation that would make rent withholding legal, and he found a group of lawyers willing to represent striking tenants on a pro-bono basis. Gray's movement prompted CORE chapters throughout the city to start organize rent strikes of their own and impelled the press to give the movement prominent coverage. This media attention helped convince the tenants in the building I was organizing that they could form a council and communicate directly with the landlord without fear of eviction, especially since they knew that CORE would provide them with free legal representation. After several meetings, they drew up a list of demands and asked me to deliver it personally to their landlord. I dutifully showed up in the landlord's office in my best suit and began sparring with him over whether he or the tenants were more responsible for the condition of the building. To my utter astonishment, he concluded the meeting by agreeing to put a lock on the front door, fix the roof, and seal up all the rat holes in the hallway and individual apartments, all of which he did shortly thereafter. For a few years at least, tenants in this building lived in healthier, safer conditions. (It was ultimately torn down and replaced by public housing.)

Nothing I had ever done gave me more personal satisfaction than getting this building repaired. I now had an experience that contradicted my parents' arguments about the immorality of the nonwhite poor as well as their pessimism about political action. This experience also helped me maintain a critical posture toward the education I was receiving at Columbia. The tenants I had organized were the kind of people that Columbia was systematically removing from Morningside Heights, pushing them into already crowded communities like East Harlem. It was hard enough being poor and dark skinned in America without the added indignity of living amid rats in decaying buildings. "Universities should be helping vulnerable people, not forcing them into ghettoes," I started to tell anyone who would listen.

Little by little, these political passions began to dominate my life, spilling over into my coursework and my personal relationships. I had a girlfriend at the time, a tall, black-haired Barnard student named Robin who came from a conservative Jewish family in Atlanta, as well as several female friends who were in Columbia's CORE chapter. These women became intellectual and political companions, and my experiences with them transformed my ideas about the boundaries of male-female relationships.

By the end of sophomore year, I was starting to enjoy the political ferment and cultural experimentation that the civil rights movement helped to stimulate on campuses throughout the United States. From Columbia to Berkeley, fighting social injustice and challenging traditional values appeared to go hand in hand. The brilliant folk singers Danny Kalb and David Bromberg hung around Columbia CORE, played at our parties, and did benefits for Southern civil rights organizers. Marijuana seemed to be a part of this rebellion. Since no one I knew in Brooklyn ever used marijuana, I hesitated to try it, but one of my CORE friends introduced me to the drug in the privacy of his apartment. Treating the whole experience as a kind of sacrament, he turned the lights down, put on a jazz record, and brought out a large water pipe that had marijuana in a bulb at the top. At each inhalation, the pipe gurgled as smoke passed through the water. Soon time appeared to slow down, sounds became distorted, and I became ravenously hungry. As

I walked up Broadway back to my dormitory, I was convinced the police would see that I was high and arrest me. When I got back to my room, I lay down on my bed and watched the ceiling spin. I enjoyed the sensation enough to repeat it every couple of weeks.

Amazingly, my academic performance actually improved during this period. As I ventured beyond the required sections of the Columbia curriculum, which were often taught by graduate students, I encountered pedagogy of breathtaking quality. Two brilliant young teachers made a lasting impression on me: Edward Said, an English professor, and Paul Noyes, a historian who taught eighteenth- and nineteenth-century European history. A dark-haired, well-built man of about thirty years of age, Said fixed a piercing stare upon any student whose attention wavered and whose body language failed to suggest a profound personal investment in European literature and philosophy. He would yell at students for having shirts unbuttoned, slouching in their chairs, or failing to participate in class discussions. Of Palestinian ancestry, Said, at this stage in his career, was an evangelist for the Western intellectual tradition he would later critique in *Orientalism*. He treated ideas as transcendent, almost holy, the only things that kept history and personal experience from devolving into chaos, and he persuaded his more impressionable students to struggle with the books he assigned as though their lives depended on it. In one sleepless night, I produced a paper for his course titled "Diderot and Kierkegaard as Interpreted through Hegel's *Phenomenology of Mind*," which almost met Said's exacting standards even though I could not understand what I had written three months later.

Paul Noyes made an equally powerful impression. Six feet, two inches tall, with long, flowing hair, Noyes paced the lecture hall as he spoke and kept a class of over one hundred spellbound with stories of war and revolution and portraits of people who changed the course of history. He could make you visualize the corrupt noblemen of France's ancien régime, angry peasants marching to reclaim their land, Napoleon's armies becoming bogged down in the Russian winter, Lenin rushing back from Switzerland to command the revolution. At a time when the civil rights movement was challenging centuries-old traditions of white supremacy in the United States, Noyes's lectures on the toppling of old regimes in France and Russia had a powerful resonance. It was easy to see organizers of the Student Non-Violent Coordinating Committee

(SNCC), then conducting voter-registration drives in Mississippi, as lat-ter-day heirs of the *narodniks* who tried to bring revolutionary ideas to Russia's peasantry in the late nineteenth century. Like many students in the course, I saw the study of the great European revolutions as pro-foundly relevant to my own life, or at least to the life I wanted to lead. During the spring semester I spent two weeks in the New York Public Library going through the minutes of the Paris Commune, which had seized control of the French capital in 1870, all in the original French, and imagined myself fighting and dying on the barricades with the com-munards. Through the power of Professor Noyes's rhetoric, and with the inspiration of books he assigned (including Isaac Deutscher's biogra-phy of Stalin and George Lefebvre's *History of the French Revolution*), I came to see writing history and making history as integrally connected.

For students of my generation, the civil rights movement brought politics and ideas to life in a new way. Nothing like it had existed in the United States for decades, at least since the New Deal and the indus-trial labor movement of the 1930s. Everywhere you looked, conflicts over the political, economic, and social status of African-Americans shaped the ways in which Americans voted and gauged their place in the world. Civil rights issues, northern and southern, dominated news-paper headlines and evening news broadcasts. Sit-ins in southern busi-ness districts, voter registration drives in remote southern towns, con-flicts over school integration and job discrimination in northern cities, and debates over the passage of the 1964 Civil Rights Act made all but the most apathetic white Americans aware that while the United States was busy presenting itself as the "defender of the free world," African-Americans in our own country did not enjoy basic constitutional rights. In Richard Hofstadter's *The American Political Tradition*, which I read in sophomore American history, I came across a quote from the abolition-ist Wendell Phillips that seemed to epitomize the contemporary strug-gle for racial justice: "None knows what it is to live until they lay their life as a sacrifice on the altar of some great cause." Wanting the grandeur of this modern crusade to spill over into my own life, I became a civil rights partisan, determined to raise the awareness of my peers about the nation's legacy of racial inequality. When the Columbia tennis team drove to Florida in the spring of 1964 for its annual two-week practice session at Rollins College, I called my teammates' attention to symbols of the southern social order visible along the highway: signs demanding "Impeach Earl Warren"; fields being plowed by black farmers using mules, not tractors; small, ramshackle, wooden sharecropper houses with crops coming up to their porches; restaurants where every patron was white. Throughout our travels, African-Americans interacted with us only as servants or menial workers. Shattering this pernicious social system seemed to be a formidable undertaking

Later that spring, this observation was borne out in the most tragic and personal manner. My hitchhiking partner from camp, Andy Goodman, was murdered in Mississippi as he tried to register black citizens to vote during a SNCC-sponsored campaign called Mississippi Freedom Summer. Among the first of nearly a thousand white college students to enter the state, Andy had been kidnapped and killed by members of the Ku Klux Klan, along with a black Mississippi resident, James Chaney, and a veteran SNCC activist, Michael Schwerner. If a person as kind and gentle as Andy could lose his life for the mere act of registering black people to vote, then Mississippi, and by extension the United States, harbored racial hatred of terrifying proportions.

That summer another series of events reinforced my perception that racial fears and divisions were tearing America apart. After years of talking about it, my entire extended family decided to leave Crown Heights for Queens. My parents moved to Rego Park, and my Uncle Mac and Aunt Esther, accompanied by my grandmother, moved to beachfront apartments in Rockaway. Although they claimed that these decisions were prompted by the death of my grandfather Charlie and the marriage of my cousin Stephen, I knew that the changing racial composition of Crown Heights must have been a contributing factor. Why else would my parents give up a two-bedroom apartment for a one-bedroom, leaving me without a room of my own, or my Uncle Mac move to a place that was much farther from his job? The apartment complexes they moved into were in all-white neighborhoods far from major areas of black settlement. They featured excellent shopping and large numbers of Jewish residents from similar backgrounds. The Crown Heights apartments they vacated would be rented by African-Americans, Afro-Caribbeans, or Hasidic Jews of the Lubovitch sect, whose religious leader had settled in a house on Eastern Parkway. I was suddenly separated from the familiar places of my youth, the ball fields and the alleys, the handball courts and hoops, the benches and stores and sidewalks, to take up residence on a couch in my parents' living room in an unfamiliar neighborhood. My emotional distance from my parents was now compounded by physical displacement. I felt like an exile in my parents' house. My commitment to civil rights, at least in my own mind, had set me on a collision course with my family.

When I returned to college for my junior year, Columbia CORE, more than ever, was at the center of a kaleidoscope of activities, from protesting University expansion to raising money for southern voter-registration drives, from demonstrating for jobs for African-Americans at the World's Fair in Flushing Meadow Park to working with local 1199 of the Drug and Hospital Workers to unionize nursing homes in New York City. I still played on the tennis team, I still belonged to a fraternity, but CORE became the focus of my campus life. I helped organize a CORE basketball team that challenged, and beat, the Columbia ROTC chapter, and I started taking my dates to CORE meetings rather than fraternity parties. Some of my athlete friends implied that I had less than honorable motives for my civil rights activism. "We know you're in it for the girls," they would say with a wink. "We hear those CORE girls are really wild."

The growing cultural division on campus between student protesters, who were predominantly Jewish in background, mixed in gender, and bohemian in style, and the athletes participating in contact sports, who were all male, predominantly Catholic, and prone to defend university authorities as a matter of principle, became even more apparent when CORE organized a large on-campus movement to support a unionization drive by university cafeteria workers. The political issue—whether one supported black and Latino cafeteria workers in seeking higher wages and union recognition—became confused by resentments about the values and appearance of the protesters. When the cafeteria workers went on strike and CORE members marched on the picket line with them, some conservative athletes made disparaging comments about the length of their hair, the sloppiness of their dress, their unathletic appearance, and their presumed sexual promiscuousness and preference for marijuana rather than alcohol. In response I started marching on picket lines in my varsity "C" jacket.

I also tried to engage the athletes I knew, some of whom I played basketball with on a regular basis, in discussions about the strike and civil rights in general. Most of them were urban and suburban Catholics whose families had worked hard to pull themselves out of poverty. Like

Crown Heights, their own neighborhoods were experiencing an influx of African-Americans, and their residents felt the pressure of ethnic succession acutely, especially because many of them owned their own homes. It deeply offended them that the northern civil rights movement had targeted de facto segregation by advocating open housing and school busing. They believed they had the right to protect their investment in their homes by keeping their neighborhoods and schools white. If African-Americans experienced social and economic discrimination, they argued, it was a problem for them to conquer through hard work and self-help, the way the Irish and Italians had done. "They've got to earn their equality," was a comment I often heard. In their eyes, offering sympathy for African-Americans, or asking for special government help, disturbed the Darwinian competition through which individuals and groups found their place in a free society. They believed that prejudice, as opposed to legal discrimination, was a natural human instinct that governments should challenge only for rare and compelling reasons. Whom somebody hires, lives with, rents to, or socializes with were private decisions, not subjects for government regulation.

Their arguments, which were perfected by conservative intellectuals of the day like William F. Buckley and Barry Goldwater, were coherent and challenging, even though they expressed a far more optimistic view of the power of markets to dispense justice than I could accept. But some of their opposition to the civil rights movement seemed more visceral than cerebral. The prospect of African-Americans penetrating their neighborhoods, workplaces, and intimate social circles genuinely *upset* them. They seemed to view African-Americans as different from whites—more primitive, more sexual, less capable of rational thought—and feared they would destabilize the communities they entered. Moreover, the same individuals who feared racial integration also despised white men who adopted a countercultural style and women who flouted traditional sexual mores and gender roles. Brought up to believe that sex and friendship were mutually incompatible and that "good girls" remained virgins until they were married, they felt threatened by an emerging morality that allowed for sexual experimentation among men and women who were friends and social equals. The idea of the beatnik-protester as romantic hero, more attractive to women than the hypermasculine white athlete, evoked rage and envy.

Conversely, I welcomed many of the cultural changes that my conservative classmates feared, and my friendships and romantic relationships illustrated this. During my junior year, I became romantically involved with two Barnard students who came from very different backgrounds, but were equally drawn to the political and cultural ferment on campus. Barbara was a language and theater major from Brooklyn, a dark-haired woman from a lower-middle-class Jewish family who seemed to explode with energy and creativity. Amy was a history major from Connecticut, a tall blonde whose quick wit and a disciplined mind had been honed by an upper-middle-class Protestant family and an elite prep school. With both of these talented women, I found common ground in the dazzling array of rallies, meetings, lectures, and concerts that civil rights movement had brought to Columbia. Sharing this energy and idealism was a joy and a privilege.

My academic interests were also strongly influenced by the values of the civil rights movement. During the fall semester of my junior year, I did a participant-observer study of a family on East 111th Street whose twelve-year-old son I tutored twice a week. This experience taught me how to describe physical settings, evaluate personal feelings and cultural biases, and record social interactions among the people I was studied. It also introduced me to the methodology of cultural anthropology and allowed me to maintain ties with the East Harlem community where I had spent much of my sophomore year.

Additionally, my research for an American history class that year proved pivotal in my decision to study the history of race relations on a graduate level. My instructor in that course was Walter Metzger, a teacher who was legendary for the quality of his lectures and the fifty-page research papers he required. A tall, elegantly dressed man from a wealthy German-Jewish family, Professor Metzger veiled a passion for liberal ideals behind lectures that were precise, ironic, and sharply argued. The nation's leading expert on academic freedom, he was one of the few historians at Columbia whose course syllabus directed attention to race relations. One book he assigned during the fall semester, C. Vann Woodward's *Origins of the New South*, alerted me to a paradox of African-American history that I had never previously encountered. For some thirty years after the Civil War, Woodward pointed out, African-Americans in the South voted, competed for public office, and possessed civic and legal equality; the segregation codes and patterns of political exclusion that blacks were fighting during the fifties and sixties had been created at the turn of the century.

The fact that segregation was a twentieth-century phenomenon and not a direct outgrowth of slavery fascinated and disturbed me and prompted my research paper on the subject. In the process, I stumbled upon a remarkable source, the *Proceedings of the Alabama Constitutional Convention of 1901*. This document was three feet high and two feet wide, and it consisted of some four hundred pages that crumbled in my fingers. In it people argued about eliminating African-Americans as a force in Alabama politics and trying to create a white-supremacist social order within a color-blind constitutional system. African-American leaders warned their white colleagues about the threat this would pose to the hopes and aspirations of their people and to the character and values of the whites who cynically denied them equal protection of the law. While I was still not a fluent or comfortable writer, the material was so compelling that I was able to produce fifty pages that allowed the voices of turn-of-the-century Alabamians to be heard. Professor Metzger returned the paper with a comment that I should consider a career as a historian. I went on to write a senior thesis under Professor Metzger on the Harlem rent-strike movement of 1963 and 1964 that would help pave the way for my graduate work and my subsequent academic career.

By the time I entered my senior year at Columbia, civil rights and race relations had become the central passion in my life, the organizing principle of my activism, my social life, the focus of my scholarship, and my plans for a future career. But this new identity rested on a powerful paradox. The classrooms where I learned history and the CORE meetings I attended had a minuscule black presence, and with the exception of my work in East Harlem, my life was almost entirely devoid of sustained contact with black people. This would soon change.

4   Meeting Ruthie

LEON TROTSKY once said, "You might not be interested in history, but history is interested in you." Many young Americans discovered this, to their sorrow, when they were called to fight a war in a country they had never heard of against an enemy they could not see. I discovered it when I became romantically involved with an African-American woman and found myself violating one of the most powerful racial taboos in the United States. In the 1960s, interracial relationships were still illegal in many states, and many white Americans regarded them as immoral, and even horrifying. Nothing could prepare a young white person, even one who was a civil rights activist, for the undisguised looks of disapproval and even hatred an interracial couple regularly elicited when they walked arm in arm down the street or sat together on the subway. Nothing could prepare a child for the hysteria of parents who saw his love interest as the source of family humiliation and who regarded marriage across the color line as a symbol of social death. And nothing could prepare a person for the racial stereotypes that came pouring into one's mind in moments of intimacy or in the conflicts that inevitably arose when people lived together in close quarters. Studying racism could be challenging. Contesting it through political action could be difficult and discouraging. But being the object of racial hatred and experiencing the power of racial feelings in one's own subconscious mind, day in day out, was far more elemental, something no academic experience could really train you for.

When I met "Ruthie," who would become my companion for six years, I was not an activist seeking to defy tradition; I was a young man looking for female companionship. Ironically, we met through a chance encounter at a party, not at a CORE meeting or a civil rights demonstration. Since the summer of my junior year, I had gone out with several women, but none of the relationships had lasted. Unattached and restless, I showed up one cold night in January at a party hosted by friends on the Columbia basketball team. The team was the only truly interracial group in the entire university, and when members threw a party, word went out to black students at several local schools. Of about seventy people at the party, maybe a third were black. It was the largest group of African-Americans I had ever seen at Columbia. Taking stock of the other partygoers, I found I knew most of the men but only a few of the women. After having a drink, I introduced myself to an attractive African-American woman of medium height and asked her to dance. We spent an hour and a half dancing together in the darkened room. During the slower and quieter songs, we managed to exchange some minimal information. I found out that her name was Ruthie, she attended City College, and that she knew one of the men who threw the party, but not much more. After several drinks and many slow dances, I began to feel the force of physical attraction more strongly than I had in a long time. And by the way we were clinging to one another, it was clear that Ruthie felt the same way. A voice in my head said, "Mark, you're becoming attracted to a black woman," but it was the voice of curiosity rather than caution. We ended up going to her apartment on West 99th and collapsing into bed. At first, nerves, alcohol, or perhaps some demon that my parents had planted in my racial unconscious got in the way, and I couldn't perform. But the excitement of the occasion and the kindness of the woman I was with gradually eroded these barriers. When I woke up the next morning, I looked at Ruthie with curiosity and gratitude. As the morning light illuminated her features, I realized she was the best-looking woman I had ever been intimate with. I wanted to see her again, and her warm, affectionate manner suggested mutual interest. Before leaving, I arranged to take her out the following weekend. Walking back to Columbia, I felt as though an important missing piece in my life had fallen into place.

In the following days, I tried to sort out my thoughts. I knew from studies of American history and talks with southern students in the Columbia dorms that interracial intimacy could bring out the worst in white Americans. White southerners viewed "social equality"—their term for interracial socializing—as a grave threat to the fabric of civilization. African-American men had been lynched for participating in consensual sexual relations with white women, and in one highly publicized incident, the Emmett Till case, a black teenager was lynched in Mississippi merely for whistling at a white woman. While northern whites lacked elaborate theories about interracial intimacy, they did seem to believe that close ties with African-Americans threatened their social status. I never met an interracial couple in all my years in Brooklyn, either among my parents' generation or my own. But on the Columbia campus, these taboos were slowly receding. Several of the black basketball players at Columbia dated white women, apparently without incident, and an interracial couple of long standing was a part of my social circle. Knowing this couple allowed me to feel that dating a black woman would not create problems within my group of friends, or draw much attention on campus.

Nevertheless, in my next meeting with Ruthie I felt an undercurrent of tension and excitement that probably would not have been present if she were a white woman. Because we had become intimate without a great deal of conversation, and because I had never had a close friend who was African-American, I found Ruthie mysterious. On our first few dates, I encouraged her to talk about herself, and in the process, get more of a context for our physical attraction. A beautiful woman with a reserved manner, Ruthie did almost nothing to call attention to her appearance. About five feet, seven inches in height and weighing 125 pounds with dark brown skin and medium-length hair that she straightened and parted with a "hot comb." Ruthie had classic West African features set off by the high cheekbones of an Indian ancestor. She could look regal, and even intimidating, but she lit up a room when she smiled. Modest in her choice of clothes—usually jeans or inexpensive jumpers— she had the manner of someone who had worked hard all her life and had no time for frills. Ruthie had grown up as one of nine children in an industrious African-American family in rural Georgia, and she still showed the marks of her southern upbringing. Her father, who operated under the protection of a white patron, had built a successful construction business in the face of great hostility from poorer whites; her mother was a deeply religious person who read voraciously and wanted her children to get an education. Ruthie, who had been sent to live with a sister in the Bronx after graduating from high school, was the first person in her family to attend college. She had started at Bronx Community and had transferred to City College, where she was a part-time student. She held two jobs, one as a counselor at a Police Athletic League center in the South Bronx and the other as a personal assistant to the director of an educational foundation on the Upper West Side. She lived in an apartment with three white roommates, all of them City College students.

I quickly saw that Ruthie had more experience crossing the color line than I did. Although she had grown up in a segregated environment, many of the people she now interacted with were white. And I was not the first white man she had dated. She had been in a relationship with a white Columbia law student for nearly a year, and had broken it off when he expressed interest in marriage. By the time we had gone out together three or four times, we both realized that something special was happening between us. I marveled at the way Ruthie could put me at ease, and I was thrilled that a woman I found so beautiful was responding to me in this way.

Ruthie answered my questions about her life with the thoughtful air of someone who was bridging two cultures. She spoke with deep affection of her mother, who had sparked her interest in learning and encouraged her to escape the parochialism of her small southern town, but she was not sure her parents would approve of our relationship. "When you go up North," her mother had told her, "you will find white people who are willing to help you, but they will never accept you as part of their family, so be careful not to get hurt."

Although Ruthie did not necessarily agree with this, she made it clear that she was not about to let herself get seriously involved with any man, especially a white one, unless he was educated, ambitious, and comfortable around black people. I often sensed that she was listening to the details of my life and trying to decide whether I was the kind of person she wanted. The fact that I was Jewish seemed to reassure her, or at least give her a reference point for understanding my racial liberalism. Her favorite English professor at Bronx Community College, her much-respected employer at the educational foundation, and her best female friends in New York were all Jewish. She saw Jews as an intermediary group between antagonistic races, a people whose history made them critical of racial prejudice and more willing than most whites to accept blacks as co-workers and friends.

As Ruthie and I grew closer, we drew comfort and support from a large network of friends. My three roommates, Jewish intellectuals whose self-deprecating humor and references to Freud, Marx, and foreign films now seem like material for a Woody Allen script, enthusiastically welcomed Ruthie into our social circle. Supportive of our relationship as a matter of principle, they appreciated Ruthie both as an audience for their madcap humor and as a confidante with whom they

could discuss personal problems. Ruthie's roommates were equally welcoming. Like many City College students, they were earthy, street-smart
individuals from working- and lower-middle-class families, and they
welcomed me as a kindred spirit despite my Ivy League pedigree. Since
two of Ruthie's three roommates were dating black men, the interracial
dimension of our relationship was hardly an issue. I enjoyed being in
their apartment and listening to their vivid, bawdy descriptions of the
men they knew, complete with clinical descriptions of their bone structure, muscle tone, and the length and shape of their penises. In the
spring of 1966, a time when the nonviolent civil rights movement had
reached its peak, Ruthie and I could not have found a better social network for an interracial relationship than white Jewish college students
living on Manhattan's Upper West Side.

Ruthie's sister, Darlene, treated us with equal warmth. Darlene sold
flowers at a hotel in midtown Manhattan and moonlighted as a barmaid
in the Bronx, and she lived in an apartment building just east of the
Grand Concourse and just north of 167th Street. In her neighborhood,
art deco apartment houses were rapidly being abandoned by their middle-class Jewish residents and rented by black and Puerto Rican families with lower incomes. Its streets and sidewalks were crowded with
people of various ages, races, and ethnicities: old Jewish women carrying groceries or sitting on folding chairs, black girls in pigtails playing
double dutch on the sidewalks, black and Puerto Rican boys chasing one
another through the street while their teenage brothers listened to music
or threw footballs, young mothers sitting on stoops with their babies,
sturdily built men walking to and from the subway in work uniforms,
and colorfully dressed hustlers conducting business and telling stories
in front of neighborhood bars. When Ruthie and I walked through this
neighborhood, nobody gave us a second glance.

Darlene's building, a six-story walkup with marble hallways, had
seen better days. Its halls were dirty, its walls cracked and peeling; the
apartments needed new windows. But Darlene's one-bedroom apartment was spotlessly clean, smelled of delicious food, and had been dec-
orated with a flamboyance that matched the appearance of its inhabi-
tant. Darlene was five feet, nine inches tall, with perfectly symmetrical
features, smooth brown skin, long legs, and a large bust that she showcased with expensive, brightly colored outfits with plunging necklines.
She was breathtakingly beautiful in a totally different manner than

Ruthie, who played down her attractiveness with shapeless, functional clothing. Darlene had the style of a showgirl or film star, someone who made a living from appealing to the fantasies of men. A high school dropout, she regarded her beauty as her one marketable asset. Darlene was one of the kindest and most generous people I ever met. She cooked for us, introduced us to her friends, gave Ruthie presents, and made us, as a couple, feel appreciated and loved. Several times a month, Ruthie and I would come to her house, eat delicious, southern-style dinners of chicken, ham, and collard greens, and spend the night on the king-sized bed in her bedroom, which was adorned with expensive mirrors, artificial flowers, and plush curtains and carpeting. Whatever happened to us in the outside world, Darlene's apartment remained a reliable safe haven.

As Ruthie and I spent more time in public places, we increasingly came to appreciate the hospitality and tolerance of those who cared for us. Going about our daily lives, we became targets for an expressive variety of hate looks, contemptuous comments, murmurs of astonishment, and occasional threats. Once, on a subway bound for the Bronx, an old Irish man seated next to us started muttering "nigger lover" under his breath. I tried to ignore him, but he kept saying it louder and louder, until I stood over him with a raised fist and said, "You'd better shut up or I'll knock your teeth out." When he saw the anger in my eye, he moved, but his actions were disconcerting, especially since none of the other passengers had done anything to rebuke him. We were also the repeated targets of hate looks and comments from older Jewish women, who appeared to blame Ruthie for taking an eligible Jewish boy off the market. Once, on West End Avenue, a Jewish woman spat on the ground when she saw us and said, "Ugh, disgusting! I bet your mother must be ashamed of you!" Down-and-out black men, who lived in sizable numbers in residence hotels on the Upper West Side, also felt free to comment. "Hey baby, what you doin' with that white man when I can satisfy all your needs," they would call out to Ruthie as we walked by. One of the most intimidating groups we had to contend with were white working-class teenagers and young men. Once, in Greenwich Village, a group of tough-looking young white males surrounded us and started shouting insults. A policeman forced them to disperse before any punches were thrown, but the incident left me frightened and shaking with rage.

After a number of these encounters, I walked through the city with a chip on my shoulder, ready to fight anyone who invaded our space. No one ever physically attacked us, but I found it difficult to walk down the street with Ruthie in a carefree manner, especially outside of the Columbia area or Darlene's multiethnic Bronx neighborhood. The level of hostility directed at us sometimes overwhelmed me, my mind veering between paranoia and vigilance. But I refused to let the retrograde attitudes of strangers drive me from away a woman I was falling in love with. If we ever broke up, I told myself, it would not be because I was afraid to stand up to racism.

To my horror, I soon began to realize that the racism I abhorred in others also lurked within me, planted in my unconscious by years of living in a society that systematically devalued the abilities and accomplishments of African-Americans. One day when Ruthie was out shopping, I found a paper that she had written for an English course and started reading it. To my surprise, and great relief, it was written in clear, grammatically perfect prose and was filled with sharp and original comments. But why had I been surprised that Ruthie was an excellent student? Her reluctance to join in intellectual debates with my roommates led me see to her as someone who was better suited to dealing with the practical realities of life than with history, literature, or social science. Worse yet, I had seen her through the lens of an insidious racial stereotype—that blacks were slower, less academically gifted, less suited for abstract thinking than whites. Seeing beyond these stereotypes, I realized, would take tremendous effort. As Malcolm X had recently observed in his *Autobiography*, racial injustice could not be ended merely by changing racist laws. White supremacy lived in the conscious and unconscious mind of every American, white and black. Uprooting it might take centuries of sustained effort.

These unsettling encounters with racism occurred at a time when my confidence as a student was at an all-time high and my professors were encouraging me to pursue an academic career. Three years of composing term papers had taught me to write clearly, if not fluently, and to approach historical research with diligence and persistence. When the leader of the Harlem rent-strike movement, Jesse Gray, refused to be interviewed for my senior thesis, I methodically tracked down all of his assistants and found out that Gray had a wealthy Jewish press agent who coordinated his media campaign and knew every detail of the

Harlem movement. When I showed up at this man's apartment on West End Avenue, he looked me over carefully, invited me to sit down, and gave me so many valuable details that my arm hurt after two hours of taking notes. My thesis supervisor was impressed with the information I had obtained and encouraged me to continue interviewing my inform- ant, who seemed quite eager to go on. However, the next time I visited his apartment, this gentleman greeted me wearing a bathrobe and lit- tle else, and he held the entire two-hour interview with his legs and chest barely covered. I was dazzled by the quality of the information though somewhat perplexed by his appearance. On my next visit, he wore the same scanty attire and started asking about my personal life. When he found out I played tennis for Columbia, he asked if he could come to one of my matches and showed up as a spectator wearing a long fur coat. A more alert person might have figured out that he was gay and interested in me sexually, but I was so preoccupied with my research and so naïve about homosexuality that I just pressed him for every scrap of information as though nothing else were going on. The thesis I wrote helped me win an award and several fellowships that paid for four full years of graduate school.

Ruthie, who followed each detail of this research, took great satis- faction in the honors that came my way. Passionate about education, proud of her own difficult journey from rural Georgia to City College, Ruthie displayed great joy in telling her sister and roommates about my academic accomplishments. Each of us had a mission: Ruthie to carve a path to higher education and professional status, I to become a scholar who would explore America's race problem. As our missions merged, and our pride in one another grew, our emotional connection deepened powerfully.

By the end of my senior year, I was falling in love with Ruthie. The more time we spent together, the more attached to her I grew. I was entranced by her beauty and moved by her determination to create a better life for herself and her family, but I was also more at ease with her than any woman I had ever known. We felt comfortable lying next to one another in bed, sitting at the dinner table, walking through the park. Proud of being pioneers in challenging racial barriers, we also enjoyed moments of quiet intimacy and communal celebration. Our social life was rich and varied, consisting of dinners with family and friends, long conversations about our futures, and parties, movies, and concerts. Because so many friends supported us and nurtured us, we had time and space to enjoy one another without the pressures of the outside world constantly intruding on our relationship. We became confidants as well as lovers, able to share problems and insecurities as well as the activities we enjoyed. We felt stronger together than each of us did alone.

Nevertheless, racial tensions were never far from our consciousness. If falling in love was not a conscious political act, sustaining and defending our relationship *was*. Fully aware that we were challenging one of the country's most powerful taboos, we dared to hope, rather naïvely, that couples like us might be the wave of the future. At the time our relationship started to become serious (the spring of 1966), virtually all of the hostility we experienced was coming from whites. Many black people still viewed interracial dating as an extension of the civil rights movement; and their support, however short lived, contributed to our sense of optimism. Personally and politically, things seemed to be going our way. I had just accepted a four-year fellowship to Columbia graduate school in history and had found a summer job with a new educational program—Upward Bound—that was located on the Columbia campus. Ruthie needed about a year and a half to complete her degree and had numerous connections for jobs in social work and teaching. I was thinking of Ruthie as someone I might marry, and decided, with some trepidation, that it was time to tell my parents about my feelings for her.

In early June 1966, several weeks before my graduation, I took the subway to Rego Park to talk to my parents. In retrospect, my timing probably was not good. A year earlier my father had been diagnosed with Hodgkin's disease (cancer of the lymph system) and had just gone through a rigorous program of chemotherapy that had pushed the disease into remission but left him severely weakened. My mother, at 60 years old, found her job at Eli Whitney Vocational High School increasingly stressful, and she blamed the defiant behavior of the school's large group of black and Puerto Rican students. Since they had left Crown Heights, my parents' negative feelings toward blacks had only deepened in the face of riots in Watts and Harlem, and the growing racial tensions in New York City's public schools. I anticipated that they would respond negatively to the news that their son had an African-American girlfriend, but that did not deter me. My decision to tell them about Ruthie stemmed at once from a need for parental approval and a powerful element of defiance. For the first time in my life, I was financially independent. No matter how much my parents disapproved of my political activities or choice of friends, they no longer had the economic leverage to influence my life. In telling them about this deeply personal matter, I was challenging them to respect my autonomy.

My mother, one of the toughest people I knew, responded to my announcement by threatening to commit suicide. "How could you do this to me?" she asked over and over again. My father, uncharacteristically subdued, deferred to my mother's histrionics. "Your mother will never accept this," he kept repeating. As my mother tried to make herself pathetic to appeal to my sympathy, I observed her with cold anger and clinical detachment. In her mind, my association with a black woman negated our family's ascent into the middle class and undermined the prestige of my academic accomplishments. Among the second-generation Jews who were her friends and neighbors, "blackness" appeared to carry a stigma that no level of personal accomplishment could erase. I was threatening everything she had worked for her entire life. When I tried to point out that my mother might actually *like* Ruthie if she got to know her, that they were both ambitious, hard-working people with strong family loyalties, she refused to listen. But by the end of our conversation, my mother had retreated from her threat of suicide and assumed a bargaining stance more suited to her personality. She would continue to recognize me as her son, but she would refuse to acknowledge Ruthie's existence. If I wanted to see her and my father, I could visit them at their apartment, but only on the condition that I never talk about Ruthie or mention her name to anyone they knew.

By refusing to recognize Ruthie's existence, my parents hoped to force me to find a partner more suited to my status and position. The next day my mother sent me a letter spelling out their arguments against the relationship, which, she claimed, were based on class and culture as much as race. Refusing to mention Ruthie by name, she warned that "the girl [her term for Ruthie] is really very young and has no background and culture." She predicted a dire future if I did not "make a complete break now." "You are a brilliant catch," she concluded. "I know you want eventually to have a family life, but if you continue, you are really alone."

My mother's letter only deepened my commitment to Ruthie. I was hardly surprised by her appeal to guilt and self-interest, but her attacks on Ruthie's character were unfair. Ruthie herself seemed more subdued. She was obviously upset by my parents' posture, but not surprised. She urged me to have empathy and stay in contact with them. She told me she was perfectly happy to keep our relationship as it was and had no desire to get engaged or married in the near future. Her comments calmed me but did not change my sense of the situation. Through the deepest impulses in my character—my need for love and acceptance, my professional ambitions, my intellectual curiosity, and my competitive instincts—I had been drawn into a battle against racial divisions and prejudices that were deeply embedded in American culture. My parents had aligned themselves, at least in my mind, with racists and bigots, and nothing could erase my bitterness at what they had done. But I was also energized by their opposition. Conflict, whether in sports, politics, or personal relations, always got my juices flowing. I had long prided myself on never walking away from a fight and now, through forces beyond my control, I had been drawn into one of the greatest moral conflicts of my generation as a *full participant*. I was no longer a sympathetic liberal whose involvement in civil rights took place in the security of all-white enclaves: I was a person living on the boundary between black and white communities, someone whose daily life was touched by racial prejudice and whose personal happiness was invested in the struggle to overcome it. I was not alone. Many Americans, black and white alike, were stretching socially constructed definitions of racial identity that limited their development or prevented them from associating with anyone they pleased.

That summer Ruthie and I found a new community among a group of predominantly black high school students who lived on the Columbia campus as part of an experimental, federally funded program called Upward Bound. I had helped write the proposal for the Columbia program, which was called "Double Discovery." We recruited several hundred students from inner-city high schools throughout New York City to take college-level courses on the Columbia campus while making full use of the athletic facilities and cultural programs. The goal was to take talented students from low-income families and acclimate them to a college atmosphere while also exposing Columbia students, who were the program's counselors and administrators, to the culture and outlook of youngsters from New York's poorest neighborhoods. During its first summer, the program worked exactly as we had hoped. For the first time in its history, Columbia's campus dormitories housed large numbers of African-American students whose language and values bore the mark of the city's streets.

As a counselor in the program, I first encountered the students at an opening dance in the Columbia Student Center. I was dancing the "frug" with an African-American woman from Barnard, bouncing up and down in my usual fashion, when I noticed that a group of students had formed a circle around me and were laughing hysterically. When I asked what was wrong, they said that I looked funny jumping up and down like a jack in the box, and they offered to teach me a more graceful and rhythmic style. For the next hour, to the accompaniment of songs like "Ain't Too Proud to Beg" and "It's the Same Old Song," several young women in the program helped me "blacken" my dancing by substituting lateral for vertical movements, snapping my fingers in time to the music, rotating my hips, and shaking my shoulders and head. They were as generous about sharing their dance style as I hoped to be about sharing my academic skills.

I formed an immediate bond with the students in the program, especially the young men I supervised in the residence halls. My New York street bravado, which often offended people from comfortable backgrounds, helped draw these inner-city youngsters closer to me. When they saw me throwing elbows on the basketball court, gyrating on the dance floor, or losing my temper when disciplining another student, they saw a familiar figure, someone whose insecurity and aggressiveness reflected the experience of growing up male in working-class New York City neighborhoods. They had all been taught to hide their sensitivity beneath a façade of toughness. If you wanted to reach them, you had to appeal to their pride, to get them to believe that there was some gift inside them that needed to come out. Helping them find those gifts became my mission for that summer. I cajoled them, bribed them, followed them around to dances and ball games, even talked to their girlfriends in an attempt to get them to take their work seriously. When that failed, I asked Ruthie, whom I often brought to the program, to use her skills as a counselor to get them to open up.

With Ruthie's help, I formed a particularly deep bond with two students I supervised. One was Paul, a strikingly handsome, sensitive-looking African-American boy from the Jamaica section of Queens. His mother, a soft-spoken single parent who had given birth to Paul when she was fifteen, had a serious drinking problem. Paul was desperate for adult guidance. Initially wary of me, Paul started to trust me when he saw Ruthie and me together. By the middle of the summer, he was relating to us as surrogate parents, sharing with us his troubles at home, his adventures with females, and his academic problems and aspirations. Ruthie, in particular, became Paul's confidante and confessor, the person he talked to about everything that bothered him. Nor was this an isolated development. The more I brought Ruthie to events at Double Discovery, the more I realized that she had charisma with adolescents, something that made the most confused and troubled teenagers want to be with her and please her. Every time we appeared together on campus or attended a special event, crowds of students of both sexes would gather around her, asking her questions and telling her stories.

Even William, my most talented and ambitious student, responded to Ruthie and me together better than he did to me alone. Arguably the best student in the program, William was the child of a hard-working Jamaican woman who had reared him and his sister while pursuing a career as a registered nurse. William had excellent academic skills, a gracious manner with adults, and compassion for his fellow students who had difficulty in their lives. He became best friends with Paul, and the two spent most of their time together. For William, who had lacked a strong male influence in his life, my connection with a black woman he admired allowed him to use me as a guidepost for his aspirations. Destined for a professional success (he later became a television news executive), William bonded with Ruthie and me as a couple and told us he hoped to emulate our relationship when he became an adult.

Ruthie and I had many great moments with these young people, but one that remains etched in my memory is a trip we took to a teach-in against the Vietnam War in a Connecticut park. The atmosphere was relaxed and festive. With student draft deferments still intact, the war had not yet touched us personally, and we paid more attention to our picnic lunches and to Smoky and the Temptations playing on our portable record players than we did to the political speeches. In this pleasant setting, the students, who were predominantly black, and the counselors, who were predominantly white, felt completely at ease with one another, all unaware that the forces of history would not be kind to everyone there. One of the counselors, Ted Gold, a short, sweet-tempered Columbia student who loved the Knicks, would join the Weather

Underground at the height of the Vietnam War and die in a townhouse explosion in Greenwich Village while trying to build bombs. Paul, whom Ruthie and I virtually adopted, would bounce from school to school and relationship to relationship, never finding the economic or personal stability he seemed to crave. Keith, the most brilliant and politically sophisticated student in the program, would live most of his adult life as a homeless person in the area near Columbia, participating in campus movements but never finding a full-time job. At that moment, however, there was little sense of impending disaster. The integrationist dreams of the civil rights era seemed to come alive in our communal solidarity. In this crowd of inner-city teenagers and antiwar activists, Ruthie and I felt at peace.

5   Contested Territory

THE BLACK POWER movement began in 1966, with Stokely Carmichael's speech at a June civil rights march in Mississippi, and it became one of the most controversial episodes in the history of the civil rights movement. When SNCC and CORE turned themselves into all-black organizations, asking long-time white activists to leave their ranks, their actions implied not only that integration was an idea whose time had passed, but that friendship and personal intimacy between blacks and whites had become obstacles to black liberation. Black nationalist sentiment had been steadily growing since the late 1950s, but its dramatic articulation by heroes of the civil rights movement spread its influence to some of the most educated and assimilated segments of the black population. Elijah Muhammad and Malcolm X had initially built the Nation of Islam, the country's most influential nationalist organization, by recruiting on street corners and in prisons. But when the Howard University–educated Stokely Carmichael, in full view of the national media, called on blacks to take control of their own organizations and let America feel the wrath of a unified black community, his message struck a chord not just with battle-hardened civil rights workers; it also reached teachers and social workers, doctors and lawyers, playwrights and professors who felt integration and upward mobility had severed them from their roots and prevented them from fully excercising their leadership skills.

As the Black Power ethos spread from the civil rights movement to the black intelligentsia, it put a tremendous strain on interracial friendships as well as interracial organizations. When African-Americans demanded space to define their own goals and find their own voice, relations with white colleagues, friends, and even marriage partners sometimes cracked under the pressure. The political and cultural creativity unleashed by Black Power, reflected in an explosion of new organizations and new styles of dress and artistic expression, had a bittersweet quality for whites close to the black community. Some, especially those in CORE and SNCC, were forced to find new organizational outlets, but many others were also left wondering whether they could sustain interracial relationships and continue to play a role in the struggle for racial equality.

For nearly a year following Carmichael's speech, Ruthie and I were insulated from the effects of this powerful movement. Outside of Harlem, a politically aware black neighborhood that had been the scene of a riot in 1964, working-class black New Yorkers remained largely indifferent to separatist sentiments. In the neighborhoods surrounding Darlene's apartment, we never had to worry about hostility to our relationship. Darlene's neighbors and friends were hard-working people whose passion for food, music, and good times left little room for drawing color lines. When everyone sat down for dinner or hit the floor to dance to James Brown, nobody seemed to care that Ruthie and I were a mixed-race couple. We encountered a similar atmosphere when we visited James and his mother in South Jamaica, or William and his mother in the Sands Project in downtown Brooklyn. We felt little tension walking the streets and were warmly welcomed into people's homes.

Sensitive to the politics of public space, Ruthie and I consciously sought out communities where we could socialize comfortably. Columbia, for the moment, was one of those. In my first year in graduate school, I found a cohort of radical students who welcomed Ruthie and strongly encouraged my interest in African-American history. Among the hundred men and women entering Columbia's master's program in American history, several white students had backgrounds in the civil rights movement or an intellectual interest in political movements for racial justice. In a social history seminar taught by Robert Cross, I met two people in the class ahead of me planning to do dissertations on African-American history, William Chafe and Harvard Sitkoff. Each would later write major works in the field. In my own class, I became closest to Laura Foner, a former civil rights worker whose father, Philip Foner, was the author of several well-known books on African-American and labor history. For Laura, who had done voter registration with SNCC in Mississippi, race was the central moral and political issue in American life, and we spent many hours discussing how to do our historical work in a manner that advanced the cause of racial equality.

I also found a mentor on the Columbia faculty in the person of James Shenton, a charismatic professor of nineteenth-century American history who gave moral and financial support to a generation of Columbia student activists. A middle-aged, single man who lived with his mother in New Jersey, Shenton used his substantial inheritance to take his students to dinner in elegant New York restaurants and help them through personal crises. As a lecturer, Shenton had no equal on the Columbia faculty. Using humor, drama, and a powerful speaking voice, he brought the great conflicts of the Jacksonian era and the Civil War to life in his classes and encouraged his students to test their historical vision by participating in movements for social change. His words had special meaning because he lived by the principles he espoused. Shenton was one of the few Columbia faculty members to support the unionization of Columbia's cafeteria workers, and in 1965 he flew to Selma, Alabama, to march for voting rights. He became my confidant, someone I could talk to about my relationship with Ruthie, my problems with my parents, and my attempts to reconcile history and political activism. I needed such encouragement because my master's supervisor, William Leuchtenberg, an esteemed historian of the New Deal, saw my political enthusiasms as an obstacle, rather than an asset, to my scholarly work. A red-faced, sandy-haired man with a hearty manner and the cold efficiency of a corporate executive, Professor Leuchtenberg encouraged research in African-American history but was skeptical that I could maintain the appropriate scholarly distance from my subject matter. He allowed me to do my master's essay on the Southern Tenants Farmers Union (STFU), an interracial sharecroppers' union that arose in Arkansas in the depths of the Depression, but warned that I would have to prove to him that I could write about this subject without turning my essay into a platform for radical socialist ideas. My research for this project required a visit over the Christmas break to the Southern Historical Collection in Chapel Hill, North Carolina, where the Southern Tenants Farmers Union papers were housed.

Those ten days at the University of North Carolina gave me a great deal to think about. The deserted campus, with its tall trees, beautiful lawns and walkways, and colonial architecture had an air of southern gentility that thinly masked the painful legacies of slavery and segregation. The staff at the Southern Historical Collection, like everyone else I met at the University, was gracious and hospitable, but they worked in an environment where racial hierarchy was taken for granted. The entire research staff of the library was white; all its cleaning staff was black. The same pattern prevailed in Chapel Hill's small business district, where I went for meals. The stores and restaurants, housed in one- and two-story brick buildings or wood-frame houses, had friendly and relaxed white employees who interacted with the public while black cleaning personnel and kitchen staff hovered in the background. Although the business district had been desegregated several years before, only whites patronized the stores. Chapel Hill's race relations seemed frozen in time. The speech and body language of its African-American service workers, at least to my northern sensibilities, seemed extracted from a Hollywood plantation epic. If you asked them a question, they replied with a deference so patently exaggerated that you wondered whether they secretly wanted to murder you. After ten days of being addressed as "boss" and "captain" by black building personnel and restaurant workers, and being asked, "How are y'all today" by white librarians, waitresses, and store owners, I started seeing images of lynch mobs, cross burnings, and white-robed Klansmen, and I wondered how my gracious white hosts would react if Ruthie and I walked around campus with our arms around one another. For the South, Chapel Hill was liberal and cosmopolitan, but the accumulated weight of three hundred of years of white violence and paternalism still shaped the way its black and white residents interacted with one another, and I felt like an alien in their midst, someone whose personal life challenged the basic principles of their social order.

Fortunately, my research in the Southern Tenants Farmers Union archives exposed me to a very different narrative of southern history, a fascinating story of black and white farmers trying to overcome segregation and accumulated racial grievances to achieve a better life for themselves and their families. In 1934 a group of black and white sharecroppers in rural Arkansas united to formulate a common response to the crop-reduction programs of the New Deal, which were driving them to the edge of starvation and threatened to force them off the land. Such interracial meetings, which had not been seen in rural Arkansas since the 1890s, were attacked by local landowners but supported by the Socialist Party, which sent organizers to the area to help these farmers create a union. For the next six years, this union fought an uphill battle against night riders, sheriffs, and economic trends that were destroying the viability of cotton agriculture. In the face of terror and intimidation, the union organized cotton pickers' strikes, fought for a fair share of the government farm subsidies, lobbied Congress and the Roosevelt administration to build homes for evicted sharecroppers, and helped draw the attention of the nation to the lives of its poorest farmers. The records of the union, which consisted of organizers' reports, testimony from government hearings, and correspondence between sharecroppers and union and government officials, offered a heart-rending picture of poor, uneducated people simultaneously struggling to feed their families during a devastating economic crisis and trying to overcome racial barriers that some Americans believed were the law of nature and the will of God. In a section of Arkansas where almost a hundred African-Americans had been murdered just fifteen years earlier, in an incident known as the "Elaine Massacre," former members of the Klan and former followers of Marcus Garvey stood up at union meetings and said that neither group could progress without the help of the other.

These Arkansas sharecroppers, and the radical organizers who risked their lives to help them, belonged to a tradition of resistance that could be traced back to the abolitionists and the Underground Railroad. They had said no to one of the dominant mythologies of the region and their nation: that blacks and whites were two different peoples condemned to be enemies. That they did this in rural Arkansas at the height of the Depression was not just an inspirational model of courage in the face of race hatred; it also suggested that movements that united working-class whites and blacks on the basis of common economic interests represented a powerful weapon against segregation. As I pondered the contrast between the harsh and violent history of the STFU, and the quiet beauty of the Southern university town where I was staying, there was no question which tradition I was drawn to. I far preferred the uncertainties and dangers of a grassroots struggle for racial and economic justice to the genteel paternalism practiced by Chapel Hill's business leaders and academics. If I drew any lesson from this research, it was that America's radicals, not its liberals, would have to lead my generation's effort to transcend the nation's racial divisions.

When I returned to Columbia, I started working with several community organizations seeking to prevent Columbia from constructing a new gymnasium in Morningside Park. Columbia's plan to construct a private athletic facility in a public park separating Harlem from Morningside Heights had outraged community activists, who feared that this might be the first step in a university strategy to transform Harlem into

a white middle-class neighborhood. Since Columbia CORE had dissolved following the transformation of its parent body into an all-black
organization, I joined the movement to stop the gym through a community organization that ran tutoring and tenant-organizing programs
out of an office on West 104th between Amsterdam and Columbus
Avenues. Located less than ten blocks from the Columbia campus, this
neighborhood, which adjoined a large low-income housing project, was
almost entirely black and Puerto Rican.

Around this time, the antiwar movement on the Columbia campus
also attracted my attention, but my participation in it was initially
ambivalent. Deeply preoccupied with race, I disliked seeing student
energies diverted into foreign policy issues. But by the early months of
1967, Vietnam had intruded so powerfully into the lives of America's
young people that no politically conscious person could ignore it.
Nearly half a million American soldiers, largely drawn from America's
poorest neighborhoods, were now fighting in Vietnam, and their death
tolls approached one thousand a month. American air power and chemical warfare were devastating the Vietnamese countryside and killing
many civilians. Student draft deferments, which had allowed most college students to view the war from a safe distance, were gradually being
phased out. A war in a country eight thousand miles away, against an
enemy who posed no direct danger to the United States, now threatened
to pull me away from my work, my friends, and everyone I loved. Pre-
venting communist guerrillas from creating a unified Vietnam was not
a cause I was willing to die for. It also did not justify killing and maim-
ing Vietnamese peasants, siphoning funds from antipoverty programs,
distracting attention from America's racial issues, and exploiting the
patriotism of America's most vulnerable young men. Frightened, I
started to talk with friends about the draft and I began participating in
antiwar activities on the Columbia campus, most of which were sponsored by the Columbia chapter of Students for a Democratic Society
(SDS).

In doing so, I had to fight my discomfort with the political style of
the SDS leaders, who seemed so caught up in Marxist rhetoric that the
human dimensions of the Vietnam crisis were eclipsed. Immersed in a
theoretical discourse influenced by the émigré philosopher Herbert
Marcuse, they often seemed condescending when speaking to a large
audience. But they were also among the first at Columbia to speak out

against the war and to identify targets on campus that could be a focus of antiwar sentiment. They demonstrated against the Reserve Officers Training Corps (ROTC), which trained students to become junior military officers upon graduation; the Dow Chemical Company, a manufacturer of napalm; the Selective Service; and the Institute for Defense Analysis, a campus "think tank" funded by the Department of Defense. They were tireless and courageous, and when they held a march and rally on the Columbia campus in early spring 1967, I decided to participate. To distinguish myself from the SDS members and show that even athletes could oppose the war, I marched in an interracial contingent of thirty athletes who carried signs saying "jocks for peace."

The march took place in a menacing atmosphere. While four hundred chanting demonstrators, most of whom were not SDS members, marched around Columbia's main quadrangle, a hundred football players and wrestlers shouted insults. Their faces red with anger and veins bulging from their necks, these hecklers called the protesters cowards and faggots, challenged them to fight, and at one point chanted, "Jews and niggers go back to Russia." I had never before seen such anger directed at demonstrators at Columbia, even during the CORE-led cafeteria strike, and it offered a sobering picture of the social divisions the war inspired. In culture and class background, Columbia's football players were far more representative of mainstream America than most Columbia students. In outer-borough New York neighborhoods and in working-class communities throughout the country, antiwar protests were still seen as a form of treason and, worse yet, a betrayal of the young men from neighborhoods like theirs who were doing most of the fighting. On a single afternoon, we got a small glimpse of how divisive Vietnam would be. For those of us who opposed the war, it offered frightening evidence of how much people hated us outside of our safe haven in Morningside Heights.

What were our choices? Most people I knew did not want to see their lives swallowed up in hatred and rage. They certainly did not want to die in a remote jungle battlefield, but they also didn't want the atmosphere of the battlefield to dominate their lives in the United States, turning them into unthinking patriots or hard-edged political ideologues. For many young people, saying no to the war meant refusing to be brutalized by its influence, refusing to turn hard, cold, and bitter, and refusing to turn their backs on dreams of social justice and racial harmony.

People who felt this way expressed themselves by growing their hair long, wearing colorful clothes, and putting on beads and long earrings. They celebrated sexual pleasure and communal love, they experimented with LSD and marijuana, and they listened to music that satirized a society that had gone mad with war. By the spring of 1967, several thousand people in the Columbia area had incorporated countercultural symbols into their personal appearance, and one could find tens of thousands of similarly dressed young people in neighborhoods throughout the city, especially Greenwich Village and the Lower East Side.

Ruthie and I both felt more powerfully attracted to this spontaneous cultural movement than to organized antiwar protests. With whites having been expelled from CORE and SNCC, and racially mixed student organizations gone from the political landscape, the counterculture emerged as the nation's most powerful, if idiosyncratic, practitioner of integrationist cultural politics. Although most people who joined the counterculture were white and middle class, its music and symbolism were racially hybrid. Black musicians like Jimi Hendrix and Sly Stone, who fused funk and rhythm and blues with free-form improvisation (and created the first popular musical groups that were racially mixed), did much to shape the movement's personality, as did white artists like Janis Joplin, who modeled themselves on black blues singers. With men growing mustaches and beards, women dispensing with makeup, hair spray, and constricting undergarments, and both sexes draping themselves in loose, colorful clothing (and in some settings dispensing with clothing altogether), interracial couples hardly stood out as symbols of unconventional behavior. Because people in the counterculture viewed interracial love as a symbol of personal freedom, the movement's growth gave Ruthie and me camouflage in public places, a welcome relief from stares and hate looks. It was liberating to be in a large crowd of people whom mainstream America regarded as "freaks" and who regarded interracial intimacy as normal and natural, something to be celebrated in public rather than hidden in shame.

Ruthie's personal entrée into the counterculture came through a flamboyant, white, red-haired Oriental-studies major named Carol who rented in a room in Ruthie's apartment. A student at Columbia's School of General Studies, Carol had many male admirers and a theatrical sense of life. She and Ruthie loved to walk arm and arm up Broadway or West End Avenue, titillating men with their physical beauty and the striking contrast of hair and skin. Carol touched a joyful side of Ruthie that rarely came out in public, an "in your face" spirit of defiance hidden within the Georgia church girl. When the three of us got high together, a blissful smile would spread across Ruthie's dignified features and she would dissolve into giggles, the pressures of a difficult life temporarily forgotten. For some people, these moments of fantasy and escape became peak experiences, the main thing that made life worth living. For Ruthie and me, they were brief interludes that made the burden of defying racial prejudice less weighty. When Carol came back from the record store with the Beatles' new *Sergeant Pepper* album, and we lit up joints and listened to "A Day in the Life," we had no illusions that we were stopping the war, banishing racism, or healing a divided nation. But we did feel bound together in a sacrament of resistance, a refusal, at least for that moment, to allow fear and hatred to dominate our lives.

These journeys into the counterculture, interestingly, did not alienate Ruthie and me from her extended family or make us less comfortable in a working-class African-American milieu. Since African-American folk culture provided much of the counterculture's inspiration, our travels between the Upper West Side and the Bronx had an interesting symmetry. Ruthie and I still spent a great deal of time with Darlene and with her sister Cora, who had recently rented an apartment in a four-story walkup next to Claremont Park, a beautiful slice of greenery carved out of a Bronx hillside between Webster Avenue and Grand Concourse in the east 170s. On blocks densely packed with small apartment buildings, wood-frame houses, and a smattering of two-family brick homes, a growing population of black and Latino families coexisted with elderly Irish and Jewish couples, who used the park for strolling, playing chess, gossiping, and enjoying the view from hillside benches, where you could see several miles of the East Bronx. The neighborhood was relatively crime free and extremely tolerant of racial differences. Ruthie and I felt completely at ease holding hands in the street or in the park, as much as we did anywhere in the Columbia area.

A tough-talking but warm-hearted woman who had two young children and weighed nearly 250 pounds, Cora made us delicious dinners of fried chicken, ham, collard greens with neck bones, potato salad, and chitlins, the last of which she cooked for twenty-four hours and served with hot sauce. After the food came the music, featuring soul singers like James Brown, Joe Tex, Wilson Pickett, and Otis Redding. We danced while drinking scotch, bourbon, and sweet wine.

The friends of Cora and Darlene who came to these gatherings often moved between the legal and the underground economy. People in this black working-class community—numbers runners, truck drivers, nurses, salesclerks—found they sometimes had to break the law in order to live a decent life. Cora's live-in boyfriend, Gilbert, who drove a truck for a liquor company, described matter-of-factly how hijacking was part of his job. Once a week, Gilbert told us, someone would approach the cab of his truck, put a gun to his head, and politely ask him to relinquish his load. Sometimes they would take liquor, sometimes the whole truck; but if they did the latter, they would give him carfare to get home. The whole pattern seemed to reflect some arrangement between the trucking company and organized crime, and Gilbert viewed it as part of his job. Discussions of the numbers were also a constant among Ruthie's sisters. One of Darlene's boyfriends, Samuel, worked as a numbers runner, and people liked to tell him their schemes for hitting a number, which could come from dreams, children's birthdays, the weather, or something they saw on their way to work.

The matter-of-fact approach to sex I encountered here also threw me off balance. Many of Cora and Darlene's friends seemed to delight in talking about sexual escapades. To be in the midst of conversations where sexuality was described as a source of pleasure, humor, and theatrical self-promotion made me uncomfortable, especially given my reluctance to succumb to historic racial stereotypes. One evening, while seated in Cora's living room, I overheard a loud conversation, probably staged for my benefit, between Cora and an equally heavyset friend over how to handle a philandering husband or boyfriend. "You and I can get a man anytime we want to," the friend told Cora. "Men like women with meat on their bones. All I have to do is show a man my titties," she said proudly, "and he'll run after me like a dog in heat. You do the same thing the next time Gilbert runs out on you, and he'll come back with his tail between his legs."

Ruthie and I, anxious to invest our relationship with an air of respectability, rarely participated in this banter, even at the risk of appearing puritanical. We also saw dangers in an uninhibited approach to sex, feeling that it easily spilled over into violence. Cora and Gilbert, who had two young children in their home, sometimes got in terrible fights over Gilbert's escapades. Once we had to hire a cab to take Gilbert to the hospital after Cora smashed him over the head with a glass bottle, creating a cut that required twenty-five stitches. Incidents like these made us glad we were monogamous.

Our involvement in this earthy milieu evoked powerful and contradictory emotions. In an environment where few people had graduated from high school, our educations and professional aspirations made us the objects of good-natured teasing. But no one ever attacked us for crossing the color line. Cora and Darlene's friends seemed to be rooting for us to succeed, both as individuals and as a couple. Although many of them bore the scars of difficult lives (literally as well as figuratively), they did not seem beaten down and depressed, or filled with rage and resentment. Through religious faith, through celebration and the pursuit of pleasure, through a capacity to express powerful emotions in a theatrical manner, these southern-born black folk managed to keep the demons unleashed by racism and poverty from destroying their lives. As for Ruthie and me, our evenings in the Bronx offered a welcome relief from the tensions of challenging racial barriers. Amid sexual banter and rough language, and some sobering episodes of violence, we experienced a generosity and tolerance for human frailty that middle-class white Americans, except for those immersed in the counterculture, seemed to lack. When Ruthie and I slow-danced, in crowded Bronx living rooms, to Otis Redding's "I've Been Loving You a Little Too Long," I felt surrounded by a love so strong it brought tears to my eyes.

If Ruthie and I could have remained frozen in those moments, we would have been spared a great deal of unhappiness. But the powerful emotions unleashed by the Black Power movement, and the anxiety these feelings evoked among white liberals and radicals, soon confronted us with difficult choices. In June 1967, when we moved into the Columbia dorms to begin working with Project Double Discovery for a second summer, Ruthie and I had our first sustained exposure to racial tension in a university setting. In its second year of operation, the program had hired a large number of black counselors, most of whom had just completed their freshman year at Columbia and were part of the first large cohort of black students to enter the school. This class contained three times more black students than any previous one, and their backgrounds were quite different as well. Many had grown up in working-class neighborhoods, attended public schools, and had little exposure to elite culture and white paternalism. Columbia's neoclassical atmosphere and its efforts to remake minority students (blacks, Jews, Italians) in the mold of white elites offended and infuriated them, especially in a time when integration had come under attack as a cultural ideal.

Tensions had come to a head that spring, when ten black freshman, most of whom were football players, decided to form a chapter of the national black fraternity, Omega Psi Phi. Initially, the Columbia administration refused to recognize this organization on the grounds that black fraternities were a relic of segregation. After long and heated negotiations, the administration finally recognized the Omega chapter, but was shocked to discover that the fraternity, as part of its hazing ceremony, placed a "Q"-like brand on the right arms of its members to recall the experience of slavery. The issue might have faded if the Columbia humor magazine, *The Jester,* had not published a satire on the new black fraternity, comparing its hazing rituals to the initiation rites of African tribes. After futile attempts to persuade the Columbia administration to censor this issue of the magazine, which it refused to do on free-speech grounds, members of the fraternity broke into the *Jester* office, removed all copies of its spring issue, and burned them. To many white students, this action, coupled with the branding ritual itself, marked the Omega members as outlaws who had no respect for their fellow students or the traditions of the university community. In a university where the protection of free speech was accorded an almost sacred significance, no one in the white student population rallied to Omega's defense.

When the Double Discovery program hired eight of the Omegas, the ill feeling sparked by this incident inevitably spilled over into the program's atmosphere. The "Qs," which is what the Omegas called themselves, started work with a powerful sense of group solidarity and a heavy dose of "attitude." Suspicious of the white counselors in the program, they kept themselves apart in social situations and spoke to one another in black vernacular speech that their co-workers had difficulty understanding. They also walked and moved in an aggressive, slightly menacing manner that was common among kids from tough neighborhoods, but which seemed to intimidate the white counselors, perhaps because it triggered unconscious racial fears or exposed their own physical insecurities. The fact that the Omegas were athletes, and most of the white counselors were small and physically timid, made for some amusing racial theater. When the Omegas sat in a large group on the wall outside the Columbia student center, you could see the white counselors, and other white students, lower their heads and speed up as they passed by. The Omegas' presence set a tone of racial division that had been absent the previous summer. The white staff of Double Discovery, some of whom were SDS members and all of whom were integrationists, did not know how to handle the new situation. Most had joined Double Discovery because they wanted a multiracial experience, but they felt uncomfortable expressing their concerns to black co-workers who seemed so filled with anger. They retreated into their own social networks, leaving the staff divided. The Omegas were on one side, and the rest of the staff, black and white, who felt comfortable working and socializing in an interracial setting, were on the other.

Almost alone among the white counselors, I refused to accept this incipient division. As a supervisor in the program, I needed the respect and cooperation of all the black staff members, and as the white boyfriend of a good-looking black woman, I felt uncomfortable in a racially polarized atmosphere. I decided to try to get to know the Omegas better. Every time I saw them together, I would sit down in their midst and start talking to them about students in the program. I found them more friendly than their public persona suggested. Not only were they receptive to talking about the students in the program, many of whom I had known from the summer before, but they were easily engaged in sports talk. When I started talking about professional and schoolyard basketball, especially the great African-American players I had seen growing up in Brooklyn, they became noticeably more comfortable in my presence. What some scholars call "homosocial bonding" started to kick in. The second time I sat with the Omegas, they invited me to join them in a full-court basketball game in Riverside Park.

I interpreted this invitation both as a friendly gesture and as a test of my ability to function comfortably in a black-controlled environment. By the late 1960s, basketball had become a cultural space where ordinary power relations between blacks and whites had been reversed. From the city schoolyards to the NBA, basketball had become an African-American male cultural terrain, a place where black players set the standards of excellence that all other players aspired to. When black men and white men played on the same court, there was often an undercurrent of racial competition. Not only was the basketball court a vehicle for African-

American expressive artistry, it was also a place where blacks sometimes used their skill to dominate and humiliate whites. It was also a terrain that I was personally comfortable in because my style of play defied racial stereotypes. I was not the kind of white athlete that sports journalists praised, a cerebral player who used skill and wits to compensate for physical deficiencies. My ball handling and shooting skills were the weakest part of my game, but I could touch the rim from a standing position, do double pumps while driving to the basket, and use my strength and jumping ability to play defense and get rebounds. When the game began, I saw my chance to blend into the group as an effective and useful player. I contested every rebound, dove onto the pavement for loose balls, played hard physical defense, and scored several times on drives and offensive rebounds. When the game was over, I felt like I had earned some respect. Amid high fives and slapped palms, I was invited to join the Omegas at the Columbia student cafeteria, where they regaled each other with fraternity stories while I sat silent, exhausted, and happy.

For the rest of the summer, I spent a great deal of time with this cohort of African-American men—more, in fact, than I did with any of my white colleagues. It was a new experience for me to be a lone white male in a group of black men. It was easiest during basketball and touch football games, where I could lose myself in the clash of bodies, but I sometimes felt awkward and tongue-tied amid the verbal jousting at parties, meals, and bull sessions. I was comfortable talking with the Omegas about the students in Double Discovery, whether we were discussing teaching methods, figuring out which girls were going out with which boys, or trying to crack a theft ring that targeted expensive knit shirts from the Blye Shop on Fifth Avenue. But when the black counselors engaged in "race talk," there was little I could do but listen. Here, the subjects ranged from the hazing practices and rituals of different black fraternities to the churches they attended in their neighborhoods back home, to the clubs they visited and concerts they attended, to the way white people responded to them on campus and off. In their vignettes and stories, they portrayed white people as arrogant, dishonest, deceptive, manipulative, frightened of blacks, and above all not to be trusted. "When someone yells, 'Get the niggers,'" a popular counselor liked to proclaim, "the white guy who says he is your friend will yell, 'Where are they?'" "These motherfuckers think they know us," another counselor often said. "They don't know shit."

Why did I stay there when the Omegas were "dissing" white people? Why didn't I challenge their blanket racial generalizations, or call their attention to the many white people who did not fit their stereotypes? In part, I remained silent out of cowardice. Making fun of or denouncing white people, for this group of black Columbia students, was a communal bonding activity, and I could not challenge it without jeopardizing my own social acceptance. I was like the Jewish neophyte in a Protestant law firm who remains silent in the face of anti-Semitism. I wanted to belong so much that I was willing to subject myself to verbal abuse if it wasn't directed at me personally. But I also kept quiet out of curiosity. By making myself inconspicuous, I got an uncensored version of what some black Columbia students really thought about whites, or at least what they liked to *say* about whites when other blacks were around. Much of what I heard upset me, but I also found the style of discourse, its combination of rage and humor, vulgarity and intellectual acuity, extremely compelling. As someone with a large amount of suppressed anger, I appreciated the way the Omegas externalized their rage through mockery and fantasies of revenge.

Even though I was an outsider in their world, I had much in common with the Omegas. Like me, most of them were athlete-intellectuals, boys who came from working-class neighborhoods and who had had to fight neighborhood bullies to compensate for their high grades and ambitious parents. They felt even more uncomfortable at Columbia than I did, but refused to let their discomfort undermine their plans to become doctors, lawyers, and college professors. Beneath their machismo and paranoia (which was certainly no greater than my own), I saw idealism, curiosity, and a deep concern for black people less fortunate than they. I also identified with their frank pride in their strength and athletic ability, a trait that I rarely saw among white male intellectuals and political radicals. Unchecked by a feminist consciousness, I enjoyed discussing politics and sports with men who wore muscle shirts and tank tops, and walked around campus trying to turn the heads of women and impress other men.

However, my interactions with the black counselors at Double Discovery never attained the ease and naturalness that Ruthie's did. Ruthie responded to the black counselors from Columbia and Barnard as though they were long-lost members of the same family. The pleasure she found in their company was so natural, powerful, and wholehearted that it made me jealous. I started to see something in Ruthie that I had never noticed before, a craving for black companionship on her own social and intellectual level; and now that she was finding it, I wondered where I fit in. When it came to Double Discovery students, my race mattered little; Ruthie and I still worked together as a team, and we regularly took students to Ruthie's apartment on our days off. But with the black Columbia students, even the ones I liked, I sometimes felt like Ruthie's appendage. I spent more and more summer evenings going with her to black student parties, which proliferated after black enrollment increased. There Ruthie and I encountered reactions ranging from cold indifference to polite tolerance. Among educated African-Americans, black solidarity seemed to be the dominant mood, and Ruthie felt far more welcome among them as an individual than we did as a couple.

The growing repudiation of interracialism by upwardly mobile blacks began to cast a shadow over our relationship. As I moved in with Ruthie that fall, joining her in the apartment on 99th Street, I wondered whether her new friends would eventually undermine her feelings for me. Ruthie claimed that her love for me and her attraction to black nationalist student activism could coexist, but I wondered if that were true. Among politically active white students at Columbia, and among young people in the counterculture, interracial solidarity still had great appeal, but Ruthie was no longer willing to spend most of her time in a predominantly white environment. I now had to fight for our relationship in a segment of the black community that I knew little about and one that was not receptive to my presence. With racial tensions rising throughout the country, and the war in Vietnam commanding more people and resources, I felt pressure, anxiety, and fear for the future.

6   Ball of Confusion

MANY SCHOLARS of postwar America have singled out 1968 as a defining moment in American political and cultural history. They cite war, assassinations, race riots, campus takeovers, gaping generational and racial divisions, and the fracturing of the Democratic Party as evidence of a political and cultural crisis that traumatized individuals and shattered families. That year my life was also in turmoil. I experienced my first arrest, the death of my father, and a traumatic separation from Ruthie during a building takeover at Columbia. Embittered by the assassination of Martin Luther King, Jr., the escalation of the war, and growing racial polarization throughout American society, I was pessimistic about prospects for peaceful change in the United States. By the early summer of 1968, I had thrown myself into radical politics and joined SDS.

The one overriding sentiment I can recall from that period is the feeling that my life was out of control. Vietnam had a great deal to do with that. For my generation of young men, the war could turn prospects for school, career, and family into a choice between combat, prison, exile, or resistance. I also experienced the tense racial climate in a deeply personal manner. Through Ruthie, I found myself drawn deeper into an African-American community that was redefining its place in American life and reevaluating its cultural philosophy. I was now the live-in white partner of a black woman who was increasingly active in black student organizations and who had recast her appearance to express pride in her African ancestry. Like many people influenced by the Black Power movement, Ruthie let her hair grow out naturally, and she began wearing clothing and jewelry imported from West Africa. To be able to claim African features as beautiful was especially liberating for Ruthie because she was much darker and more African looking than the models and beauty queens featured in popular magazines like *Jet* and *Ebony*. When Ruthie stepped out of the house wearing a brightly colored African top and a two-inch-high afro, she seemed to glow with beauty, happiness, and a new self-confidence.

The cultural changes that made Ruthie feel more attractive made me feel more vulnerable. Prior to the rise of Black Power, Ruthie had been too dark-skinned to attract the attention of the few African-American males at Columbia and City College. But now that black had become beautiful, African-American students and professionals were suddenly very interested in her. Everywhere she went, good-looking black men gravitated to her, flirting with her and asking her out. The competition made me jealous. I had a strong suspicion that Ruthie would have never dated me, much less fallen in love with me, if we had met me *after* the emergence of the Black Power movement.

Fortunately for me, Ruthie was not one to break up a relationship when it ceased to conform to the latest political fashion. She was deeply loyal, and she remembered how I had stood up to my parents when they had demanded that I leave her. But the pressures of justifying her ties to me in the face of rising nationalist sentiment began to take its toll. The playful, irreverent woman who had enjoyed getting high and going to "be-ins" gave way to a politically serious person with a strong sense of social responsibility. Wary of spending too much time with our white friends, Ruthie insisted we center our social life around her family and the students in Double Discovery, where we could simultaneously enjoy the company of accepting black people and use our skills to help solve problems. When her mother became seriously ill during the fall of 1967, Ruthie assumed the role of social worker and surrogate mother to her younger siblings. She invited one of her brothers from Georgia, Thomas, to stay with us in a spare bedroom until he found a permanent place to stay. When Thomas found his own apartment, she invited three youngsters from Double Discovery to stay in that room on weekends or when they were having conflicts with their parents. Ruthie and I placed our time, our money, and our skill in dealing with public bureaucracies at the disposal of these young people. We cooked for them, helped them with their homework, consulted with their teachers, parents, and guidance counselors, took them to the movies, and tried to help them find jobs. Outside of the privacy of our bedroom, Ruthie and I now spent little time alone. Increasingly, we comported ourselves as a team of social workers shuttling back and forth between the West Side and the Bronx. Between Cora and her children, who always seemed to be the victims of some disaster, and the Double Discovery students we had assumed responsibility for, we never knew when a 3:00 A.M. phone call would require us to visit a police station or a hospital.

Although I was proud of what we were doing, I found this life stressful. Being around people who lived on the edge of crisis made it difficult to study or write in our apartment, sending me to the Columbia library much more than I liked. I also faced difficult issues surrounding my own racial identity. Increasingly, my whiteness had become a source of embarrassment to Ruthie. On several occasions, I heard her describe me to black friends as someone who "seems to be white, but really acts black" or is "blacker than most black people." She was not the only person to make such remarks. The girls in Double Discovery would often tell Ruthie "he's just like a nigger" after watching me dance and play basketball. But not all black people were willing to grant me "honorary brother" status. When I went to black student parties at Columbia as Ruthie's partner, my skin color felt like a badge of shame. Nothing I did on the dance floor or said in conversations could make me feel welcome. I could never forget my whiteness, as I could with Ruthie's relatives or the students in Double Discovery. Columbia's student nationalists had turned blackness into a mark of status much as my parents had done with whiteness.

Under the press of these experiences, I started to think about race in unconventional ways. One thing I knew for sure, I did not want to go back to being "white." My relationship with Ruthie had been the single most important experience in my life, a powerful stimulus to my intellectual and emotional growth. Spending my life in settings where black people were not welcome, or where black culture was not honored, had no appeal to me. But as black nationalism spread, whole sections of the black community were becoming off-limits to me. In order to preserve my status as a racially indeterminate person (or a white boy with soul?), I needed to find places where fluid racial boundaries permitted blacks and whites to be equally comfortable. Borrowing a term from the Vietnam War, I told people I wanted to live in an "interracial DMZ" (demilitarized zone), a place where people could set aside racial hostilities and create new identities based on a fusion of different cultures.

My heterodox ideas about race received a sympathetic hearing from fellow graduate students at Columbia, many of them veterans of the civil rights movement. At a time when gender had not yet become a major political issue, questions of race and class were the central preoccupations of radical students in the graduate history program. In my classes and seminars, I belonged to a cohort of about twenty men and women, all of them white, who were interested in transforming historical writing to give more attention to the experiences of racial minorities and working-class people. We studied together in the library, ate lunch together, went for drinks in the West End bar. We passed around books and articles by independent Marxist scholars like E. P. Thompson and Eugene Genovese, plotted ways of challenging our professors, and tried to figure out how we could best protest the war in Vietnam. Convinced that a more democratic approach to historical writing would be a foundation for a more democratic society, we discussed ways of putting our own research at the service of the movement.

One vehicle for our efforts was a new magazine called *Radical America*, edited by Paul Buhle, an American history graduate student at the University of Wisconsin. During my first year in graduate school, Paul heard about my undergraduate thesis on the Harlem rent strikes and asked permission to publish it in *Radical America*'s second issue. I agreed and subsequently became the journal's New York representative, placing it in bookstores and soliciting articles and subscriptions. Paul was animated by a missionary zeal about the history of American radicalism. He wanted to help the current generation of student activists understand how radical movements of the past had dealt with racial tensions, class divisions, and ideological conflicts. He was particularly interested in reexamining the history of socialist and communist parties in the United States, which had been erased from popular memory during the McCarthy era and had been written about by scholars unsympathetic to their goals. My master's thesis on the Southern Tenants Farmers Union, a racially integrated organization developed by American socialists, fit Paul's editorial vision perfectly. Paul published it, encouraging me to push its implications further and become *Radical America*'s expert on the racial policies of the American Left.

This intellectual mission gave me standing among my fellow students as well as strength to endure the cultural dissonance in my life. Every day I shuttled between Columbia and a residential environment so bizarre and picaresque it would have challenged the descriptive abilities of a Charles Dickens. Prior to the gentrification projects of the 1970s, West 99th Street between West End Avenue and Riverside Drive was known as one of the most dangerous blocks on the Upper West Side. Its three large single-room-occupancy hotels accommodated single men and women, who could rent rooms by the week or month, usually with no questions asked about their backgrounds or habits. One of these hotels, the Hamilton, housed harmless pensioners; but the other two, the Harvard and the Fablan, contained a remarkable array of people rejected and discarded by society, including alcoholics, heroin addicts, prostitutes, car thieves, muggers, and at least ten transvestites, all of whom seemed to congregate in the street in front of the two establishments. These residents rarely missed a chance to make comments to the more reputable residents of the block on their trips to and from school, work, or shopping. Nearby stood an eight-story apartment building that housed at least fifty Spanish-speaking families from Puerto Rico and the Dominican Republic. The children of these hardworking immigrants used the block for stickball, football, basketball, and jump rope, side-stepping rusting car parts, broken wine bottles, used condoms, and discarded heroin works while they played. Across from this immigrant haven stood 317 West 99th Street, the eight-story elevator apartment building where Ruthie and I made our home. With its spacious apartments and marble hallways, this building seemed a relic of a bygone age, but its population of teachers, artists, actors, and students, and a few retirees, had the worn-down look of people for whom every trip outside their apartments had an element of danger. Everyone in the building seemed to know one another and look out for one another. Other than the superintendent, Angel, Ruthie was the only nonwhite tenant, but she was welcomed as a fellow combatant in the struggle to maintain a dignified existence amid the surrounding chaos.

Life in Ruthie's apartment, while much safer than life on 99th Street, offered an equally vivid mélange of cultures. In addition to our teenage houseguests, Ruthie and I had two other roommates, both of them white: my college friend, Michel, a graduate student in French history, and Ruthie's old friend Ruby, who had lived with Ruthie for three years. Michel spent most of his time in the library and at his girlfriend's place, but Ruby, a social worker who was the child of prominent American Communists, helped give our apartment its unique ambiance. An attractive, pale-skinned woman whose silken black hair hung to her waist, Ruby slurred her speech and changed her verbs to sound African-American, and she dated only black men. Bright and generous when she was sober, Ruby, when drunk, had a propensity to get into screaming matches with her boyfriends that started in our apartment, moved into the hallways, and ended in the street. Don, Ruby's major love interest, claimed to have been close to the Black Panther Party in California, and he also added excitement to our lives. A short, dark-skinned man with few teeth, an engaging smile, and a gift for storytelling, Don loved to regale us with tales of his years in street gangs, time in prison, and his contacts with the Panthers and the Nation of Islam. Don had many ways of making money, few of them legal, but he derived his success more from charm than intimidation. He was an excellent cook, a good housekeeper, and an astute critic of all forms of popular music. He was also good company when you were feeling down. If I was feeling overwhelmed by graduate work, angry at my parents or Ruthie's nationalist friends, or worried where Ruthie and I would find the money to pay our bills, I could get high with Don and feel better. Don had seen a lot of trouble in his life and knew just what to say, and what music to put on, to make my problems seem manageable.

Living on 99th Street represented the closest thing to an interracial DMZ that I had ever experienced. With a lot of hard work, Ruthie and I created an atmosphere in our apartment where white and black people of widely different backgrounds could come together as friends. Perhaps the best example of this was when we found a roommate for Ruthie's brother Thomas, a shy nineteen-year-old whose country manners made him an easy target for hustlers and street people. The person we matched him with was Ted Clay, a twenty-two-year-old white Princeton graduate from Louisville who had consulted with me when writing his senior thesis and who wanted to live in New York. A direct descendent of Henry Clay, who got an allowance from his wealthy parents, Ted was tall, painfully thin, soft-spoken, and as unsophisticated as Thomas. Within one month of his arrival in New York, he was mugged three times. Never was there an odder couple than the scholarly looking child of southern aristocrats and the country boy from Georgia. Neither knew how to cook, clean, balance a checkbook, or find their way around New York. Neither had experience in finding or holding a job. But they were two of the sweetest, most considerate people you would ever want to meet. Even after they got their own place, they were a fixture at our apartment, especially at dinnertime. With a lot of help from us, they got through their first six months in the city without getting evicted, stabbed, or robbed of all their possessions. Theirs was an interracial pairing that worked.

The lifestyle Ruthie and I created was not conducive to saving money. It was not unusual for us to feed seven or eight people a night, and if we had extra money, we often spent it on Ruthie's relatives or the Double Discovery students who came to our apartment. But although living from paycheck to paycheck (or in my case, fellowship check to fellowship check) could be stressful, the communal atmosphere of our apartment provided a welcome refuge from the troubles of the world and could offer much-needed comfort for someone going through a personal crisis.

I would need a heavy dose of such support in late January 1968, when my father suffered a relapse of Hodgkin's disease. Hospitalized in the cancer ward at Memorial Sloan Kettering on the Upper East Side, my father slowly wasted away, day by day, over the course of three months. An almost daily visitor, I sat by his bed and discussed my courses, my research plans, the state of national politics, the progress of his disease, the effectiveness of his treatments—everything and anything but my relationship with him or my relationship with Ruthie. My father's courage in the face of pain and impending death moved me greatly. Every day, no matter how ill he felt, he would prepare a lesson plan for the substitute who was handling his physics class at Jamaica High School. He kept up this ritual until the day before he died. My mother, in turn, stayed in the hospital around the clock. She nursed him, comforted him, and made sure he had the best care possible and never once cracked under the strain.

My parents' valiancy in the face of death only dramatized for me the depth of their racial feeling. Even while I was making daily pilgrimages to my father's bedside, my parents refused to acknowledge Ruthie's existence or offer any indication that they accepted my feelings for her. I was crushed by their stubbornness, but refused to show my emotions and plead for a reconciliation. Instead, I performed my filial duties with as much dignity as I could muster, swallowing my pain at the personal and communal tragedy that had descended upon our family. People at the hospital often praised me as an attentive, loyal son, but I grew increasingly melancholy about the implacable force of my parents' prejudices and my father's deteriorating health. I would return home each day drained and despondent. If Ruthie happened to be there, she would give me a smile, a hug, and words of encouragement. If she was out, our roommates or the kids who stayed with us would join me at the dinner table or in front of the television, aware that I needed company. At a time when the emotional gap between me and my parents had become particularly depressing, my friends provided the comfort I craved from my biological family.

Whenever someone talks of the permanence of racial barriers, the mutual support and empathy between the diverse residents of that 99th Street apartment leaps into my mind as a rejoinder. Nothing symbolized this more than our collective response to the assassination of Martin Luther King. On an April evening in 1968, I returned from visiting my father to find a group of people sitting around a television screaming in anguish and crying hysterically. On the television screen, grim-faced reporters told of the fatal shooting of Dr. King at a motel in Memphis and of the riots that had broken out in black communities throughout the country. Between the news reports they played clips of King's speeches; the visions of racial harmony and justice he invoked seemed to be mocked by the day's events. Yet in that apartment, that night, King's vision still lived. The five people sitting around that television set—me, Ruthie, her brother Thomas, Mike from Double Discovery, and Steve, a white student from California who had been dating Ruthie's friend Carol—all responded as though a source of hope and inspiration had been taken away. For all of us, King was a spiritual leader, a person who had set a standard of love and sacrifice that had given us the courage to challenge ancient hatreds and taboos. His death left a terrible emptiness and an anger we did not know what to do with. When we heard crashing sounds coming from the street below, we all ran downstairs to join whatever was happening. But it was not the beginnings of a riot: it was a group of fifty black teenagers from the projects on Amsterdam Avenue marching down the street banging on garbage-can covers and singing "We Shall Overcome." We ran into the street to join them, picking up can covers of our own, and marched with them through the streets of the Upper West Side, slowly moving in the direction of Times Square. By the time the group, by now composed equally of blacks and whites, had reached 72nd Street and Broadway, it had picked up nearly five hundred people and acquired its own police escort. At Times Square, the group dissolved into a mass of thousands of restless people, some making speeches and holding animated conversations, most just standing around looking lost. Our own small group took the subway home and went to bed. The next day's news reports focused on the riots that had taken place in fifty American cities, the violence seeming to repudiate the principles that King had lived by. What

King had meant to working-class black people, and to whites who identified with the civil rights movement, seemed to get lost in this parox-
ysm of rage, but I had seen first-hand that his dream of harmony and
reconciliation still lived.

One week after King's death, my father died. I went through the
funeral and the seven-day period of mourning as if in a trance. I felt a
dull ache inside me the whole time, but whether it was pain at losing
him, or pain that we had never achieved a reconciliation, is hard to say.
To the hundreds of people who came to offer sympathy, I kept up the
pretense of filial duty, but I could not wait to get back each night to my
real home on 99th Street and to be among people who loved and
accepted me for who I was. Being at my mother's apartment in Rego
Park for seven days in a row was excruciating. Ruthie's existence created
a barrier between us that not even my father's death could bridge. Both
of us were too proud and too stubborn even to broach the subject, and
an unbearable tension filled the air the entire time we were together. I
played the role of dutiful son and ambitious doctoral candidate for her
friends and relatives, but hated every minute of it. I was convinced that
if they knew I had a black girlfriend, these warm and generous Jewish
teachers, civil servants, and small business people would have seen me
as a threatening figure, someone whose life choices mocked their quest
for social acceptance and their triumph over poverty and anti-Semitism.

The deaths of my father and Dr. King hastened my move toward
radical politics. I had been arrested for the first time in February 1968,
when I joined a small group of Columbia students and Harlem residents
to perform civil disobedience at the site of the new Columbia gym
planned in Morningside Park. My motives for getting arrested, however,
had more to do with seeking a rite of passage than with ideological
commitment. When student deferments were officially ended and a lot-
tery was held to determine young men's eligibility for the draft, two of
my best friends from graduate school decided to go to jail rather than
register. I was deeply moved by their convictions but had no way of
matching their sacrifice, having won a draft number high enough to
place me out of immediate danger. Instead, I decided to find a way of
getting arrested on behalf of another issue I cared about. When I heard
of a demonstration in Morningside Park sponsored by community
organizations from Harlem and the West Side, I decided to join it even
though I had no confidence that we would stop the gym from going up.

Only thirty protesters showed up at the demonstration, ten of them Columbia students who had been active community organizers. After half an hour of chanting, we approached the fence surrounding the construction site and tried to tear it down; New York City police soon pried us away and arrested us. As we were taken off to the criminal courts for arraignment on charges of disorderly conduct, I felt as if I had passed a kind of citizenship test. Even if the gym still went up, I had preserved my self-respect by getting arrested in protest of Columbia's abuse of power and contempt for Harlem residents.

Two weeks after King's assassination, protesters once again raised the issue of the gym, this time with far more support and a stronger under-current of rage. In an unprecedented step, Columbia SDS and Columbia's Student African-American Society (SAS) called a joint rally at the sundial in the center of campus to demand that Columbia stop construction of the gym, rescind the suspension of six student demonstrators who had staged a sit-in at the president's office during an antiwar protest, and sever Columbia's ties to the Institute of Defense Analysis. Nearly five hundred students came to this rally, a far larger number than I had ever seen congregate on the campus, and heard speakers from both organiza-tions denounce Columbia as a racist institution that rode roughshod over its nonwhite neighbors and gave its students no voice in campus gover-nance. There was an unruly, bitter edge to the rhetoric of the speakers and the mood of the crowd. SDS's new leader, Mark Rudd, had shed the orga-nization's cerebral image and had adopted a combative, confrontational style. After King's death, he had interrupted a memorial service in the Columbia chapel and denounced Columbia president Grayson Kirk as a hypocrite, using words from a Leroi Jones poem, "up against the wall motherfucker, this is a stickup." At this rally, both he and Bill Sales, the black student organization leader, were urging the crowd to follow the example of students at black colleges, who had been seizing buildings to press their demands. When the speeches ended, Rudd and Sales led the crowd in a slow march up the steps of Low Library, where President Kirk had his offices. I rushed to the front of the line to assure my presence in any confrontation, even though I had no idea what the strategic objective of the demonstration was. King's death, and the bitter experience of my father's funeral, had put me in a fighting mood.

As the first marchers approached the doors to Low Library, we faced a line of fifteen campus security police with their billy clubs in ready position. Given the size and mood of the crowd, we probably could have overpowered them, but someone yelled "To the gym site!" and the entire march changed direction and headed across Amsterdam Avenue to Morningside Park. There we tore down hundreds of feet of fencing surrounding the site before enough police could arrive to stop us. After construction ceased for that day, and the demonstrators had accumulated a sizable police escort, someone yelled "Let's take a building!" and we started back for campus. The crowd then filtered into Hamilton Hall, the major undergraduate classroom building. It was completely unguarded since it had no research facilities and no administrative offices other than the college dean's. As three to four hundred demonstrators milled about in the main alcove of the building and took turns giving speeches, the leaders of SDS and SAS tried to decide what to do. One thing was clear: although occupying Hamilton Hall had *not* been the original objective of this protest, it gave us leverage over Columbia that no group of student protesters had ever had.

For a couple of hours, the protest became a speak-out on Columbia policies, as demonstrators took turns talking about university expansion, the gym, and the war. I spoke briefly about the protest's historical context, describing the many unsuccessful efforts by community organizations and CORE to prevent Columbia from displacing low-income residents in Morningside Heights, and recounting my arrest at the gym site two months earlier. "For the first time in my six years at Columbia," I told the crowd, "the forces opposing university expansion have the upper hand. Let's not leave this building until we get some serious concessions." However, by late afternoon the fragile unity between SAS and SDS was unraveling. Black student leaders thought the protest had become undisciplined and wanted to barricade the building with a core of committed activists. One month earlier, some of the SAS members had participated in a building occupation at Howard University led by the Student Non-Violent Coordinating Committee, and they believed the same tactic could work at Columbia. The white students wanted to keep lines of communication open with the rest of the campus. The racial division in the building was exacerbated by rumors that black activists from around the city, led by militants from SNCC, were smuggling guns into Hamilton Hall and preparing for a shootout with New York City police. Two weeks before, a black student had been killed by police in the town of Tuskegee, Alabama, triggering huge demonstrations at the black college in that community, and SNCC activists were allegedly coming to Columbia to seek revenge for his death. These rumors were difficult to verify because SAS had started meeting separately from the rest of the protesters and closing its meetings to whites. What started out as a united protest had turned into a tension-filled standoff, with black students in one side of the building and white students in the other.

These tensions were complicated by the presence of a small group of African-American men, not Columbia students, who circulated through the building with a conspiratorial air. Late that afternoon, a friend and I were approached in the bathroom by a black man in his late twenties who asked, "Are you ready to die today?" We looked at one another in astonishment and replied, "We hadn't really thought about it." After a long pause we added, lamely, "We might consider dying, but most of our friends aren't ready to take that step." We left the bathroom in a daze, wondering what was going on. This protest was veering out of control. There was little communication between SAS and SDS and few signs of solidarity between black and white students. The SAS leadership, reinforced by black students from other campuses and organizers from SNCC, had seized control of the demonstration, infusing it with a deadly seriousness that left most white students feeling helpless. Without consulting the SDS leadership, they had barricaded the college dean, Henry Coleman, in his office and refused to let him leave. Even the most militant in SDS seemed stunned by this action. Never in their wildest fantasies had they thought about taking an administrator hostage. For the first time in their lives, Columbia's white radicals were experiencing the full force of the black community's anger, and the experience left them badly shaken.

The Columbia administration also seemed paralyzed. Normally decisive in dealing with student protests, Columbia now faced a phalanx of African-American students, supported by black activists from off campus, who had control of its most important classroom building. Rooting them out by force not only risked a gun battle, if the rumors about firearms turned out to be true, but also had the potential to trigger rioting in Harlem, especially since the construction of a gym in Harlem's largest park was the protesters' major focus. Although I resented SAS's open contempt for white protesters, I recognized that their tactics would probably do more to stop the gym than anything done in a spirit of interracial harmony. To gather my thoughts, and get away from the atmosphere of racial animosity, I left the building early in the evening to get dinner. When I returned, the entire situation had changed. The black students had ordered all whites out of the building and had barricaded its entrances, leaving only a small, carefully guarded opening for the people of whom they approved.

Exhausted by the day's events, I returned to 99th Street to get some sleep, only to get another shock. Ruthie, who was there waiting for me, announced that she had gotten a call from the leaders of SAS and was going to join the occupation of Hamilton Hall. She packed some clothing and left the apartment in great excitement, gratified that the SAS had invited black City College students to participate in the demonstration. I felt devastated by her departure. The most important protest in Columbia history, something that I had welcomed with enthusiasm, now challenged some of the principles around which I had organized my personal and political life.

The next day I returned to campus to discover that the white students pushed out of Hamilton Hall had occupied and barricaded two other buildings, the most important of which was Low Library, the main administration building. Radical graduate students were also making plans to occupy Fayerweather Hall, the main center for graduate programs in the liberal arts. I was invited to participate in the occupation of Fayerweather, but I could not bear to be cooped up there while Ruthie was occupying Hamilton Hall. I decided to play a role in the protest that allowed me to move between buildings, giving me the flexibility to observe what was going on in Hamilton Hall and, if possible, to communicate with Ruthie. I became part of an SDS logistical force that brought food in and out of buildings, carried messages between SDS leaders and SAS, and sought to deal with a large gathering of angry students who wanted to expel protesters from the buildings.

In the first days of the building occupations, there seemed to be almost as many students opposed to the protest as supported it. A large group of white Columbia athletes, most of them football players, assembled daily outside Low Library and Hamilton Hall, shouting insults at the demonstrators and threatening to storm the buildings and drag them out. On the third day of the protest, they formed a picket line around Low Library to try to prevent food deliveries. In response, SDS organized a cadre of radical athletes and neighborhood teenagers, which I joined, to break their blockade. We broke through their line at several points and got enough food through to keep the protesters extremely well fed. In addition, several highly respected athletes, including the best player on the football team, started discussion groups at local fraternity houses to explain the issues that led to the protest and persuade most of the athletes to remain neutral. With their help, the counter-demonstrations gradually fizzled.

As demonstrators dug in for a long occupation, the race issues that had fueled the protests remained in the forefront. The students in Hamilton Hall, aware that fear of unrest in neighboring Harlem was their greatest weapon, recruited famous black militants to speak at their rallies and encouraged black people from neighborhoods surrounding Columbia to come to campus. In a demonstration of political solidarity that would be difficult to duplicate today, black students from Brandeis High School on West 84th Street marched up Broadway to Columbia to show support for the Hamilton Hall protesters. At various times, SNCC leaders Stokely Carmichael and H. Rap Brown, and Harlem street activist Charles Kenyatta, spoke with megaphones from the second-floor balcony of the building, threatening to "burn Columbia down" if it tried to build the gym. Their rhetoric, reinforced by a substantial community presence, probably did a great deal to restrain counter-demonstrators from trying to storm Hamilton Hall. It also prompted soul-searching among many segments of the Columbia community. It was impossible not to be impressed by the level of passion that black students and their allies brought to this protest. Their anger was awe-inspiring, but so was their discipline, their solidarity, and their willingness to sacrifice for a cause that affected the people of Harlem more than it did them. Alone among the Columbia protesters, the black students had support from an entire neighborhood.

This student-community alliance also set the stage for a huge growth in white student support for the protest, on and off campus. With Columbia officials paralyzed by the fear of provoking a race riot, white protesters were able to seize and hold four buildings—Low Library and Mathematics, which were controlled by SDS; Fayerweather, which was controlled by radical graduate students; and Avery, which was controlled by students from the School of Architecture and Planning. Moreover, white radicals from throughout the city, and in some cases the country, were arriving to support the protest. Tom Hayden spoke at a large outdoor rally and the Grateful Dead gave an impromptu concert in front of the Columbia student center, while SDS members from City College and NYU and members of the "Motherfuckers" from the Lower East Side, a radical street-fighting group, were among those occupying Mathematics Hall. With nearly a thousand people occupying buildings and several thousand more attending impromptu rallies, and with university operations entirely paralyzed, the Columbia occupations, supported by a student strike, had become the most powerful and effective student protest in modern American history.

The racially bifurcated character of this protest raised some difficult issues for me. The militancy of black students, fueled by the Black Power movement, had given this demonstration the power to neutralize Columbia's enormous wealth and influence. Even if the university rejected the protesters' demand for amnesty, everyone realized that the gym project was dead, and that Columbia could no longer displace low-income tenants while pursuing its own expansion. But the very passions that had made this movement so effective also had the power to shatter my relationship with Ruthie. It was sobering, to say the least, that in the midst of the most important political action I had ever been involved in, we couldn't talk, much less share our thoughts and feelings. If blacks and whites had to mobilize separately to launch an effective challenge to institutionalized racism, as the Columbia experience suggested, where did that leave interracial couples like Ruthie and me? And once separated, how would blacks and whites be brought back together? I respected the Black Power movement but also regarded it with profound ambivalence. The dynamism of black Columbia protesters could not erase the memory of the magical experiences I had had with Ruthie or the friendship and solidarity I experienced with her family, students in Double Discovery, and people in our apartment on 99th Street. Somehow, I would have to find a way of reconciling nationalism and interracialism, of defending the legitimacy of interracial love and friendship while still supporting organizations and movements that used nationalist strategies to advance the black community's interests.

When the strike finally ended, however, the racial divisions on campus had hardened. The Columbia administration only intensified these divisions by making a separate deal with the black students in Hamilton Hall, allowing them to leave the building voluntarily through underground tunnels just before the New York City police moved in on the other four buildings. That evening, when the New York police forcibly ejected demonstrators who were occupying Low Library, Fayerweather, Mathematics, and Avery Hall, and violently dispersed hundreds of peaceful observers as well, almost no African-Americans became involved in the mayhem. Columbia thereby managed to end the building occupation without provoking riots in Harlem, although the indiscriminate beatings administered by the police during the bust probably did more to radicalize white Columbia students than the demonstrations themselves. Many Columbia students remained "on strike" for the rest of the semester, and membership in SDS and a newly formed radical graduate student organization swelled to huge proportions. But the black students at Columbia maintained a separate organization with an agenda quite distinct from that of radical white students, concentrating on the development of black studies courses within the Columbia curriculum and the improvement of Columbia's relations with the Harlem community.

In the aftermath of the strike, I joined SDS and immediately became drawn into a fierce internal debate on the politics of black nationalism. The main leadership faction of SDS, led by Mark Rudd and Lewis Cole, believed the Columbia strike provided the model for a revolutionary challenge to an American government that was losing control of its empire at home and abroad. They thought that if white radicals followed the lead of militant blacks, as they had at Columbia, they could build a movement that could end American efforts to control Third World economies and redistribute the nation's wealth in a manner that insured greater racial justice. However, they faced a severe challenge to their leadership from SDS members associated with the Progressive Labor Party, a spinoff of the Communist Party that had taken China's side in the Sino-Soviet dispute. Progressive Labor leaders argued that black nationalism was reactionary and that no revolutionary organization could be built with separate black and white wings. They wanted SDS to challenge SAS's separatism and try to recruit black Columbia students into interracial organizations. Convinced that the Progressive Labor position would discredit SDS in the black community, Rudd, who had been a counselor in Double Discovery the summer before, asked me to use my knowledge of African-American history and the history of the labor movement to argue that the nationalist impulse was a progressive force in African-American life and that white radicals had to learn to work with it. While Rudd and Cole used Marxist theory to justify their position, particularly the essays of Stalin and Mao Tse-tung on the national and colonial question," I drew upon the experience of the American Communist Party in the 1920s and 1930s, which had taken the position that African-Americans were a "nation within a nation" and had tried to achieve a balance between nationalism and interracialism.

In the course of my research, I kept up a running correspondence on black nationalism and the left with Paul Buhle, my editor at *Radical America*. Paul also saw race as the central issue facing SDS and indeed all American radicals who wished to build a movement to transform American society. We agreed with one position taken by the American Communist Party: that the best way for white radicals to undermine the force of nationalism was by challenging white racism. As an oppressed nationality, African-Americans had the *right* to form separate organizations and were fully justified in not trusting whites. If white radicals wanted an integrated society, they would have to prove, through their actions, that they were worthy of the black community's trust. Adding weight to this theoretical approach was the fact that the Communist Party had created one of the most integrated organizations in American history, a place where blacks and whites not only organized together politically but socialized, dated, married, and raised families. In short, the party's moral recognition of the legitimacy of black nationalism, and its division of labor between black and white radicals, ultimately helped it create a viable multiracial organization.

The more I examined the Communist Party experience, the more I realized that it was futile for me as an individual, or for SDS as an organization, to challenge black nationalism directly. My friends and I were in no moral position to tell African-Americans that they should trust whites or work in integrated organizations. Nevertheless, the impact of black nationalism on my own life was quite painful. Ruthie returned from Hamilton Hall feeling a great sense of accomplishment but also with a distinct air of sadness. For the first time, she told me, some of the black men at Columbia were telling her it was time to break up with me, even though they liked me personally. I didn't know what to say. I tried to show my love for Ruthie by doing extra chores around the house, controlling my temper, being more tender and considerate in our lovemaking, but I felt like I was swimming against the tide. Both of us were now spending more time going to political meetings, but these meetings were sharply divided by race. As nationalist sentiment intensified and spread, I feared that our love might fall victim to political and social pressures.

Although my personal life was in turmoil, the racial tensions I was experiencing gave depth and focus to my historical studies. Increasingly, I found that African-American history helped give me perspective on current issues. Radicals in the past had faced many of the problems my friends and I were encountering. If Depression-era Communists could reconcile nationalism and interracialism, maybe our generation could also. I was determined to stay suspended between black and white worlds and share what I learned with anyone who wanted to listen. History would be my refuge, my inspiration, my shelter in the storm.

7   Nowhere to Run, Nowhere to Hide

By THE SUMMER of 1968, defending interracial harmony, at least on the American left, often seemed a quixotic project. With the civil rights and antiwar movements dividing into black and white factions, it was difficult for political activists to extol the virtues of an integrated society without appearing to discourage self-assertion and self-discovery by African-Americans. While I publicly defended the right of African-Americans to control their own organizations and communities, I tried to locate my personal life within a racially diverse atmosphere while the nationalist firestorm ran its course. My social life, family activities, and recreation largely took place in multiracial settings. From the classrooms of Double Discovery, to the basketball courts of Riverside Park, to the homes of Ruthie's relatives in the Bronx, to our communal apartment on 99th Street, I tried to spend as much time as possible in places where blacks and whites felt comfortable together.

African-American history played a central role in this project. The more I studied black history, the more I became convinced that it was impossible to understand American history without incorporating its African-American component, an insight W.E.B. Du Bois had offered more than sixty years earlier and that all too few white scholars had chosen to pursue. Black people were deeply embedded in all of the social processes that made the American nation, from conquest and settlement to westward expansion and industrialization, and they had a powerful influence on the development of the American political system and culture. Making this knowledge part of the teaching of American history could help democratize American academic culture and have a role in healing racial divisions.

My immersion in African-American history helped me to keep a foothold in the black community at a time when many liberal and radical whites were leaving it. In the summer of 1968, I was invited to teach a black history course in Project Double Discovery that had been taught the summer before by Eric Foner, a brilliant young Columbia graduate student and protégé of Richard Hofstadter. Foner had recently been hired by the Columbia history department, despite his support of the building occupations, and had been assigned to teach the first African-American history course at Columbia College the following spring. He was spending the summer doing research. Armed with syllabi and suggestions from Eric, I tried to figure out what kind of material would reach the politically aware inner-city high-school students in my Double Discovery class. For additional help, I turned to the person I knew who had the greatest knowledge of African-American history and culture, Una Mulzac, owner of the Liberation Bookstore on 131th Street and Lenox Avenue in Harlem. A tall, light-skinned woman with a salt-and-pepper afro, Una had spent many years in the Progressive Labor Party but had left when that organization repudiated black nationalism. Her store was a trove of works of history and literature by authors from Africa and the African diaspora, as well as books on Marxist philosophy and literature on world revolution.

Una advised me to avoid textbooks and concentrate on memoirs of famous protest leaders, which would help my students see African-Americans as agents of historical change. In addition to *The Autobiography of Malcolm X*, she recommended *The Life and Times of Frederick Douglass*, Booker T. Washington's *Up From Slavery*, W.E.B Du Bois's *Souls of Black Folk*, and an anthology containing short pieces about Nat Turner, David Walker, John Brown, Marcus Garvey, and Martin Luther King, Jr. I purchased the books she suggested and then spent an hour talking with her about the Columbia strike, Vietnam, and the Progressive Labor Party's efforts to take over SDS. If I had any doubts about the appropriateness of a white person teaching African-American history, Una helped lay them to rest.

Nervous when I arrived to teach my first class, I was reassured to see many familiar faces, students I had supervised as a division leader or met on the basketball court and at Double Discovery dances. The class was all black, equally divided between men and women, but I tried to proceed as though my whiteness was no barrier to a shared sense of mission. I approached the students as co-conspirators, telling them that we were embarking together on an adventure to recover a lost history and that they were going to learn things in this class that they probably never heard about in school. If they did their work seriously, they could then go on to teach others. This appeal to communal responsibility seemed to register. Through television, movies, and contact with black political organizations active in their neighborhoods and schools, they knew that African-Americans were redefining their place in American society and that the rest of the country was coming to recognize this change in the social landscape.

I decided to organize the class around a debate format, assigning short passages about African-American leaders and having the class discuss the issues those leaders faced. Should Nat Turner have killed every white person in his path? Should Booker T. Washington have supported segregation? Was Marcus Garvey right in saying white Americans would never accept blacks as equals? Should Malcolm X have left the Nation of Islam? I also assigned essays on these topics, the best of which would be published in a class magazine that we distributed to everyone in Double Discovery. The material, the debate format, and the possibility of a more public hearing for their work made for a lively, and sometimes tumultuous, classroom atmosphere.

That summer as before, Double Discovery students welcomed Ruthie and me into their lives without hesitation. They seemed to follow Ruthie everywhere, asking for advice about personal matters or just wanting to be near her. Despite the growing popularity of nationalist ideas and organizations, not one of them displayed any hostility to our relationship. The parties Ruthie and I threw that summer were well attended by Double Discovery students, who seemed comfortable socializing with our black and white friends so long as they could control the musical selections and set the tone on the dance floor. With our record player basting soul and rhythm and blues and our refrigerator filled with bottles of sweet wine—Scuppernong, Boone's Farm, Manischewitz Concord Grape—people danced together with reckless abandon and in combinations unchecked by age, race, or gender.

The tensions surrounding our relationship in the Columbia community, however, continued to escalate. I soon discovered that Ruthie no longer felt comfortable bringing me to SAS parties and other events hosted by black organizations. One evening, when she was getting dressed to go to one of these events, I asked why she couldn't take me. "Stop it, Mark! Stop it right now!" she replied, bursting into tears. "This is too much pressure. I can't take it anymore. Everybody's trying to tell me what to do. I don't want to choose between you and my friends. We've been through a lot together, but I have this other life too. Please don't ask me to give it up!"

As she started to weep uncontrollably, I reached out my arms and held her. She was shaking and shivering with fright. After half an hour of reassurance, Ruthie went off to the party, but the conflict remained unresolved. Ruthie's deep desire for companionship with other politically active black students, something I understood in theory but resented in practice, was creating issues that both of us had difficulty handling.

Little by little, these tensions chipped away at some of the trust and intimacy that made our relationship so special. When Ruthie went to SAS gatherings, I would sit around our apartment in a fit of jealous rage, wondering if she was going to discard me for one of the men in the organization. If she came home late, I would accuse her of cheating on me, an accusation that would provoke bitter sarcasm from Ruthie, whose public and private persona was far less sexual than mine. "You're crazy!" she would scream at me. "Just because you think about sex all the time, you think everyone else is the same way. Why don't you go sleep with one of those little white girls you hang around with all day? Then you won't bother me so much." Once that summer I almost did. At an off-campus party, I started slow dancing with a white history graduate student I was attracted to, and sparks began to fly. We ground our bodies into one another for nearly an hour without pause, and if either of us had given any sort of signal, we would have ended up back at her apartment. But no matter how mad I was at Ruthie, I could not humiliate her by going to bed with someone she knew. Betraying our relationship for revenge or sexual pleasure was not a step I was ready to take. But that did not stop me from screaming at her, cursing her, and, on one occasion, throwing her clothes out the window, a gesture Ruthie matched by bombarding me with pork chops and chicken wings from the refrigerator. Although we always made up after these theatrical episodes, we had begun to pay a price for refusing to accommodate to racial divisions

These issues, however, were soon dwarfed by health problems and family emergencies that beset Ruthie, none of which were racial in origin. While eating dinner at our apartment late that summer, Ruthie suddenly began spitting up cupfuls of blood. When we rushed her to St. Luke's emergency room, doctors told us that a blood clot in Ruthie's lung had burst and that she had been an hour away from bleeding to death. The hospital staff was able to stop the bleeding and stabilize her condition, but they kept her there for five full days of tests. Their explanation of what had occurred was chilling. The blood clot, doctors told us, probably had been caused by the birth-control pills that Ruthie had been taking for the past two years. These pills had been marketed by drug companies and distributed by physicians without sufficient warning of their side effects. Ruthie had not only suffered a life-threatening blood clot, she also sustained some heart damage, and her physical condition would have to be carefully monitored for the rest of her life. When she came home from the hospital, she was in great need of comfort and care. Guilty that my jealousy and anger had added to her stress, I tried to submerge my own physical and emotional needs and nurse her back to health.

At first, Ruthie's illness seemed to ease the atmosphere of crisis that had invaded our relationship. The five-day hospital stay, during which I kept a vigil at her bedside, dramatized the powerful emotional investment we had in one another and made the political and cultural ties she felt to her comrades from the Hamilton Hall occupation seem less significant. Nevertheless, we were not the same couple we had been two years before. We still felt bound together by shared values and mutual respect, but much of the optimism had vanished from our relationship, along with the passion and physical excitement. Ruthie returned from the hospital physically and emotionally spent, and I had to defer to her fragility in ways I found painful. The innocent couple who thought their love would change the world had been replaced by a pair of survivors; stubborn, resilient, determined to hold on to our principles in the face of hardship and tragedy.

In these circumstances, our apartment on 99th Street assumed even greater significance as a place where the racial tensions of the larger society could be temporarily put aside. After Ruthie returned from the hospital, a steady stream of visitors came by to comfort her and show their concern. The sheer diversity of the people who cared about Ruthie—from our building, from her family, from Double Discovery—was simply astonishing. The Australian sculptor who lived across the hall, the gay British art critic who lived below us, our Dominican superintendent, Angel—all visited regularly, adding a cosmopolitan, international element to the multiracial group who congregated in our apartment. This communal display of affection moved me deeply, making it even harder to imagine separating myself from Ruthie, even though our physical relationship had lost its joy and spontaneity.

We were also bound together by affection for two new roommates we acquired that fall, Bruce Hazard and Wendy Wisner, who almost instantly became our closest friends. Bruce, a recent Princeton graduate, had gotten a job teaching inner-city teenagers in an Urban League street academy in Harlem, and he was still experiencing the shock of adjustment to New York City. Brought up in a white middle-class family in rural New Hampshire, and educated in the pastoral elegance of Princeton's campus, he found the eclectic atmosphere of 99th Street and the anger and passion of Harlem's residents challenging. But Bruce had grown up doing hard physical labor on a working farm, and he was tough, resourceful, and difficult to intimidate. He was also thoughtful, direct, and completely free of snobbery or racial prejudice. Ruthie immediately felt comfortable in his presence. Like Ruthie, Bruce preferred to express himself through small, practical gestures rather than lengthy talk. Bruce also had a number of skills that improved the quality of our lives, from cooking quick, inexpensive dinners, to washing dirty dishes quickly and efficiently and driving vehicles with a standard shift. We liked to talk with him about teaching and listen to him sing and play the banjo; I enjoyed playing basketball and football with him in Riverside Park.

Wendy, a senior at Sarah Lawrence College who quickly became an equally valued companion, was also white. The product of an elite Washington family—her father had been a founder of the CIA—Wendy had been brought up on a Maryland plantation farmed by white sharecroppers and staffed by African-American and French servants. But she actively rebelled against her upper-class upbringing. A powerfully built woman with limitless energy, Wendy was much happier shoveling manure in a barn or hiking in the wilderness than dressing up for a cocktail party or formal dinner. Our apartment became a place where she could spend time with Bruce, escape her mother's nagging, and be in the company of people who enjoyed her eccentricities. Ruthie quickly became Wendy's confidante and big sister, somebody she could turn to for advice on clothes, jewelry, her love life, or her problems with her family. In turn, Wendy's sharp tongue and wicked sense of humor made Ruthie laugh at a time she desperately needed cheering up.

With Bruce and Wendy's arrival in our apartment, the class and cultural diversity of people who came to visit us became even more dramatic. In an apartment where the daughter of the founder of the CIA
slept in a room down the hall from the daughter of the labor editor of
the *Daily Worker*, the newspaper of the American Communist Party, it
was difficult to predict who might show up at our door. On any given
day, we could have working-class black kids from Brooklyn and the
Bronx, draft resisters from Tennessee, or Jewish Marxists from SDS sitting next to friends of Bruce and Wendy with surnames like Hewitt,
Delacorte, and Morgenthau. An abhorrence of the Vietnam War, a belief
in racial equality, and an affinity for the drug culture temporarily produced an atmosphere in which common styles of dress, speech, affect,
and musical tastes muted class and cultural boundaries centuries in the
making.

Bruce and I also spent time together in the colorful and tempestuous
multiracial community that formed around the Riverside Park basketball courts between 110th and 112th Streets. In New York City, where
basketball had the status of a secular religion, each schoolyard tended
to have a distinct personality. Some outdoor courts, like the ones on
West 4th Street in Manhattan, and at Nostrand and Newkirk Avenues
in Brooklyn, attracted college players, pros, and top high school
prospects; others, like the one on Amsterdam Avenue and 99th Street,
were used exclusively by teenagers. But the courts on 110th Street
attracted a polyglot, largely adult constituency that included school
teachers, employees in local stores, Columbia graduate students, and a
significant number of actors and writers who lived on the West Side. On
weekday afternoons at 3:30, and on weekends at 9:00 A.M., the "regulars" started gathering and choosing sides for half-court and full-court
games. The quality of the games was usually modest; few of the participants had played college basketball, some of the players were over
thirty, and the vast majority of the action took place "below the rim."
But the verbal byplay that accompanied the games was breathtaking in
its inventiveness and variety, shaped by an undercurrent of racial tension in a group equally divided between blacks and whites.

Amid the shoving, banging, and maneuvering for position, there was
a racially charged competition over who had the right to interpret the
action on the court. Many of the college-educated black men who played
at Riverside deeply resented the white players, coaches, and media com-

mentators in professional and college basketball who assumed white superiority in the mental aspects of the game and who treated blacks as raw physical specimens in need of constant direction. In response, they perfected the role of the African-American basketball-philosopher, someone who, invited or not, told other players where to go and what to do, clinically assessed their strengths and weakness, and offered commentary on basketball and life when resting between games. If a white player accepted their leadership and showed respect for their views, these men could be quite gracious. But if a white player of lesser ability tried to boss them around, they would insult him, humiliate him, refuse to pass him the ball, and make sure he was not picked in subsequent games. At the Riverside Park basketball courts, displays of white racial arrogance of the sort taken for granted in much of America would guarantee you a seat on the sidelines.

Once I learned the complex racial etiquette, I enjoyed playing at Riverside Park. Since I was more of a raw athlete than a skilled, well-coached player, I could easily join in the communal mission of challenging racial stereotypes. If I played hard, jumped high, pulled out an occasional acrobatic show move, and kept my mouth shut, the basketball philosophers treated me with respect, making sure I got picked when people chose up teams and inviting me to sit in on the after-game discussions. I also became friends with Milton Brown, the best player in the park. Milton was a doctoral candidate in education whose brilliant play and volatile temper kept everyone on their toes. About five feet, ten inches tall and weighing 175 pounds, with light brown skin and a reddish afro, Milton had great quickness and leaping ability, excellent ball-handling skills, a fierce will to win, and firm opinions about how the game should be played. Milton never stopped chattering from the moment he stepped onto the court. He teased and insulted opponents, told his teammates when to pass and when to shoot, and berated them if they were selfish or lazy. Some people hated his arrogance and feared his wrath, but I found that playing with him moved my game to a higher level.

To be sure, not all my experiences at Riverside Park were so positive. One of the regulars at Riverside was an African-American radio personality and journalist named Ethan Kile, who had a loose tongue, a terrible temper, and limited basketball skills. About six feet, three inches tall, with extremely pale skin, reddish hair, and thick glasses, Ethan got into screaming arguments with other players almost every time he came to the park. I generally kept out of his way, but one afternoon we became the target of one another's racially charged resentments. Ethan and I were on opposite sides of a full-court basketball game in which a downstairs neighbor and I were the only white players. Suddenly he got angry at my friend, who was a very poor player, and started calling him a "honky computer brain." Furious that he was using race to attack an essentially defenseless person, I decided to teach him a lesson and told my friend to let me guard Ethan. Every time I got the ball, I took him to the basket and pulled out my best array of spins, double pumps, and hesitation moves. To provoke him further, I elbowed him sharply in the stomach and ribs every time we jockeyed for position under the basket. Before long Ethan was calling *me* a honky, and when he finally snapped and started throwing punches at me, I sent him sprawling to the ground with a single left hook. That ended the game. As I was getting dressed to go home, Milton Brown approached me and said, "I'm glad you hit him. He had it coming." Although Milton's support was important to me, the incident left me shaken. Ethan was someone whose professional work I respected and to see him resort to race baiting saddened me. My own role in the incident also raised disturbing issues. When I punched Ethan, I was clearly releasing a great deal of pent-up resentment against race-conscious black men, whom I blamed for the troubles between Ruthie and me.

These tensions also spilled into my political and intellectual life, driving me toward positions that were increasingly extreme. As much as I loved historical research, my anger about the racial issues I confronted every day was too great to be satisfied by recovering and reinterpreting African-American history and analyzing how past radical organizations had dealt with America's racial divisions. Throughout the fall of 1968 and the spring of 1969, I veered erratically between my doctoral work at Columbia and participation in street actions and campus takeovers organized by SDS. Having persuaded Richard Hofstadter to serve as my doctoral advisor, and published two articles in *Radical America*, I seemed poised on the edge of a modest academic career. But I was fascinated by the evolution of SDS leaders into professional revolutionaries and their efforts to form alliances with black organizations who practiced armed self-defense. I still marched in peaceful protests against the war in Vietnam; I still participated in the radical caucus of the American Historical

Association and the steering committee of the Socialist Scholars Conference; I still took on writing projects for *Radical America*. But when the
opportunity arose, I participated in building seizures at Columbia and
the University of Chicago and joined militant street demonstrations in
New York City that targeted draft boards, corporations engaged in war
research, and officials of the Johnson and Nixon administrations.

While I cannot speak for every SDS member who made the transition from student radical to "street-fighting" revolutionary, I felt at the
time, and still feel now, that anxiety about America's racial crisis played
as large a role in that transformation as anger at the Vietnam War. Even
with SDS chapters on hundreds of American campuses, many SDS leaders felt frustrated by their inability to intervene on the side of the black
community in the violent racial conflicts that were occurring in many
American cities. The uprisings that followed King's assassination, the
militarization of urban police departments, the rise of gun clubs and
law-and-order candidates in white urban neighborhoods, and the rapid
growth of the Black Panther Party, a grassroots black organization that
preached socialist revolution and armed self-defense, caused many SDS
leaders to feel that campus organizing put them on the sidelines in the
country's most important political conflict. In their heart of hearts, most
SDS leaders I knew were romantic integrationists who identified powerfully with African-American culture. They listened to black music,
rooted for black athletes, and felt deeply wounded by the separatism
and hostility of black activists on college campuses. To them, transforming SDS into a phalanx of off-campus militants allied with black
revolutionaries represented an opportunity to show African-Americans
that *some* whites were willing to stand by them in a time of maximum
danger. To preserve the possibilities of an integrated society, they had
to turn themselves, as Mark Rudd put it, into latter-day "John Browns."

Nothing did more to speed the migration of SDS off college campuses than the growth of the Black Panther Party. The Panthers' mix of
revolutionary humanism and street-corner bravado, forged in community colleges and prison libraries, mesmerized white student radicals
and stirred their imaginations. Here were courageous men and women
from the nation's toughest black neighborhoods who believed that white
radicals had a role to play in the struggle for black emancipation. Unlike
black student unions on college campuses, whose alliances with white
student radicals were often perfunctory at best, the Panthers welcomed

white participation in campaigns to free arrested or imprisoned Panther leaders, and they conducted aggressive fund raising among progressive whites for their newspaper and community programs. Following the strategy Malcolm X endorsed following his break from the Nation of Islam, the Panthers kept their own organization exclusively black, but enthusiastically sought alliances with white, Latino, and multiracial organizations who endorsed their goals.

But an alliance with the Panthers carried unanticipated political costs. The Panthers' socialist and internationalist principles, their rejection of race hatred as a principle of political mobilization, and their commitment to serving poor and working-class people—reflected in the children's free-breakfast programs and the community health clinics they sponsored—coexisted with a romantic identification with African-American street criminals and an open-ended, and sometimes incendiary, commitment to armed self-defense. One year after Huey Newton and Bobby Seale founded the Panthers in 1966, they attracted national attention by organizing armed patrols to monitor the Oakland police and picketing the California state legislature with guns in hand. Given the brutality and lawlessness of police forces in black communities, the Panthers' project for "policing the police" proved to be a brilliant strategy for building a following. But as the Black Panther Party grew into a nationwide organization, with chapters in almost every large city, some of its leaders began to move beyond advocating self-defense and to extol the gun as the preeminent symbol of black freedom. In the process, the distinction between using firearms to repel aggression and employing them as existential symbols of self-assertion sometimes became blurred. Wherever party chapters were established, gun battles, raids, and indictments seemed to follow. Although most of the violence that enveloped the Panthers was government initiated, the result of attacks by local police and a pernicious FBI counter-intelligence program (code-named Cointelpro), which used informers, infiltrators, and provocateurs to maximize conflict and paranoia among the party members, all too many Panthers contributed to the resulting turmoil, seizing upon party directives to "pick up the gun" as a license to beat wives and girlfriends, torture political opponents, and commit robberies to fund the movement.

The sacrificial heroism of individual party members, many of whom were jailed on serious charges or died in shootouts with police, made it difficult for white radicals to evaluate, much less criticize, this complex movement culture. Impressed by the Panthers' courage in challenging abuses of police power and desperate to find any black radical organization that would ally itself with whites, some SDS leaders began to anoint the Panthers as the vanguard of a multiracial revolutionary movement developing in the United States. By the spring of 1969, hundreds of SDS members around the country, loosely linked in a "Revolutionary Youth Movement Caucus," were working closely with Black Panther chapters in their local communities and incorporating Panther slogans and rhetoric into their political work. Regional SDS offices organized defense campaigns for Eldridge Cleaver, Huey Newton, and Bobby Seale; raised funds for the Panthers' free-breakfast programs, and in one city, Chicago, created a Pantherlike organization called "Rising Up Angry" that sought to organize white working-class youth against racism and police repression. Under Panther influence, SDS activists from upper-middle-class and middle-class backgrounds adopted the language and affect of working street toughs and Panther neighborhood organizers. They wore leather jackets and work shirts, studied martial arts, used Panther slogans like "Power to the People," and referred to police as "pigs" and the government as the "pig power structure." But the relationship also involved extralegal activities and a much higher quotient of risk than SDS activities ever had before. In early 1969, friends in SDS asked me to help Panther spokesperson Eldridge Cleaver escape the country to avoid imprisonment for murder. After West Coast SDSers spirited him into Canada, I was supposed to stay with him in a Canadian safe house until arrangements could be made to get him to Cuba. I turned this assignment down because I felt I was being watched by the FBI, but the request certainly got my attention. As the SDS national leadership moved to embrace revolutionary strategies and objectives, the demands on members began to grow.

Not everyone on the left regarded this development positively. Many college SDS chapters were more concerned with stopping the Vietnam War than with joining a revolutionary movement under the leadership of the Panthers. Moreover, almost all of the radical historians I worked with, ranging from bitter ex-Communists like Eugene Genovese to visionary idealists like Paul Buhle, warned me that talk of revolution and armed struggle was more likely to provoke repression than accelerate social change. But despite my own doubts that revolution was possible in the United States, I welcomed the SDS shift toward off-campus organizing. From bitter experience, I knew that hostility toward blacks was far more deeply entrenched among whites in neighborhood and workplace settings than on college campuses. The prospect of thousands of campus militants challenging white racism in its most malignant manifestations and trying to create alliances between working-class whites and blacks seemed both noble and extremely difficult. If nothing else, it would show African-Americans that at least *some* whites were willing to relinquish a comfortable existence to confront America's most difficult internal problem. As American Communists had argued forty years earlier, nothing could undermine the emotional and political basis of black separatism more than a massive mobilization of whites to challenge white supremacist practices and defend black victims of injustice. If it took revolutionary rhetoric and utopian fantasies to get people to make this sacrifice, I was willing to go along. What some people saw as revolutionary posturing I saw as gestures of racial reconciliation, and I was not about to stand on the sidelines while SDS leaders tried to draw white-working class youth into antiracist coalitions and antiwar organizing.

I was also attracted by the aura of power and excitement that surrounded SDS on campus and off. In early 1969, SDS had strong chapters at state universities and city colleges as well as schools like Columbia, and had started to reach beyond its core constituency of Jewish intellectuals and "red diaper babies." In cities like Chicago, New York, and Boston, it had opened offices in downtown business districts and could bring thousands of people together for street demonstrations on a single day's notice. Joining this organization seemed like being part of a great national fraternity engaged in a mission of social change. I took many trips that confirmed the widespread influence of SDS, but one made a particularly powerful impression, a visit to Chicago during which I stayed with my old college friend Louis, who was an SDS leader and a graduate student at the University of Chicago. During my five-day visit, I spent time at SDS national headquarters, engaged in long discussions about race, and attended SDS-led protest meetings on the University of Chicago campus.

Chicago was a violent, rigidly segregated city, but its economy had been built around basic industries like meat packing and steel, and it had a radical working-class tradition that dated back to the Haymarket

Affair and the Wobblies. When Louis and I took the elevated train from Hyde Park to the SDS office on West Madison Street, I saw a city sharply divided between run-down residential neighborhoods and a sprawling downtown business district patrolled by angry-looking policemen. An air of menace hung in the streets, but also an air of romance. In the neighborhood surrounding the SDS office, which was Chicago's skid row, you could almost see the ghosts of radical organizers who had gone before us—the Haymarket martyrs, the Wobblies, the leaders of the 1919 steel strike, the Communists who brought the CIO to Chicago's biggest factories. In fact, vestiges of this working-class radical tradition still seemed to be alive and well. Chicago had the strongest and best-organized chapter of the Black Panther Party in the country, led by the scrupulously honest and charismatic Fred Hampton. It had helped build small youth organizations modeled on the Panthers in white working-class and Latino neighborhoods. There was a Young Patriots organization in a white Appalachian neighborhood, a Young Lords organization in a Latino neighborhood, and the SDS-led Rising Up Angry, active throughout the city with white working-class youth. Linked by common hatred of the war, the police, and the rigidly tracked Chicago school system, these organizations reflected the spread of an anti-authoritarian spirit from college campuses to working-class communities, and they suggested that high schools, community colleges, and even the military could be targets of radical organizing.

I participated in a sit-in at the University of Chicago during the last day of my visit, one provoked by the university's urban renewal policies and its complicity with the war in Vietnam. After a series of brilliant speeches by SDS leaders, hundreds of white students surged into the main classroom building and started barricading doors and windows and writing flyers that explained their actions. A festive spirit took hold in the once-sterile atmosphere of classrooms and offices. Students hugged each other, sang, held impassioned political discussions, and talked about their families, their studies, their plans for the future. Total strangers became friends. At two o'clock in the morning, I found myself in a room filled with desks, file cabinets, and sleeping protesters, making love to a young woman I had just met. An erotic energy seemed to pervade the demonstration, providing an exhilarating complement to its political seriousness. At that moment, SDS seemed to be a catalyst for multiple forms of generational rebellion.

When I returned to New York I became more involved with SDS at the campus and regional level. SDS's New York regional headquarters were in a shabby industrial building in a neighborhood now called Soho. In these offices, I met SDSers from many local universities, including City and Brooklyn Colleges, NYU, Fordham, Lehman, and Hunter. I also met SDS members attached to no college at all. The sense of power and intellectual excitement there was as great as in Chicago. Most of these people saw their movement as related to Third World liberation struggles at home and abroad, and they had a powerful emotional identification with black militants in the United States. They envisioned SDS as one component of a multiracial revolutionary movement led by a politically aroused African-American community. The organization contained a number of strong and articulate women who used their influence to raise questions about the exclusion of women from power in the movement and society. Without rejecting SDS's emphasis on Third World struggles, they called attention to the numerous ways women were devalued and exploited by the men they interacted with. At the time I did not view women as oppressed in the same way that I felt blacks and the Vietnamese were. I associated oppression with poverty, colonialism, and racial persecution, and it was hard for me to see college-educated white women as victims. But their demands for a fair share of power seemed reasonable, and I supported a women's liberation platform in SDS, even though the issue did not have the same emotional appeal for me as the struggle against racism. My convoluted response, fairly typical among men in SDS, showed deference to SDS's women cadre, who constituted at least half of the organization's active members, but little understanding of the incendiary issues radical feminists had begun to raise regarding male-female identity, power, and sexuality, as well as the accepted division of labor in the family and society.

SDS's growing preoccupation with race cemented my involvement in the organization. Although most of my white SDS comrades led more segregated personal lives than I did, and assumed that black and white radicals would work in separate organizations for the foreseeable future, their emotional identification with African-American culture and their concern with overcoming racial divisions was as strong as mine. Hunger for acceptance by African-Americans was a powerful undercurrent in their lives and a driving force in their political work, pushing them into actions with escalating levels of risk.

Even before the fateful summer of 1969, such pressures almost ended my career as a graduate student. In February 1969, as I was walking onto the campus for my oral examinations in American history, Mark Rudd and Lew Cole approached and warned me that they were going to occupy and barricade Fayerweather Hall, the building where my examinations were being held. "Oh, shit," I replied. "Can't you take another building?" "Sorry Mark, we can't," they answered. "But if you'd like, we'll let you stay while we throw everybody else out." An hour later, I walked into a seminar room in Fayerweather and faced a committee that included my two closest friends in the Columbia history department, James Shenton and Eric Foner, and two distinguished older faculty members with moderate political views, Richard Hofstadter and Dwight Miner. As they started to ask me questions, I heard people running through the halls, slamming doors, and smashing furniture. The commotion came from above and below us and from the hallway outside, but nobody so much as knocked on our door. I answered the questions my mentors asked me with as much aplomb as I could muster, but I was getting some very strange looks. After I passed the exam (I *had* actually studied pretty diligently for five full months), I offered to escort my committee out of the building. All the outside doors had been barricaded shut, so I took them to the student lounge, where thirty or forty demonstrators were holding a meeting, and, with the aid of several SDS members, carefully helped them out through an open window five feet off the ground. Several hours later, I returned to the building in my street clothes and remained inside until the occupation ended.

My role in this episode came back to haunt me two months later, when I was helping SDS secure and barricade another building. As SDS prepared to occupy Philosophy Hall, several conservative students grabbed and pushed me as I tried to close the main door. When they squirted me with Mace, I lost my temper and started throwing punches at the person nearest me, sending him to the ground and clearing enough space to allow me to slam the door shut. Unfortunately, my little tantrum was caught by a CBS cameraman and transformed into a thirty-second segment on the evening news. The next day, the main disciplinary officer at Columbia, Proctor Kahn, came up to me and announced that Columbia was initiating proceedings to expel me from graduate school. Upset by this news, I immediately went to John Mundy, the chair of the graduate history program, and asked him to intercede with the administration. Mundy, whose office had been trashed by protesters while my orals were taking place, was decidedly unsympathetic. "If you want to play Christ, you're going to be crucified," he told me bluntly. I next went to Richard Hofstadter, my dissertation supervisor, and several alumni supporters of the Columbia tennis team, and managed to persuade them to write letters asking Columbia to exercise leniency on the grounds that I could be a productive scholar and a solid citizen if I calmed down. Their letters must have had some effect because the graduate dean invented a new disciplinary category to deal with my case: "permanent censure." I was allowed to remain in graduate school, but was subject to immediate expulsion for any new violation of university rules. The word "censured" was stamped in big red letters on my permanent transcript.

This episode shook me, but did not drive me out of radical politics. Curtailing my participation in protests at Columbia, I intensified my involvement in New York regional SDS, which was forming collectives and affinity groups to organize off-campus actions. Increasingly, SDS was gravitating toward Leninist models of organizing, which emphasized the creation of small groups of disciplined revolutionaries rather than loosely structured mass organizations. I became involved with an entirely white Upper West Side collective composed of college graduates, over half of them women. We went to numerous demonstrations together, ate some communal meals, and spent a great deal of time discussing strategy for the SDS national convention in Chicago, where we expected to wage a war for control of SDS against people from the Progressive Labor Party. The Progressive Labor Party position—that all nationalism was reactionary—made it difficult for SDS to sustain an alliance with the Black Panther Party, a relationship we viewed as essential to SDS's transformation from a student organization into a revolutionary force.

In retrospect, one could find humor and pathos in the spectacle of graduates of Columbia, NYU, Wellesley, and Wisconsin trying to model themselves on revolutionary Communists in the Third World. Although our theoretical icons, figures like Ho Chi Minh, Che Guevara, Mao Tsetung, and Regis Debray, had all begun, like us, as middle-class intellectuals, they had organized for revolution in societies where the majority of people were impoverished peasants. The projection of revolutionary possibilities in a society as wealthy as the United States required a vivid imagination and a strong element of hubris. To put it bluntly, most of us became revolutionaries because we believed that a society with as violent a record of suppressing people of color as the United States, which was killing hundreds of thousands of people in Vietnam and using brutal force against black freedom fighters at home, *ought* to have a revolution. Whether or not "objective conditions" existed for such a movement here (in terms of popular discontent or government weakness and instability), we viewed revolutionary politics as a way to bear witness against injustice and to share the sacrifice of African-American militants and Third World revolutionaries.

Being among people who displayed such devotion to a cause was seductive and compelling, especially with so much instability in my own life. That summer my relationship with Ruthie ran into new difficulties when she decided to go to Georgia for three months to nurse her mother through the last stages of terminal cancer and to prepare her two younger siblings to attend school in the North. Soon after her departure, Bruce and Wendy moved into their own apartment, leaving me on 99th Street with three other roommates, one of whom was Paul, my former Double Discovery student. With Ruthie in Georgia, Nixon in the White House, the war still raging, and my career at Columbia in jeopardy, the SDS collective became my surrogate family, a place where I found emotional support as well as intellectual and political energy. We helped draft resisters and deserters, raised funds and attended protests for imprisoned Black Panthers, held demonstrations at draft boards and recruiting stations, and took to the streets to protest New York appearances by Nixon administration officials. For the moment, these activities seemed realistic and constructive.

Our mobilization for the Chicago SDS convention seemed to display the power and seriousness of the movement we had built. New York SDS rented four buses to take us to Chicago, and the appearances of the 150 people who boarded them showed how much the movement had changed since that first antiwar demonstration I attended in the spring of 1967. Most were veteran political activists in their early and mid twenties, and they projected the toughness and physical confidence of people who had been in numerous street demonstrations and confrontations with police. The women and men alike moved with swagger and attitude. Many wore leather jackets and heavy boots, or army fatigues. Some had had martial arts training, and others had been

instructed in street-fighting techniques. We looked formidable and pos-
sibly slightly dangerous, a bit like a left-wing motorcycle gang. When
we stopped for food in the middle of the night at a truck stop near
Akron, the truckers who were eating there did not know what to make
of us. We didn't look like teenagers from their neighborhoods, we did-
n't look like college students, and we didn't look like hippies. But there
we were, 150 strong, seated at tables next to them, and they wanted to
know what was going on. As we tried to explain our politics, we were
able to find some common ground in opposition to the war and hatred
of the politicians and businessmen who appeared to benefit from it.
"They ain't such bad guys," one trucker was overheard to say. "It's just
that they want to overthrow the government."

When we got to Chicago, however, things started to unravel. Of the
fifteen hundred people assembled, slightly more than half were associated with the Revolutionary Youth Movement (RYM) caucus. To isolate
and humiliate members of the Progressive Labor Caucus, the SDS
national leadership had invited representatives of the Black Panthers
and the Young Patriots, who swaggered around the convention in black
leather jackets and berets looking as intimidating as possible. The intellectual level of the proceedings was not impressive. The cult of working-class machismo and revolutionary bravado quickly transformed
discussions of strategy and ideology into chanting contests. Worse yet,
the main Panther speaker, whose charisma was supposed to sway the
convention toward a dramatic repudiation of Progressive Labor, gave
an offensive and embarrassing speech about how women could help the
revolution through their "pussy power" and then became outraged
when women in the audience groaned and hissed. After denouncing the
convention as a bunch of "counterrevolutionary white punks," he
stormed off the stage in anger, leaving the multiracial unity that RYM
leaders hoped to encourage in shambles. When the RYM leaders finally
engineered a vote to expel Progressive Labor and create a purer and
more disciplined version of SDS, most in the audience felt demoralized
and drained. Those of us who supported the RYM position dutifully
moved into an adjoining hall to found the new organization, but we
hardly felt confident about the future. The inability of the group we had
anointed our "vanguard" to acknowledge the moral and political legitimacy of women's liberation placed our whole revolutionary strategy
in question. Were we making a revolution for blacks and the Vietnamese,

or were we making a revolution for ourselves? Where did our own visions of a better, freer life fit in our strategic calculations and our relationships with other groups fighting to transform American society?

When we returned to New York, we found that the destruction of the old, loosely structured SDS had created more problems than it solved. The unity of purpose we hoped to achieve did not materialize. The many goals we had set forth in the RYM caucus—implanting our movement in the working class, creating alliances with revolutionary black organizations, showing solidarity with the heroic Vietnamese people, advancing the cause of women's liberation—were not amenable to simple strategic formulas. In fact, these objectives often appeared to clash, and divisions *within* the RYM caucus started to become as sharp as those involving Progressive Labor. In the resulting confusion, some people became desperate. That summer some of my closest friends decided to take violent measures to jump-start the revolution that they saw escaping their grasp.

8　Bringing the War Home

DURING THE FALL of 1969, my closest friends in SDS became trapped in an ideological and emotional whirlwind. Adopting a dramatic new political strategy that assumed the possibility of a black-led revolution in the United States, they now called themselves Weatherman (after a line in Bob Dylan's "Subterranean Homesick Blues") and set about purging their lives of friendships and material comforts in order to match the sacrifices of African-American militants and Vietnamese revolutionaries. Within several months, through rapidly escalating acts of protest and communal intimidation, they formed an underground political organization that bombed government and corporate targets as their major method of protest. I was there when the process began and almost got swallowed up in it. I spent a month in the New York Weatherman Collective and participated in several of the cadre actions aimed at transforming its physically timid members into hardened revolutionaries.

Race represented a powerful subplot in this project. One of the most distinctive elements of Weatherman's internal culture was its use of antiracist rhetoric, particularly the slogan "smashing white-skin privilege," to mobilize its members for revolutionary violence. The Weatherman collectives were perhaps the first radical organizations in modern American history to make guilt about whiteness their primary motivating force. Participants continually invoked the heroism and sacrifice of African-American militants and Third World revolutionaries to inspire one another to take high-risk political actions and to discard any relationships, including marriages and friendships, that stood in their way. In Weatherman's mental universe, African-Americans appeared only as heroes and victims. Lacking sustained day-to-day contact with the black community, they were unable to see African-Americans as a diverse and complicated people who could not be pigeonholed into those two categories.

Weatherman had started out as a tendency within the Revolutionary Youth Movement (RYM) caucus that had expelled Progressive Labor from SDS. The people who developed the Weatherman statement, Mark Rudd and John Jacobs from Columbia, and Bernadine Dohrn from the SDS national office, believed that the main engines of revolution in the world were the people of the Third World nations and African-Americans in the United States. Unlike other leaders of the RYM caucus, they believed that the majority of white workers had been so co-opted by their jobs, houses, and pensions that they would never support revolutionary change. They wanted SDS to concentrate on organizing white working-class youth against racism and the war rather than on uniting black and white workers on the basis of economic issues. Their mistake was to tie a quite plausible analysis of white working-class conservatism to a claim that the African-American community was ripe for revolution. Citing the urban rebellions that followed the death of Dr. King, the growth of the Black Panther Party, and the rise of black student unions in colleges and high schools, Weatherman argued that a revolutionary crisis was forming in the United States. As Third World revolutions chipped away at American imperialism, white Americans would have to choose sides between supporting the black revolution or a weakened but still potent American government.

When I first read the Weatherman statement at the 1969 SDS convention, I did not dream that its authors actually *believed* that revolution was imminent. I thought they were using Marxist rhetoric to legitimate the argument that youth and racial minorities had become the primary agents of social change in the United States. But I underestimated how seriously some SDS leaders took their new role as revolutionary communists. Some of the people who began Weatherman had visited and worked in Cuba or had been among the American radicals who met with representatives of Vietnam's National Liberation Front. They approached ideological struggles and strategic planning in SDS with an extraordinary sense of urgency and consequence. In their eyes, no less than the course of world history would be affected by SDS's policies and actions.

By July 1969, the Weatherman faction decided to break with their former allies in RYM and recruit SDS members for a new organization that would use violent, confrontational tactics to "bring the war home." Dispensing with the loose-knit, decentralized structure that had helped make SDS the most powerful campus organization in American history, they proposed to build an organization of collectives whose members would live communally and operate under tight political discipline. By August 1969, they had persuaded about five hundred people throughout the country to join Weatherman collectives. Most of these members came from elite universities, and many were women. In New York City, at least half of the Weatherpeople came from SDS chapters at Columbia or New York University.

One major goal of the first Weatherman collectives was to get out of university neighborhoods and organize white working-class youth into militant antiwar protests. The New York Weatherman Collective decided to rent a house in a tough but gentrifying section of South Brooklyn bordering Prospect Park. One female collective member and I posed as husband and wife to negotiate the lease and sign the rental agreement. Once the house was secure, collective members began undergoing what could best be described as a "social class makeover" in preparation for organizing working-class Irish and Italian teenagers. Every collective member participated in martial arts training, running, and calisthenics. They purchased boots, helmets, army fatigues, and heavy jackets in preparation for street fighting. As someone who had grown up fighting on the streets of Brooklyn, I found it amusing to watch my fellow collective members, most of whom came from sheltered backgrounds and at least half of whom were women, try to adopt the toughness and swagger of working-class men. In Weatherman, machismo and physical aggressiveness had suddenly become fashionable. The women in the collective were the driving force in this transformation. Meeting in separate caucuses as well as in general collective gatherings, women approached physical training as a rebellion against traditional gender roles as well as a tool of working-class organizing.

For the first couple of weeks, I found the atmosphere of the Weatherman collective more intriguing than intimidating. Being in a left organization that valued physical toughness and in which women were stronger leaders than men was a new experience for me. Colorful and dynamic women, who had participated in student rebellions and, in some instances, had a background in theater, invested the organization's internal discussions, especially those relating to gender, with passion and intellectual excitement.

But currents of white guilt and revolutionary adventurism soon undercut Weatherman's intellectual and cultural creativity. At the national conference of Weatherman organizers, held in Cleveland in late

August 1969, Weatherman leaders took turns flagellating themselves, and the rest of the white student left, for failing to make real sacrifices for their political beliefs. In their view, while Vietnamese revolutionaries were dying to free their nation from American imperialism, and black revolutionaries were being harassed, jailed, and ambushed on the streets, white so-called revolutionaries were spending their time on marches, rallies, and building occupations rather than inflicting material damage on the institutions that ruled America. The source of their timidity, they concluded, was "white skin privilege," the array of material and psychological advantages that made white people feel that America belonged to them. To achieve any genuine solidarity with Third World revolutionaries, white radicals would have to purge their lives of the comforts and privileges that inhibited political militancy. The Weatherman organizers decided to take an extraordinary step to force its cadre to become more intrepid—to ban all monogamous relationships, gay or straight, within Weatherman collectives. From the Cleveland conference onward, no Weatherperson was to have a special emotional or sexual relationship with any individual; they had to give their loyalty, their passion, and their commitment solely to the collective and the revolution.

This policy made Weatherman dramatically different from any organization to which its members had ever belonged. The ban on monogamy not only gave Weatherman the aura of a religious cult, it also set the stage for an erasure of individuality that was conducive to mind control. Not even communist parties, notoriously aggressive in policing their members' personal lives, ever designated marriage, love, and friendship as counterrevolutionary! But there was a logic to this strategy. What better way was there to harden and toughen a group of middle-class radicals than to deprive them of nurturing relationships and make them totally dependent upon the approval of their collective? What better way to create a "new generation of John Browns" among people who had grown up in comfort and security, than to create conditions that were conducive to martyrdom?

Collective leaders, upon their return from Cleveland, imposed the new policy on monogamy and ordered a dramatic escalation of political activity. For the next two months, we would mobilize for a huge, violent demonstration in Chicago called the "Days of Rage." Several times a week, our collective would stage dramatic actions to draw white working-class youth to Chicago to "Bring the War Home." We would crash

121

rock concerts and school assemblies, show up at parks and public beaches, and hold impromptu rallies in working-class neighborhoods to build support for the Days of Rage. We would physically resist police or right-wing hecklers, even if outnumbered, to show working-class teenagers we were fighters. By winning their respect, we would attract them to our movement.

In the hothouse atmosphere of communal living, passionate political discussions, and risk-laden protest, people felt a surge of energy. The collective's first action after the Cleveland conference was to crash a rock concert in Flushing Meadow Park. Dressed in jeans and army fatigues, en masse we smashed through security guards at the entrance, distributed leaflets for the Days of Rage, and addressed the audience from the stage. Returning to 99th Street to crash for the night, we were all high from the sheer physicality of the evening's adventure and people's inhibitions were released. As we bedded down on sleeping bags and blankets on the floor of my apartment, the young woman who had been my partner during the action lay down next to me and stripped to her panties. Lonely from Ruthie's absence, I took this as an invitation to begin lovemaking and started kissing the young woman passionately, uninhibited by the ten or so people sleeping on the floor or on the bad. Paul Buhle, my friend from *Radical America*, who was staying in my apartment during a visit to New York, was among those in the room. Outraged by what was going on, he leaped up and screamed at me, "How could you do this to Ruthie?" The young woman ran out of the room, leaving me guilty and embarrassed.

The pace of activity continued unabated. Two days later, we crashed a Rolling Stones concert at Madison Square Garden, breaking through security with the same tactics we had used at Flushing Meadow. Between actions, we had impassioned discussions about the line on monogamy. Among the minority of the collective members who rejected it, I argued that if the purpose of smashing monogamy was to give up white-skin privilege, the line should not apply to interracial relationships, which did more to radicalize their white partners than any strictly political experience. "If you ask me to break up with Ruthie," I told my comrades, "I'm leaving the collective."

No one in the collective challenged my position. But when my friend Louis, who was in the national Weatherman leadership, arrived from Chicago, he advised me that my relationship with Ruthie violated

Weatherman policy. "I can't believe you can sit there with a straight face and tell me to break up with Ruthie," I retorted. "You know what Ruthie means to me and what I've had to go through to stay with her. In the name of fighting racism, you're acting like a racist." Louis regarded me sadly and told me there was nothing personal about his position. "When you're a communist," Louis said, "you follow the organization's line whether you agree with it or not. You can't destroy the collective's discipline by making your own rules." When the discussion ended, I was shaking with rage. Louis had been supportive of Ruthie and me during our earliest days together and had been a good friend to us both. Although he was simply asking me to do what everyone else in Weatherman had done, it felt like a personal betrayal. I was also troubled by his affect during this conversation. The funny, self-deprecating person I had known and loved, the passionate activist who had helped engineer the University of Chicago sit-in, had been replaced by a troubled, remote figure weighed down by political responsibilities.

The encounter with Louis pushed me toward leaving Weatherman. I decided I would do so the next time someone asked me to break up with Ruthie. But events took an unexpected turn. Our collective regularly held outdoor karate practice at 14th Street and Prospect Park West in the Park Slope neighborhood of Brooklyn, a corner that was a popular hangout for working-class teenagers who were attracted to the counterculture. One sunny Saturday in early October 1969, a group of long-haired youth congregated in the park, many of them stoned on pot and heroin. They watched as forty men and women ran in place and practiced punches and kicks, all the while screaming and chanting against the war in Vietnam. Soon our performance had attracted at least fifty onlookers. While we rested on the grass, the friendly and curious young people asked who we were, where we had come from, and why we were practicing karate in a neighborhood where almost nothing interesting ever happened. Most of them were high school dropouts and most of us had degrees from top eastern universities, but we quickly found a common ground in hatred of the war and the police. Although we listened to the same music and took some of the same drugs, they had lived harder lives. Many had done jail time at Rikers Island for petty crimes, and they were regularly harassed and beaten by local cops, who seemed personally offended by their participation in the drug culture.

An hour into these discussions, the women in our group left for our Brooklyn house, and some of the men went to a nearby coffee shop for lunch; the rest of us remained in the park talking with the neighborhood teenagers. Suddenly, two of our collective members ran back to park, shouting, "They say they won't serve us because we look like hippies." The teens showed no surprise; "Yeah, we can't eat there," they confirmed. They claimed that the police used the restaurant as a surveillance point for the park and a hangout for undercover cops. That was all we needed to hear. We leaped up, marched to the restaurant, and held an impromptu sit-in, taking over three booths and demanding menus and meals. The countermen and waiters seemed astonished. "You guys obviously ain't from around here," the manager observed, "so let me tell you once and for all—we don't serve hippies." We advised him he was violating the law and refused to move. After a five-minute standoff, two young Irish cops, one six feet tall and two hundred pounds and the other five feet ten and slightly built, swaggered into the restaurant and said, "OK, get the fuck out of here." We calmly asserted our right to service. "Officer, they can't decide who they want serve on the basis of appearance," one of us said. "Our right to be here is protected by civil rights laws." "Are you fucking kidding?" one of them replied. "You'd better get out of here, or you're going to come out on the short end of the stick." Our polite refusal to leave sent them into a rage. They began flailing their nightsticks at the people nearest to them while the waiters and the countermen jumped in and tried to eject us from the restaurant.

Within seconds we had the restaurant workers on the floor and had taken away the cops' nightsticks. When one tried to draw his gun, the most formidable member of our group, John O'Connor, who had been an army sergeant in Germany, disarmed and restrained him. Before we could regroup, four police cars came screeching up onto the sidewalk outside the restaurant, and ten officers charged through the door with guns drawn. They threw us to the floor, cuffed us, and took us to the local station house, where the entire precinct seemed to regard our arrival as a personal offense. None of us had ever experienced the "street justice" that police regularly meted out in working-class and poor neighborhoods. While they tied John O'Connor to a chair and worked him over in the station-house yard, they made the rest of us face the squadroom wall while members of the precinct whacked our legs and elbows with blackjacks and nightsticks and aimed dropkicks at our backs. "You fucking assholes," one shouted, "you're lucky this isn't Vietnam." "We ought to shoot you right now," someone else screamed. After five or ten minutes of this, we were dragged up the stairs, handcuffed together, and placed in a small holding cell. O'Connor joined us holding his side. He had two broken ribs from the beating he had taken.

For the next five hours, the eleven of us remained handcuffed together in a cell no larger than five feet by eight feet. No one read us our rights, no one told us what we were charged with, no one gave us an opportunity to make a phone call. We felt like civil rights demonstrators in a southern jail, and so we did what SNCC workers did when they were arrested—we started singing. Instead of spirituals and freedom songs, we sang old rock and roll songs, moving from the do-wop groups of the fifties to the Stones and the Beatles. Our performance seemed to amuse the police officer assigned to watch us. After a couple of hours, he took off our handcuffs, got us some bologna sandwiches, and allowed us to make phone calls to get lawyers for our arraignment. He also told us that all eleven of us had been charged with disorderly conduct and reckless endangerment, common charges for a protest demonstration. The six biggest guys, including me, had also been charged with felonious assault. Additionally, O'Connor had been charged with robbery and attempted murder for taking a cop's gun, the most serious charges made against SDS members in a New York City demonstration. "Some of you are in deep shit," the supervising officer advised us.

Later that evening, police officers brought us in a paddy wagon to Supreme Court in downtown Brooklyn to await our arraignment in night court. The court officers marched us to a holding pen and locked us in with about thirty other prisoners. Some were stringy-haired white kids who were obviously there for drug offenses, but the majority were hard-looking black and Hispanic men who seemed to regard jail as the inevitable consequence of trying to make money from the street. "You don't look like you belong here," someone told us when we walked in. When we recounted the day's events, our explanation elicited animated comments from the other prisoners. "Now you know how America really works," one black prisoner observed. "The cops make up their own laws when dealing with people like us." A powerfully built white prisoner, his arms covered with tattoos, seemed to question our sanity. "You college guys got it made," he said. "If you mind your own business and keep out of trouble, you'll all be rich. Why would you want to blow it all and be with people like us? The people in here are God's lost children." When we told him that we were revolutionaries, and that we wanted to end racism and stop the war so that people like him could get a fairer shake, he just grinned and shook his head. Very quickly, our holding cell became transformed into a political forum. Almost everyone related some of their experiences with police, judges, and prisons. The camaraderie eased our fears and lifted our spirits. By the time the judge called us into court, we were much less frightened of whatever lay ahead.

In the courtroom, we were greeted by twenty members of our collective and a bearded, bushy-haired lawyer whom they had found to represent us at our arraignment. The judge, an old-line Brooklyn Irishman with meticulously groomed white hair, looked at us, our lawyer, and our supporters as though we had all dropped down from another planet. As our lawyer read the list of colleges we had graduated from, hoping for leniency, the judge's face seemed to get redder and redder. When he finally spoke, his voice was shaking with rage. "This is a very unusual case," he said. "When people who have been given the best education our society has to offer incur charges of this kind, our country is in grave difficulty. These defendants must be prosecuted to the fullest extent of the law. I set bail at twenty-five hundred dollars for all defendants charged with felonies and fifteen thousand dollars for Mr. O'Connor. The defendants charged with misdemeanors are released in their own recognizance." These bail amounts, like the legal charges, placed us in uncharted territory. Our collective did not have the money to get us released, and so the six of us with the most serious charges were taken across the street to the Brooklyn House of Detention, where we would have to stay until somebody paid our bail.

It was at this moment that the full seriousness of our charges started to sink in. The Brooklyn House of Detention was a notoriously rough city prison, filled with tough and angry men who carried the fears and hatreds of a racially divided city. As we were searched and processed, I noted that very few of the inmates were white. The guards, however, were almost all white, thickly built men who looked and talked like the cops who had beaten us in the station house. The jail, a noisy and barren structure of metal and stone, magnified the sound of shouts and curses and closing gates. There were no windows in the processing area, and the outside world seemed far away. As we moved from room to room to get fingerprinted, searched, and cleaned, the six of us were placed in different groups, and it occurred to me that I would have to survive in this place without the support of my friends. Because I refused to shave my beard, I was sent to a special floor for difficult and recalcitrant prisoners. As I took the elevator up to my floor, my legs were shaking with fear.

My anxiety only mounted as a guard marched me from the elevator past rows of cells to the one where I would be held. Here, in one place, were the scariest looking men I had ever seen in my life. I had always thought of myself as tough, but 90 percent of these men could demolish me in short order. Would I get caught in a race war? Would I have to choose sides? Would someone try to rape me? What could I do to prevent that from happening? I decided to ask my cellmate for advice, a thirty-year-old Hispanic man who was in for armed robbery, and who had pictures of his wife and three children on the desk next to his cot. After he offered me a cupcake that his wife had baked, I asked him what I would have to do to survive on the floor. His answer did not reassure me much: Mind your own business. If somebody bumps you or lays a hand on you, jump him and beat him till the guards pull you off. Then you'll get some respect.

My first chance to test this advice came a few hours later, when we went to the dayroom for lunch and recreation. A huge, well-built white man in a muscle shirt came over and asked what I was in for. I told him that I was part of a group of antiwar protesters who were roughed up by the cops and charged with assault. "Don't worry," he said. "We'll take care of you. Nobody is going to bother you." His friendliness made me wary. Was this the first overture in a seduction? An invitation to join some white supremacist group or a white prisoners' protection committee? Then somebody switched on the television, and I saw the reason for his good humor. The New York Mets had just won their division and were in the National League playoffs. The whole day room was in an uproar. People were cheering, clapping, slapping each other's palms. The air of menace had been replaced by a powerful (if temporary) spirit of unity. Nobody argued or fought that entire afternoon. I went back to my cell feeling more relaxed than I had in two days. Maybe my luck was changing.

After two more days of bad food, good conversation, and impassioned cheering, I was bailed out. As I prepared to leave, I tried to make sense of what had happened. I had actually enjoyed my time in jail because of the transcendent powers of a pennant race, even while the potential for violence and racial conflict clearly lurked beneath the surface, ready to explode when sports-induced euphoria started to fade. When I walked through the doors of the House of Detention and into the sunlight, I felt a tremendous sense of relief. I had managed to escape unharmed from an institution that crushed people's wills and damaged their personalities. Next time I might not be so lucky.

As I took the subway home with the members of my collective who had bailed me out, I looked forward to some time off to sort out my political options. But my comrades, who had gone to their parents (and my mother) to raise bail money, had rescued me ahead of the other defendants because they had plans for me. They wanted me to play a leading role in seizing control of a student assembly at Richmond Hill High School that same week as a way to publicize the Days of Rage. I was selected to overpower the gym teacher who took care of security at school assemblies because my comrades considered me one of the stronger and more athletic people in the collective.

I felt neither honored nor reassured by this assignment. I had just spent three days in jail on a felonious assault charge that carried a one-to-seven-year sentence, and they wanted me to go right back out and do something that would almost certainly result in another serious charge. I did not want to risk spending more time in jail for a number of reasons, not the least of which was fear.

Five women in the collective undertook to change my mind. They brought me into a room and sat me in a corner while they took up different positions along the wall. I could not look anywhere without seeing one of them. They flattered me, telling me how my comrades admired my strength, fitness, and ability to fight; and when I resisted, they shifted to contempt. My machismo was a façade, they said, a ruse to extract sexual favors from women rather than a sign of real courage and commitment. Like most men, I was more bluster than substance. Most of the women were half my size, yet they were willing to risk their lives for the revolution. I was a coward and a blowhard, a weak-minded intellectual trapped inside a powerful body. Like most white men, I was a pathetic creature. Stripped of the privileges of race and gender, I became too weak to function. In the first serious challenge to my comfortable life, I had proven myself unfit for the revolution. This went on for five straight hours, as I grew increasingly upset. I respected the character and intellect of these women, and their insults contained just enough truth to hit me very hard. What they were asking me to do seemed crazy, but their rationale for attacking me was strangely on target. All my toughness and swagger could not hide one salient fact: They were willing to abandon the comforts of middle-class life to become revolutionaries, and I was not. With cruel accuracy, they made me face the distance between my words and my deeds, and that realization made me feel both helpless and hypocritical. The more they attacked, the more I tried to disappear into the corner, my arms and legs curled in a fetal position. I began crying and whimpering but would not give in to their pressure. The women in the room had somehow transformed themselves from gentle, considerate idealists into iron-willed revolutionaries, but I had no desire to imitate them. I wanted out of this group, wanted to be freed from these pressures to strip myself bare and remake my life. But to do so, I had to admit that I was not a hero, that I was a scared and cautious person who was unprepared for the rigors of a revolutionary life. When they got that admission out of me, they left me alone. As I left that room, I decided to sever all ties to the collective. I was finally out of Weatherman.

I felt like a huge burden had been lifted, but I was too angry and frightened to feel much joy. A felonious assault charge that carried a prison term still hung over me, many of my closest friends were denouncing me as a coward, and my girlfriend was in Georgia managing a family crisis and had little time or inclination to help me through my own. I called Ruthie once a week, but she seemed so drained by her mother's approaching death that I felt guilty burdening her with my problems. Lonely and confused, I hoped, in the face of much evidence to the contrary, that the passion would return to our relationship when she came back to New York.

Through this episode I had learned a valuable political lesson. Like many other radical activists, I was being asked to join a revolution in a nation where most of the people who stood to gain from such an upheaval were not ready to take such risks. Creating a cadre of white antiracist heroes to match the sacrifices of the Panthers was an appealing fantasy, but the price of becoming one of them was too great for me to pay. In the fall of 1969, the war in Vietnam was still raging uncontrollably and tensions between blacks and whites seemed grow in every sphere of American life. I wanted to address these issues, but I also wanted some semblance of a normal life, with a partner I loved, friends I could count on, and a career I was committed to. It was time for me to face the limits of my political commitments and advance the causes I espoused in ways that seemed more practical and safe.

First, however, I would have to make sure that I did not go to jail for the Brooklyn incident. Divisions among our eleven defendants complicated this task. Three of the eleven, including John O'Connor and me, had dropped out of Weatherman; the other eight remained in the collective and were rapidly accumulating additional charges. O'Connor and I decided we would need top-flight legal representation, so, on a friend's recommendation, we decided to meet with the best left-wing criminal lawyer in the city, a tough-minded old warhorse named Sam Neuberger. A sixty-year-old former Communist who draped his ample frame in expensive suits and had an office in lower Manhattan overlooking the Hudson River, Neuberger was not a subtle man. After telling stories about the important political cases he defended during the thirties and forties, he bragged to us about his lucrative practice as a lawyer for organized crime. "I defend murderers, loan sharks, gamblers, and racketeers, and I usually get them off," he told us. "My normal fee is one hundred thousand dollars. Since this is a political case, I'll give you a discount. My fee will be ten thousand dollars, paid in advance." O'Connor and I looked at one another and gasped. We were used to movement lawyers defending us for free; ten thousand dollars seemed like extortion. But we had little choice. This was a criminal case in the Brooklyn courts, and our fate might hinge on our lawyer's familiarity with the judges and district attorneys. Neuberger had that kind of insider knowledge, and we reluctantly agreed to his terms. We did insist that Neuberger defend all eleven of us together, however, even though we knew that the defendants still in Weatherman would probably never pay a cent of the legal fees. We did not want the government to play up divisions among us that might lead to pressure to turn state's evidence.

We used every possible resource to find the money for Neuberger's retainer. To get the ball rolling, I swallowed my pride and asked my mother for two thousand dollars. Although she wanted me to get my own lawyer and cut myself loose from the others, I finally convinced her that Neuberger would get the desired results no matter who else he defended. We supplemented her check with another two thousand dollars collected through fund-raising parties and personal appeals. Neuberger signed on as our legal representative in the next set of court appearances, but kept leaning on us for the rest of his retainer. We now had a capable lawyer to guide us through the city's complex legal system and keep federal agents from squeezing us to testify against our fellow defendants.

I then tried to rebuild my political life, which, because of the climate of the times, was confined within a racially divided left. No matter how much I wanted to work in a multiracial setting, my options were limited by the virtually unanimous insistence of African-American radicals that antiracist whites should work *in alliance* with blacks and Hispanics rather than join with them in common organizations. But I was also acutely aware of what could happen to a group of white intellectuals when guilt about whiteness become the guiding principle of their political life. Because Weatherman collectives were self-segregated organizations that recruited only whites, their political stance, unchecked by day-to-day contact with the black community, tended to become progressively more adventurist and confrontational. Throughout the fall of 1969, Weatherman collectives accumulated more arrests and isolated themselves from more people. Neither unaffiliated working-class youth nor members of campus SDS chapters showed any interest in the Days of Rage. In desperation, Weatherman organizers started showing up at meetings and denouncing those who refused to endorse their demonstration as "running dogs," a term Mao Tse-tung used to refer to counterrevolutionaries and cowards.

At the time, there were a large group of unaffiliated radicals in New York City who had once been active in SDS before it shattered into revolutionary fragments. Some were undergraduates, some were graduate students, and some had dropped out of school to work. A small group of us, appalled by what had happened to Weatherman, decided to create a new organization called "Mad Dog SDS," which believed in building political consciousness through mass demonstrations and educational activities rather than violent small-group actions. Like Weatherman, we wanted to create a community of interest between white working-class youth and their black and Hispanic peers, but our strategy was to move to working-class neighborhoods and work through schools, workplaces, and recreational areas to reach people and raise their consciousness. Initially, Mad Dog SDS proclaimed its existence by marching in antiwar demonstrations and protests against government attacks on the Black Panther Party, but in November 1969 we decided, like former SDSers in New Haven, Chicago, Oakland, and several other cities, to launch organizing projects in white working-class neighborhoods. We had Mad Dog activists already living and teaching in the two communities we chose, the Northwest Bronx, and the Astoria section of Queens.

Although I still maintained a residence on the Upper West Side, I decided to become part of the Bronx project. Two Mad Dog activists I liked and admired—Suzy Danielson, an intense and brilliant sociology instructor at Lehman College, and Hank Chaikin, a cheerful, sardonic teacher in the City College SEEK program—lived in the Northwest Bronx and encouraged me to help them start a group that would pool the resources of SDS chapters at Fordham, NYU, Lehman, and Bronx Community Colleges while reaching out to students at local high schools and neighborhood residents. We rented a storefront on West 184th Street between the Grand Concourse and Jerome Avenue, across from Bronx Community College, and started a community newspaper that expressed our group's distinctive political identity, which was antiwar, antiracist, and profeminist, spiced with a heavy dose of class consciousness and Bronx pride.

From the very beginning, my participation in this group was beset with contradictions. Here I was, a shell-shocked ex-Weatherman, known in SDS circles largely for my writings on black history, taking daily subway rides to the West Bronx to help local SDS members try to organize white working-class youth, a group I had had no contact with since my early years in Brooklyn. Moreover, my social life increasingly took place in an all-black setting. When Ruthie returned from Georgia in January 1970, she brought her youngest brother and sister to live with us, and I found myself once again absorbed in the life of her extended family. Ruthie's youngest brother, Dee, and her sister Annabel became our surrogate children. A high school senior and junior whom we enrolled in New York schools, both were excellent students who were curious about the city and eager to talk about college sports, music, religion, and politics.

Sadly, Ruthie looked like she had aged ten years during her ordeal in Georgia. She had lost fifteen pounds in the six months she was away, and her beautiful face looked drawn and beleaguered. At twenty-three years old, with siblings all over the country who expected her to hold the family together, two adolescents who were her sole responsibility, and a heart problem that was potentially life threatening, Ruthie was overwhelmed by concerns that most people confront only in middle age. She appreciated my help with her family responsibilities and shared many of my political ideals, but she had become passionless and remote when we were alone in our bedroom. I was frustrated by her coldness but still found it difficult to imagine living with another woman. Not only did I have vivid memories of the times when we had meant everything to one another, but I was deeply invested in the cultural and emotional connection with the black community that I had experienced ever since we became a couple. Although my need for affection and friendship was more often met by Ruthie's siblings and the Double Discovery kids we adopted than by Ruthie herself, the apartment on 99th Street was still the only real home I had, the one place I could go to find unconditional acceptance and spiritual renewal.

I longed for a way to incorporate these experiences into my political organizing, but found it difficult to do so. In the late sixties radical movement, at least in New York City, blacks organized blacks, whites organized whites, and those who challenged this division were perceived as hostile to black empowerment. Even in situations that cried out for integrated organizations, radicals of my generation lacked the courage, or imagination, to create them. The Northwest Bronx was a case in point. The community we were organizing was undergoing rapid ethnic change. The line of black and Hispanic settlement was fifteen blocks south of our storefront and rapidly moving northward. Although our immediate neighborhood was at least 90 percent white, every local school was racially integrated. We wanted to create an awareness of common interests among people of different backgrounds, but in the organizing model we followed, we presumed that African-Americans would want to join black organizations and that our job was to mobilize whites around antiracist perspectives. Anxious to avoid accusations that we were undermining black unity, we never put forward a nonracial model of political identity, even though that may have been the only realistic alternative to racial tension and white flight. Privately, I wondered if whites could become genuinely antiracist without forging ties of friendship and affection to individual African-Americans, but I lacked the courage to express this publicly. Instead, I lived a double life, conducting my political life among whites, and my social and recreational life among blacks.

That said, our Bronx project was still one of the more dynamic and constructive community-organizing efforts undertaken by a New Left organization. By taking a class-conscious approach to antiwar organizing, one hostile to the government and the military but sympathetic to the rank-and-file soldier, we managed to touch a considerable number of Bronx residents. The first meetings of the Bronx Coalition, which is what we called ourselves, attracted nearly a hundred people, many of whom had been part of antiwar groups at area high schools, colleges, and medical centers.

These meetings were radically different from those I had attended on the Upper West Side. First of all, many of the Coalition's most active members were middle-class married couples, something I had never encountered before in a radical organization. They had come to the Bronx to work and raise families, and their presence served to check some of the adventurism that had driven SDS off the deep end. The Coalition also attracted a sizable group of Bronx residents from working-class backgrounds, most of them students from area colleges. One goal of the Coalition was to make the antiwar movement a visible presence in the Northwest Bronx, and to some degree we succeeded. Among these working-class and middle-class Bronx residents, hatred of the Vietnam War had a personal dimension. Many of them knew someone who had fought in Vietnam and had died or come home seriously injured or addicted to heroin. For them, mobilizing against the war was not the outgrowth of an abstract critique of American foreign policy; it was about saving the lives of friends and neighbors. The first issue of our community newspaper, the *Cross Bronx Express*, denounced the war, not just for violating the Vietnamese people's right to self-determination but for siphoning public funds from schools, subways, and hospitals, and creating a climate conducive to violence on the streets of the Bronx.

The *Cross Bronx Express* had a bold, tabloid-like flavor and great pictures and graphics. We sold it at subway and bus stops, outside high schools and colleges, in front of department stores and supermarkets, and next to the Army recruiting center at Fordham Road and the Grand Concourse. Selling the paper on crowded Bronx street corners gave us an excellent barometer of public sentiment. When I first started hawking the paper, my favorite spots were in front of Alexander's department store on Grand Concourse and Fordham Road and De Witt Clinton

High School on Moshulu Parkway. I was afraid that some people might physically attack me because they interpreted criticism of the war as an attack on American soldiers. But the majority of people I encountered were either strongly opposed to the war or at least concerned about its impact on their lives. Of the hundreds of conversations I got into while selling the newspaper or handing out leaflets, no more than ten were adversarial. When we sponsored speakouts against the war on street corners or at local churches, the response was similar. Older Irish men sometimes heckled us, but women and young people, no matter what their race or nationality, usually gave us a respectful hearing. Because most of our speakers grew up in Bronx neighborhoods and made personal experience a reference point for their arguments, many people were receptive to our claim that the war benefited only the rich and the privileged. One of our most effective and popular programs was draft counseling. More than twenty young men from the Bronx took advantage of our unorthodox strategies to avoid conscription, which ranged from telling their draft boards they wanted to shoot officers, to feigning or acknowledging homosexuality. Although the Coalition's more intellectual leaders did talk about American imperialism and the suffering of the Vietnamese people, our basic antiwar argument usually appealed to self-interest. For most members of the Bronx Coalition, keeping people out of the war, and fighting to get American troops back from Vietnam, was first and foremost an effort to save American lives.

Our organizing proved far less effective on the question of race, which was of great concern to many residents of the Bronx. Many of the white people we worked with believed that the movement of blacks and Hispanics into their communities would bring crime, drugs, noise, racial tension, and the deterioration of housing, schools, and public services. Although churches, synagogues, and the local Democratic Party encouraged peaceful accommodation to a changing racial order, some Bronx residents resorted to violence and intimidation to try to keep their neighborhoods white. In Belmont, the largest Italian neighborhood in the North Central Bronx, black people from outside the immediate community were routinely threatened, beaten, and chased if they entered the neighborhood after dark. A few were even murdered. Black teenagers were particular targets of hostility. City buses carrying black and Hispanic students to Roosevelt and Dodge High Schools were showered with rocks and bricks when they drove through Belmont and had to be rerouted out of the neighborhood. Nothing as dramatic took place in the Jewish and Irish areas, but signs of racial hostility were abundant. The basketball courts in public parks and schoolyards were often divided by race, with grim-faced Irish teenagers playing on one and black kids on another. Racial graffiti were everywhere. Handball courts and school walls were often spray-painted with such slogans as "White Power" and "Niggers Suck," and the Cross Bronx Expressway still had some of the "Wallace Country" signs that had been placed there during the 1968 presidential election. There were a few integrated neighborhoods in the Northeast Bronx, where black and white people were friendly to one another, but those were suburban-style neighborhoods of one- and two-family houses where the majority of black residents were civil servants and professionals. In the West Bronx, where most residents lived in apartments or row houses, people were convinced that rapid racial change, coupled with disinvestment by landlords and banks, could turn their neighborhoods into slums.

Although the Bronx Coalition made fighting racism one of its major priorities, we had no coherent strategy for building solidarity across racial lines. To our credit, we insisted that racial integration did not cause neighborhood decay. Crime, drugs, and the deterioration of rental properties, we argued, were accentuated by cuts in public services and the actions of banks and landlords; they were not inherent behavioral traits of racial minorities. But we lacked practical programs to show that integration could work. Of the fifty to a hundred people who came regularly to the Coalition office, no more than five were black or Hispanic. We never made special efforts to recruit minority members, or to transform the Coalition into an integrated organization. Instead, we substituted alliances with black militants for friendships and political relationships that crossed racial lines. The first issue of the *Cross Bronx Express* was filled with pictures of raised fists and articles about the Black Panther Party, but it did little to address the problem of "white flight" or the corrosive racial tensions Bronx residents encountered in streets, schoolyards, parks, and places of business.

In the Bronx Coalition, support for the Black Panther Party was the most visible symbol of our emotional investment in antiracist politics. The heroism and self-sacrifice of the Panthers inspired and energized us but also set a standard for antiracist organizing that was easier to meet rhetorically than in real life. While we distinguished ourselves from most whites in the Bronx by rallying to the defense of the Panthers when they faced armed assaults and prosecutions by local and federal law-enforcement agencies, we also showed our immaturity by mindlessly adopting Panther slogans. One telling example took place during a march across the Queensborough Bridge to protest the indictment of twenty-one members of the New York Panthers, who had been arrested on an array of poorly formulated and improbable charges, one of which was blowing up the Bronx Botanical Gardens. In the middle of the demonstration, our contingent started chanting, under the direction of Panther leaders, something that sounded like "Power to the People, Arthur Pig." I asked the person next to me, "Who is Arthur Pig?" With a slightly contemptuous expression, he told me that we were not chanting "Arthur Pig" but "Off the Pig," Panther slang for "Kill the Police." This should have given me pause. Quite a few policemen, and many parents of police officers, lived in the West Bronx neighborhoods we were trying to organize, and chanting a slogan that targeted police for death, even metaphorically, would certainly raise barriers between us. But the entire Coalition, me included, was so desperate to show the Panthers that we stood with them against government repression that we joined in the chanting without hesitation. As we marched across the Queensborough Bridge, arms linked, with a thousand of our black, white, and Latino brothers and sisters, we were so caught up in this moment of interracial solidarity that we never questioned the rhetoric that united us, and soon we had incorporated this language into our organizing. By the spring of 1970, some Coalition leaders, including me, had begun referring to police and government officials as "pigs" in our literature, and employing "Power to the People" as a major Coalition slogan.

These rhetorical excesses revealed the limits of the Coalition's racial politics. It was certainly appropriate for us to defend the Panthers from raids and prosecutions that depended on illegal surveillance and the use of infiltrators and provocateurs. But too often we used support for Panther defendants as a surrogate for neighborhood-based programs that bridged racial barriers. There were precious few Black Panthers, or black radicals of any kind, in the West Bronx neighborhoods we were trying to organize. What we did have was a rapidly growing population of working-class African-Americans. They wanted a better life for themselves and their children, but our preoccupation with war and political repression prevented us from reaching out to them on issues like deteriorating schools and housing, which might have linked them to their white and Latino neighbors. Convinced that government attacks on the Panthers were destroying hopes for a more just society, we sent Coalition contingents to midtown Manhattan to protest the murder of Fred Hampton, and to New Haven to protest the imprisonment of Panther National Chairman Bobby Seale. But we failed to explore practical strategies for promoting interracial solidarity in our own neighborhood. Our political vision was too apocalyptic and our rhetoric too strident to address the concerns of Bronx residents about neighborhood stability. Imprisoned by our identity as white radicals in a neighborhood that whites were fleeing, we could only stand helplessly by, in later years, as the borough faced the greatest catastrophe in its history, the plague of disinvestment, arson, and abandonment that swept through the South Bronx and leapt across the Cross Bronx Expressway into the West Bronx neighborhoods we were trying to organize.

While the Coalition's organizing on race ultimately foundered on political abstractions, its struggles with gender issues became a focal point of great creativity, transforming the lives of almost everyone the Coalition touched. Unlike its efforts to fight racism, which focused on citywide and national issues, the Coalition's campaign to empower women flowed from the direct personal experience of women in the organization and highlighted every area in which they felt devalued, from work, politics, and health care to sexuality and family life. But this holistic, deeply personal approach to organizing did not come without pain and conflict. It took a women's revolt four months after the Coalition's founding to place "Women's Liberation" at the top of Coalition priorities. In February 1970, the women in the Coalition, who had been meeting in caucus several times a week, announced that men would have to leave the organization unless they agreed to a complicated list of demands, which included a fair division of child care, secretarial work, speaking, and writing; purging the organization of "macho" behavior; and opening a women's health center. This ultimatum, and the outpouring of rage that accompanied it, stunned men in the organization, who were being given this directive by co-workers, comrades, and, in some cases, wives and girlfriends.

The meeting at which these demands were presented was tense and emotional. After Suzy Danielson read the list drawn up by the Women's

Caucus, at least twenty women, some of whom had never before spoken at a Coalition meeting, stood up and described how they felt stifled and intimidated in Coalition activities. The male leaders of the organization, they complained, rarely let the women get a word in edgewise, much less shape Coalition priorities. If women's liberation were Coalition policy, they asked, then why were women in charge of typing and layout for the *Cross Bronx Express* while men wrote the editorials? Why was child care only a woman's responsibility? Why did some women members spend so much time taking care of their children that they had no time to do Pap smears and abortion counseling for women in the neighborhood? This undemocratic division of tasks not only prevented women from developing as leaders, it hampered Coalition organizing. Because the male leaders insisted on boarding the storefront windows (out of fear that they would be broken by hostile neighbors) and swaggered around in leather jackets, work shirts, and army fatigues, many area residents thought the Coalition was a motorcycle gang! How could a neighborhood woman come to such a place to talk about birth control or abortion? The boards had to come down. The women had to take leadership. The men had to learn to do child care and secretarial work so that women could open the health center that the neighborhood needed.

Like most men in the Coalition, I left this meeting in a daze. Many of the women's criticisms seemed directed at me personally. I wrote editorials and articles for the *Cross Bronx Express*. I spoke passionately and repeatedly at Coalition meetings and rallies. More pointedly, in light of the "motorcycle gang" comment, I wore muscle shirts and boots to dramatize my physical toughness, convinced that this would be an asset in organizing working-class youth. After hearing a long succession of women get up and denounce Coalition policies, I decided to approach Suzy Danielson, the woman in the Coalition I felt closest to, and ask her point-blank whether I still had a role in the organization.

Suzy was alternately tough and reassuring. "This isn't about you, Mark," she said. "Women in this organization are rebelling against things that have been holding them back all their lives, and if for the moment this makes you a target, you'll have to accept the consequences. But the changes we've called for are going to make the Bronx Coalition a stronger organization, and we want you to be a part of it. We still want you to speak and write, but we also want you to learn design and layout for the *Cross Bronx Express* and help out with child care. Starting next

Monday, you'll be babysitting twice a week. And you'll be going to men's meetings on Sunday mornings so you can discuss with your male comrades what women's liberation means for men. Who knows," Suzy concluded, giving me a hug, "maybe you'll learn something from this."

With some trepidation, I submitted to the reeducation program the Women's Caucus had designed, which led to what I can only describe as a life-changing experience. First of all, I was awed by the explosion of energy and creativity that the revolt unleashed among women in the organization. Within a month, the Women's Caucus had opened a storefront clinic that offered free Pap smears, birth-control information, and abortion counseling. They also produced an extraordinary issue of the *Cross Bronx Express*, devoted exclusively to women's liberation, containing a critique of male-dominated health professions, an essay on women's history, a pair of articles explaining why access to legal abortion was a prerequisite for women's freedom, and a powerful editorial explaining how women's liberation "was a whole new experience of women coming together to understand why . . . schools, hospitals, marriage, churches, jobs, movies, families, ads, EVERYTHING—stifles us, warps us, makes us angry, makes us feel alone, stupid, inferior." As I watched women change from silent participants in antiwar rallies into tireless advocates of women's health needs—willing to take on the government, organized religion, and the medical profession—I realized how much I had underestimated the emancipatory potential of the radical women's movement, and the complexity and breadth of its critique of American society.

I also began to see how this movement could help me confront some of my inner demons and make me a more self-critical and flexible person. Doing child care for one of the Coalition's children, an energetic, temperamental two-year-old, stretched me to my limits. Not only did I have to feed him and change his diapers, but I had to force myself to respond calmly and patiently when he cried or threw things. Caring for him for five hours at a stretch was a challenge for someone as volatile as I was. It gave me new respect for what women did all the time without notice or credit, and it even helped me learn to control my temper.

I also gained new friends in the men's consciousness group that met on Sunday mornings. Prior to these meetings, I had often gravitated to men who reveled in their physical toughness. I enjoyed practicing karate moves with the Coalition's resident martial arts experts and had spent many hours playing basketball in local schoolyards with some of the other male members. But as my machismo became a target of ridicule, and I sought to build a political identity that incorporated some of radical feminism's insights, I drew closer to two of the more mature and thoughtful men in the Coalition, Danny Coleman and Ray Reece. Danny, a short, energetic man who taught in the Lehman SEEK program, took the position that women's liberation was a necessary stage in the development of the American left and urged us to welcome the opportunity to play a greater role in family life and relinquish some of the burdens of political leadership. Danny's historical sense impressed me, and I began to seek him out for long discussions about gender, race, and the history of American communism. Ray, by contrast, appealed to a romantic, emotional side of my personality that few people but Ruthie had ever seen. At our Sunday morning men's meetings, Ray spoke more easily about his doubts and vulnerabilities than any man I had ever met. I felt myself drawn to Ray as a confidant and soul mate, someone I could talk to about my problems with Ruthie, my fear of going to prison, my worries about my place in the Coalition, and my anguish at the inability of the left to prevent the racial tensions that seemed to be tearing America apart.

These new friendships, especially the one with Ray, came at an opportune time, given the strange and frightening fate that had befallen many old friends who had remained in Weatherman. During the winter of 1969–70, the Weatherman collective decided to divide into cells and go underground, the better to do "material damage to the American War Machine." At first no one knew exactly what this meant, but within a few weeks the Weatherman leadership began issuing "communiqués" that took responsibility for the bombing of banks, corporate headquarters, and draft boards. Such acts of violence drew a skeptical response from most antiwar militants, who regarded them as premature and counterproductive. "A couple of Weather people have been making forays in this area," Dale Rosen, a historian-activist, wrote to me from San Francisco in January 1970, "sounding out the Lawyers Guild, criticizing the Tenants Union (bourgeois, white-skin-privileged organizing) ripping off guns from radical arsenals. In another time and another place, some of it might make sense, but not here and now. I just don't see the possibility of urban guerrilla attacks creating chaos sufficient to justify the costs."

The transformation of Weatherman into an armed, underground organization stunned and depressed me. Some of my best friends from college and graduate school had been caught up in this desperate initiative and were now wanted by the police and the FBI. Seeing their pictures on wanted posters brought the tragedy of Vietnam home in the most personal way. This war, which had killed and maimed so many working-class men, was now claiming future scholars, teachers, and writers.

During this period, the FBI tried to link me to Weatherman bombings. Commandeering a room in the basement of my apartment building from the superintendent, a good friend of mine, they set up bugs and wiretaps and tried to interview my neighbors; but they got little cooperation from anyone in our tight-knit building. Whenever the FBI was physically present, Angel, our superintendent, would signal me from the front of the building, and I would head to a safe house around the corner, a studio apartment rented by a woman I knew who was more countercultural than political and therefore not on the FBI's radar screen. After three tense days (during which I had a guilt-ridden sexual encounter with the woman who housed me), the FBI left, apparently satisfied that I was no longer in Weatherman, but their presence left me badly shaken. I was particularly worried about how the new Weatherman initiative would affect my impending trial in Brooklyn. Many of my co-defendants had accumulated multiple arrests since our arraignment, and at least five had gone underground. Although our lawyer, Sam Neuberger, told me not to panic, I found it hard to keep calm. Apprehensive about doing time in prison, I started drinking a fifth of sweet wine, and smoking marijuana heavily, each night before I went to bed.

Then, in February 1970, a townhouse exploded in the West Village, where a Weatherman cell had been making bombs. The explosion killed three people and sent the two survivors screaming into the streets bleeding and partly clothed. One of the survivors, Kathy Boudin, had been one of my favorite people in New York SDS; one of the people who died was Ted Gold, a former counselor in Double Discovery and a defendant in my Brooklyn case. His death nearly put me over the edge. Nowhere could you find a more improbable candidate for terrorism. Ted was small in stature and big in heart, a gentle person with a great sense of humor, a love of ideas, and a gift for working with teenagers. He had been one of the best counselors in Double Discovery and one of the best-liked persons in Columbia SDS. If a person as kind and compassionate as Ted could wind up making bombs, it seemed to me that American society was in desperate trouble. In my grief, I wrote a poem for Ted, and sent it to *Radical America*, where I had it printed under the pen name of Nelson Temple. I used the name of a young man from Double Discovery whom Ted had worked with and who later was murdered in a Bronx robbery. This pen name not only memorialized Ted's work with teenagers, but represented my way of telling Louis, who had also worked with Nelson, that I still cared about him even though he had chosen a different political path.

> I
>
> remember ted gold best
> riding to connecticut
> in a car with six
> young kids from the
> ghetto
> to a conference on the war
> Five congressmen spoke
> and we played
> smoky and the miracles on
> the portable record player
> and went swimming
> The kids have grown
> STUDENT
> PUSHER
> PANTHER
> Ted liked to go
> to the Knick games
> He had season tickets
> last year
> This year
> he is dead
> Of a bomb meant for better targets
> There will be no processions
> and the articles in the
> *Times* will have no quotes
> For those who lost before the battle
> Who found a battle
> they never really sought.

As the Weatherman tragedy unfolded, I felt an acute sense of powerlessness, of being swept up by forces of history over which I had little control. I was even more appreciative of the daily routines and personal relationships at 99th Street, fragile though they were. Although Ruthie was drifting away from me, I clung to her with fierce loyalty, doing what I could to help her younger brother and sister adjust to life in New York. My contact with Ruthie's family, who gave us love without reservation and valued our skills as educators, helped me keep my sanity during this chaotic time. Working with Ruthie's brother on his college applications, helping her sister with her high school homework, and cooking meals for the former Double Discovery students who boarded with us on a regular basis, kept me grounded at a time when American society seemed to be falling apart.

Nevertheless, pessimism and a sense of desperation crept into my political perspective. I lost confidence that my comrades and I could dramatically change the injustices we saw around us or stave off the devastating consequences of the war on poor and working-class communities. In a March 1970 editorial in the *Cross Bronx Express*, alongside a proud account of the many protests the Coalition was organizing, I presented a somber view of conditions in the Bronx and a pessimistic vision of the future:

> Look at the lives most of us live up here. Who's happy? Food prices out of control; rents, subway fares, taxes spiraling; medical expenses frighteningly higher; schools like prisons; air, water, and sound pollution; racial and ethnic antagonisms; the spread of hard drugs; the war the draft the army. . . . The time for illusions is over. We've witnessed the butchery in Vietnam. We've seen the police attacks on students and black people, street kids and workers. We've seen the cost of living skyrocket, the spread of hard drugs among our friends and children, the deterioration of our hospitals, schools, and subways. If we don't get ourselves together now, it's going to get worse and worse. Dig it. More wars, more pollution, more hate, more cops.

In the face of these conditions, the Bronx Coalition sustained a frenetic pace of activity. In the spring of 1970, the high point of radical protest during the Vietnam era, we opened a successful women's health clinic, organized numerous antiwar demonstrations, helped trigger massive strikes at Bronx high schools and at Fordham, NYU, and Lehman College following the American invasion of Cambodia, picketed in support of striking postal workers, continued to operate a successful draft-counseling program, marched for legal abortion, and tried—unsuccessfully—to discourage teenagers from gravitating to heroin and other hard drugs.

But how much these protests mitigated the effects of the war and the relentless decay of Bronx neighborhoods remained an open question. The Kent State killings following the invasion of Cambodia depressed and frightened student activists, making them more receptive to countercultural dreams than revolutionary politics. No matter what we did, young men kept dying or returning from Vietnam crippled, bitter, addicted to drugs. Heroin addiction spread. Racial tensions festered. Every day the streets seemed a little dirtier, the houses a little shabbier, the people more worried and distracted. More and more people, including some Coalition activists, spoke of leaving the West Bronx for places with less conflict and division, whether it was Yonkers, Rockland County, a commune in Oregon, or a house in Vermont. For white working-class Bronx residents, the dream was an apartment in Co-op City or a house in the suburbs; for Coalition activists, a communal life in harmony with nature was the ideal. Nevertheless, each group shared the desire to distance itself from racial tension and urban decay.

But deeply positive experiences linked me to this wounded community. If the Bronx represented the advance guard of white flight and urban decay, it was also a place where black and Latino working-class people had created more cosmopolitan and racially tolerant ethnic neighborhoods than the city had ever seen. Nowhere in the United States did Ruthie and I feel more at ease strolling and shopping than in the heavily Latino South Bronx neighborhoods where Ruthie's sisters lived. With their profusion of colors and cultures, these communities, despite their poverty, represented a vision of the future that I welcomed more than feared. So when it came to finding a teaching job after my fellowship money ran out, I took the first one that was offered at a university with a Bronx campus—a position in the Institute of Afro-American Studies at Fordham University, one of the first black-studies programs established at a private university in New York City. Some people advised me not to take this job—after all, I was white—but it seemed like a perfect complement to my organizing with the Bronx Coalition. Little did I know that the Coalition would soon dissolve, Ruthie and I would break up, and that my role as a teacher and scholar in black studies would become the focal point of a thirty-year effort to build interracial organizations and communities.

9   A White Man in Black Studies

WHEN I was hired by Fordham University's Institute of Afro-American Studies in the spring of 1970, I joined an educational experiment that was revolutionizing American campuses. The black-studies movement, which began in California in the mid-1960s, hit the New York metropolitan area with a vengeance in the spring of 1969. Black students at several area campuses took over buildings to demand the creation of degree-granting programs that offered courses on the black experience, promoted research in black history and culture, and used campus resources to help struggling local black communities and advance the cause of black liberation worldwide. The programs and departments that were created in the wake of these protests were as novel for their governing structure and nonacademic functions as for the subjects taught in their classrooms. Following the example of the pioneering black studies department at San Francisco State, founded in 1967, the New York–area programs, whether at Fordham, Princeton, or the colleges in the CUNY system, fought for expanded recruitment of black students and faculty, created cultural and educational programs for black communities off campus, and took on causes ranging from open admissions in the City University to the cessation of U.S. military aid to South Africa.

The black students who shaped these programs, most newly recruited to white universities following the urban uprisings of the sixties, consciously sought out faculty members who were longtime political activists as well as those with traditional academic credentials. Journalist-historians like John Henrik Clarke and Julius Lester, playwrights and poets like Imamu Amiri Baraka and Nikki Giovanni, and Marxist intellectuals like C.L.R. James became important figures on black studies faculties along with university-trained historians, sociologists, political scientists, and literary scholars. The intellectual atmosphere that resulted could be contentious and highly political, blurring lines between student and faculty, campus and community, scholarship and political advocacy, and artistic expression and communal therapy. This was participatory democracy on a grand scale, unleashing creative impulses and grand ideas, as well as occasional uninhibited expressions of rage and alienation, within university communities whose traditional norms of scholarly discourse left little room for such passion and political commitment.

Although I was fully aware of the black studies movement, my recruitment to a black studies faculty came about more by accident than through conscious intent. When I started looking for a college teaching position in January 1970, I had applied only to history and social science departments. Forty letters drew just three responses, all from community colleges, and I assumed that my professional life, at least for the foreseeable future, would consist of teaching introductory American history and Western civilization courses. Then, during a basketball game in the Columbia gymnasium, Bill Connolly, an Irish-American teenager whom I had befriended on the Riverside Park basketball courts, told me that his black studies teacher at Fordham was looking for someone to teach African-American history. That Bill was taking a black studies course was itself surprising; when I first met him three years earlier, he was filled with racial resentments, which had thankfully been eroded by exposure to the antiwar movement and the counterculture. But I was also intrigued that his professor, who was also the program's director, would actually ask his students for help in finding faculty and decided to send him a letter indicating my availability and interest.

My letter of inquiry was very different from the ones I sent to history departments. Realizing that one of the goals of the black studies movement was to create teaching opportunities for black scholars, I decided to acknowledge my race and save Stanley Majors, the director of Fordham's Afro-American Institute, the embarrassment of discovering that salient fact when I arrived for an interview. My letter, preserved in our department's archives, displays my ambivalence about applying for the position. "First of all, I am white," I wrote:

> This might exclude me from the program as you have conceived it, and if so I could hardly object. But if you feel there is a place for qualified whites in the program, then I might be worth considering.
>
> For the last two summers, I have taught black history courses in the Double Discovery Program at Columbia. In both instances, my classes were among the most popular in the program, and I was asked to return

by the students. Bill Wright, a Fordham student who was in Double Discovery, can testify to my abilities. I really love teaching and identify enough with black aspirations to overcome some of the obstacles that whites will inevitably have in presenting these materials.

In addition, all the research work I have done in the last five years has dealt with black history. I have written several scholarly articles on black political movements and several review essays on the writings of Harold Cruse, Rap Brown, and Eugene Genovese.

Clearly, all the build up in the world isn't going to ease your justified suspicions. If your program is exclusively by blacks and for blacks, then I have no place in it. But if you think that part of the job of black studies is to educate whites to the nature of racism in American society, then you might find me a useful addition.

I sent this letter, accompanied by my curriculum vitae, with minimal expectations. Two weeks later I received a letter inviting me in for an interview. It presented a vision of black studies that I liked. "After looking over the material concerning yourself in your correspondence," the director of the Institute wrote,

> ... I am of the opinion that your work in the area of Black Studies is quite impressive. To respond to your notion that being "white" might exclude you from our program, I would like to state that we *are* primarily interested in allowing black educators an opportunity to play a major role in the development and implementation of instruction in the area of Black or Afro-American Studies. However, we are also greatly concerned with developing an academic program centered around academicians (black or white) that are professionally capable of transmitting a knowledge of the Afro-American heritage. In other words, "whiteness" would prove to be the basis of an application rejection only if that whiteness inhibits a sensitivity to the black experience. Moreover, our courses are open to *all* students enrolled at the university.

I looked forward to the interview, which was scheduled for March 23, 1970, with great anticipation. Not only was I excited by the prospect of teaching something other than Western civilization, I was also intrigued that the person interviewing me seemed to share my political outlook and my passion for African-American history.

When I arrived at Fordham for my interview, I looked around in wonder. The university was a tree-lined refuge from the bustle of Bronx streets, its hundred-acre campus graced with beautiful old buildings, large manicured lawns, and well-cared-for athletic fields. Its Catholic heritage was revealed by the crosses hung in classroom buildings, the stained-glass windows in the library and university church, and the portraits of Jesuits on display in the administration building. It was hard to believe that this venerable institution, which had helped generations of Catholic immigrants move into the middle class, had spawned one of the most militant antiwar movements of any college in New York City and formed one of the first degree-granting black studies programs at any Catholic college in the United States. But Fordham had changed dramatically in the aftermath of the Second Vatican Council. Not only had it opened itself to major currents in American intellectual and political life, but it had invested significant scholarship money to attract African-American students, transforming itself from a virtually all-white school to one where black students represented nearly 5 percent of the undergraduate enrollment on its Bronx campus, and much more than that in its new college at Lincoln Center in Manhattan.

The office of the Institute of Afro-American Studies in 205 Dealy Hall resembled an Urban League street academy or a Black Panthers headquarters more than a college department. The walls of this former classroom, which had been divided by eight-foot partitions into three offices and a reception area, were covered with red, black, and green flags, pictures of Malcolm X, Huey Newton, and Marcus Garvey, and maps showing the United States dwarfed within Africa's borders. As I arrived for my interview and looked around in amazement, I was greeted by a slim, brown-skinned man in his late twenties who ushered me into one of the offices. This was Stanley Majors, director of the Institute, a graduate student in American history who had been assigned to administer this insurgent academic program.

What followed was less a job interview than an invitation to share an important political mission. Majors began by describing the Institute's origins in a student sit-in and its evolution into a degree-granting program administered by a student-faculty governing board. The goal of the Institute, he emphasized, was not just to promote an academic understanding of the black experience; it also aimed to promote community involvement, cultural awareness, and participation in black liberation struggles in the community, the nation, and the world. But these goals could only be sustained if the Institute's faculty won respect as teachers and scholars. Majors said he was impressed by my résumé and had heard good things about me from Will Wright, my former student from Columbia Upward Bound. He then asked what I planned to teach. Startled, I quickly came up with titles for three courses that reflected my research interests and political commitments: History of American Racism, History of Black Protest, and Afro-Americans in the American Labor Movement. Professor Majors seemed to like what I proposed. "Those should work very well," he told me. "I will present your courses and vitae to the governing board within the next few weeks. You should be hearing from us very soon."

As I left the Institute office, my head was spinning. If I read the situation correctly, I was about to be offered something very close to my dream job—teaching and writing about racism and black history among colleagues who shared my political passions and commitment to building alternative institutions. The Afro-American Institute was for all intents and purposes a "movement organization," one created and sustained by student protest, and staffed by young black scholars immersed in the political struggles of their era. Not only would my research on black radicalism be welcome in this setting, but I could easily use my position in the Institute to promote the antiracist and antiwar organizing of the Bronx Coalition. The prospect of being the only white person in a black studies program was daunting; I knew that some, and perhaps many, black students would take offense at my presence. But the cultural dissonance that I would encounter would certainly be no greater than what I would experience as the only radical in a traditional history department. On my three other job interviews, I had been greeted by clean-shaven, middle-aged white men who displayed little interest in my research and no apparent empathy for my political views. If I took one of those jobs, I would have had to live incognito, carefully hiding my political passions, my musical tastes, my communal living arrangements. I much preferred being the only white person in an Institute run by black activists to being a counterculture radical in a department of conservative historians. The Institute job, if offered, was the one I was going to take.

Three weeks later, I received a letter inviting me to join the Institute of Afro-American Studies as an Instructor. I was offered a one-year contract, at a salary of eighty-five hundred dollars, and I quickly accepted. To my great relief, none of the top administrators of Fordham College asked to interview me or did a background check on my political activities. At the time I signed my Fordham contract, I still faced assault charges, and my Columbia transcript was stamped "Censured" in bold black letters! But if anyone in the Fordham administration knew about this, it did not deter them from hiring me. The governing board of the Institute, like those of many black-studies programs created in the late sixties, had complete autonomy in hiring so long as its candidates had minimally acceptable professional credentials. Hired in May 1970, I was scheduled to begin teaching in early September of that year.

With the Fordham position secured, other parts of my life remained to be put in order. First, and perhaps most important, our lawyer, Sam Neuberger, found a way of settling the Brooklyn case without requiring us to serve any time. The opportunity arose when one of my co-defendants, Josh Schwartz, who had left Weatherman shortly after I did, was severely beaten by police during demonstrations in Manhattan protesting the murder of Chicago Panther leader Fred Hampton, who was assassinated during a police raid while lying unarmed in his bed. Schwartz's case against the police was so ironclad (the beating occurred in public in front of numerous witnesses) that Sam was able to get the Manhattan and Brooklyn district attorneys to reduce all of the Brooklyn charges to misdemeanors in return for Schwartz's not pursuing the brutality case. Early in June, Sam marched us into Brooklyn Criminal Court, had us plead guilty to simple assault, and got us released with fifty-dollar fines and no jail time. The eight-month ordeal that began in a Brooklyn coffee shop was now over.

One of the first things I did after the case was settled was return to my doctoral work. I called Richard Hofstadter, who had chaired my oral examinations, and asked if he would mentor the dissertation I planned to write on Communist Party organizing among blacks during the Depression and World War II. After congratulating me on my new job and the settlement of the Brooklyn case, Hofstadter agreed to work with me, but only after warning that he would "ride herd" on me to assure the dissertation got done. "I think this will involve some sacrifice of your political activities," Hofstadter wrote, "since it would take the energy of genius to keep three balls in the air instead of two. . . . I should add that I think I would give you precisely the same advice if I agreed entirely with your political views, and approved of your activities, instead of thinking that they are from never-never land, as I do!"

Hofstadter was joined in these sentiments by Paul Buhle, who made it his personal mission to persuade me to stop writing apocalyptic revolutionary pronouncements and return to writing history. After I sent him one particularly strident piece, in which I solemnly insisted "we must make a revolution in . . . the most powerful empire that man has ever created," even though "we will be harassed and murdered and incarcerated in an effort to stop us," Paul accused me of viewing the revolution as a football game in which I acted as the coach. "The notion of Football Coach as revolutionary leader," Paul wrote, "at this stage in society . . . is *machismo* (this is clearest in Panther-things, but clear enuf in the aping of the panthers by various factional types in the Last Days of SDS). To break with this notion, and to see yourself—as did CLR James with his people-as a *helpful* figure is one of the healthiest things you can do."

Little by little, Paul's letters began to chip away at my fascination with strategies that presumed that armed revolution was imminent, and even desirable, in the United States. In the last two years, organizations on the American left that had embraced armed struggle, most notably Weatherman and the Black Panther Party, had caused the death and imprisonment of many idealistic people, provoked fierce repression, and won little popular support. In the face of this tragedy, it felt unseemly, if not irresponsible, for me to write articles urging people to give up their jobs and material comforts to join a life-and-death struggle for political power in the United States. Moreover, since I was personally reluctant to make the sacrifices that revolutionary politics imposed, for me to insist, as I did in one piece, that "the principles of armed struggle . . . have to be emphasized and practiced in all aspects of our organizing" had the stench of hypocrisy. As Paul suggested, it was time for me to find ways of intervening in the political issues of the day that did not result in burnout or self-destruction. At his urging, I began work on a long article for *Radical America* evaluating the Communist Party's relationship to the black radical tradition in the United States, examining the party's pioneering, if not always successful, efforts to become a multiracial organization and encourage black-white unity among sharecroppers, industrial workers, intellectuals, and the unemployed during the Great Depression.

If my response to turmoil and disillusionment was to resume my academic career, many of my friends responded very differently, by leaving New York City. In the aftermath of the Kent State shootings, the back-to-the-land impulse began to assert a powerful appeal among disaffected political activists. Following a utopian impulse deeply embedded within the American radical tradition, tens of thousands of students and young professionals, most of them white, moved to small towns and rural areas in the hope of creating democratic communities that were free of racial tension, competition, and materialism. Although this migration helped spark a cultural and economic revitalization within New England and the Pacific Northwest—especially in Maine, Vermont, and Oregon—it weakened the white left in some urban areas. During the summer of 1970, three couples who were among the founding members of the Bronx Coalition shocked their friends by announcing that they were leaving the Bronx to the build new lives in less stressful settings.

The departure of these key political leaders seemed to destroy the fragile chemistry that had given the Coalition its energy and effectiveness. Most of us who remained still felt passionate about women's liberation, racism, and the war, but we wondered whether we had the energy to sustain a revolutionary organization with six of our hardest-working comrades gone. By September 1970, the Coalition had trouble attracting people to its weekly meetings, raising the funds to pay for its storefront, and publishing the *Cross Bronx Express*. Some aspects of Coalition organizing survived. The women's health project continued to grow in power and influence, leading to the foundation of the Bronx's first legal abortion clinic at Montefiore Hospital and the development of a rape crisis center. Politically active students and faculty at Fordham, Lehman, Bronx Community, and NYU continued to organize antiwar protests at their schools and send contingents to antiwar marches on Washington. A large and energetic "Bronx contingent" participated in a large demonstration in New Haven in November 1970 to demand the release of the Black Panther leader Bobby Seale. But increasingly these activities took place without central coordination. By the time my second semester at Fordham began, the Bronx Coalition was dead, and there was no longer a single organization in the Bronx that tried to address the war, the economy, neighborhood decay, racial tensions, and issues of gender and sexuality in terms of a common political framework. Among white radicals in the Bronx, the dream of a disciplined revolutionary struggle lost its appeal, giving way to countercultural visions, single-issue organizing, and a politics of the possible.

Departures from the city also eroded the interracial social life Ruthie and I had developed on the Upper West Side. Many of our close friends left New York for places like Maine and Oregon, and their departures added to Ruthie's depression. I tried to persuade Ruthie that she would be happier and more relaxed if we spent part of our summer visiting these people, but she was reluctant to leave her family for any length of time. Although she joined me for a four-day visit to Bruce and Wendy in Maine, she decided to go to Georgia rather than come on the West Coast vacation I had planned for us visiting Carol in Portland.

The trips to Maine and Portland were eye-opening reminders of how many portions of the country were touched by sixties activism. Bruce and Wendy's move to Maine was less an escape from their role as educators than its transference to a depressed rural area. When Ruthie and I visited them, we were stunned by the poverty of their surroundings. They lived in a small wood-frame house without electricity and indoor plumbing. Their immediate neighbors, the Johnson family, lived in a wood-and-tarpaper house surrounded by rusting machinery, abandoned cars, and huge piles of tin cans. But as we soon discovered, Bruce and Wendy had worked out a symbiotic relationship with the Johnsons. In return for the rural survival skills that Mr. Johnson and his older children were able to impart, Bruce and Wendy had turned their house into a second home for the younger Johnson children and worked diligently to improve their academic skills. They interacted with these energetic children in much the same way Ruthie and I had with youngsters in Double Discovery—reading to them, telling them stories, feeding them dinner, taking them to the town library and to the movies. Their house in Harmony, Maine, had become, in effect, a rural extension of the Urban League academies where they had once taught, a place where young people from poor families could find love, nurturing, and intellectual stimulation.

My trip to Portland introduced me to a more communal and, perhaps, self-indulgent version of sixties utopianism. Our friend Carol and her boyfriend lived in a section of Portland that was filled with thousands of young white people who had given up school and careers to live on food stamps, odd jobs, and the sale of marijuana. Located next to a river and a city park, their community contained blocks of small wooden houses surrounded by flower and vegetable gardens which its long-haired residents cultivated with loving care. People were friendly, hostile to the government, and receptive to almost any form of illegal or unconventional behavior. No one managed to express this unique ethos better than Carol, Ruthie's old friend from the Upper West Side, who supported her passion for travel and her activities as a leader of Portland's women's liberation by working as an exotic dancer. As she put it, "When I'm not waitressing at a 'Real New York Style Deli and Restaurant,' I'm ripping off my clothes to shake and quake.... THIS is where all my education and brain cells got me—sputtering and grinding away to make $250–300 a week. I hope Women's Lib gangs beat the hell out of every businessman and bureaucrat they meet!" During my two weeks in Portland, I happily accommodated myself to the community's unconventional mores. I spent my days smoking pot, running up hills in the neighborhood park, going to concerts, practicing martial arts, and helping Carol's boyfriend rebuild the engine of his Volkswagen bus.

But as much as I liked Portland's countercultural community, I found it hard to imagine living there. The almost complete absence of blacks in Carol's neighborhood, along with the lack of a black cultural presence in the city as a whole, made me uneasy. My personal politics, and my identity as an intellectual and a political activist, had been so deeply molded by contact with the African-American community that I could not feel comfortable living in an all-white environment, even one with progressive politics. The only utopian ideal that had ever moved me was the vision of an interracial community invoked by Martin Luther King and the civil rights movement. If the stresses of my life became too great, I could always retreat for a time to Maine or Oregon, but I knew I would eventually miss the music, the street life, and the mingling of races and cultures that made New York unique. I flew back from the West Coast in late August feeling confident about the direction my life had taken. I was ready for the challenge of teaching black studies at Fordham.

Before I began teaching, however, I wanted finally to confront my mother about Ruthie. In the two years since my father had died, my mother continued to pretend that Ruthie was not a part of my life. She refused to set foot in our apartment, never invited Ruthie to accompany me when I went over for lunch or dinner, and avoided mentioning Ruthie's name in phone calls and letters. As long as revolutionary politics dominated my life, I had not given this matter much attention. But now I wanted my mother to make at least a gesture of acceptance toward the woman I shared my life with. I wrote her a letter warning

that I would sever ties with her unless she recognized Ruthie as my partner and girlfriend and began to treat her as a member of the family.

My mother responded with a twelve-page letter that contained a
grudging invitation for Ruthie to come to dinner. The invitation was
accompanied by a ringing defense of her "middle class Jewish values"
and a bitter diatribe against the politics of the sixties: "I am a middle
class Jewish liberal women who has always been anxious to make this
a better world for everyone. I think my way is better. I'm incensed at
SDS and the Black Panthers, the use of marijuana, the loose morals, the
Afro-American teachers, the Arabs etc. I am a confirmed Zionist. . . . I'm
not religious, but I am tied up to everything Jewish."

For the first time in four years, my mother admitted that Ruthie might
be an admirable person, but she did so in a backhanded manner that
made it difficult for Ruthie to accept her hospitality:

> I take it for granted that you're in love and she may be a lovely girl. I
> would not like even a non-Jewish white girl. I lived in a dream world. I
> don't want an heroic son who has to show the world what must be done
> even if it makes life harder for him and everyone concerned. I would
> have preferred a life for you that I would share, but if it can't be, it can't
> be. . . . You can bring Ruthie to see me. I have *middle class* values and a boy
> brings his friend to his mother's house. You know that I am a good host-
> ess and that I am a lady though a nervous one. I'll talk to both of you. I
> have nothing against Ruthie or her family. They may be wonderful, but
> this is not what I hoped for.

Ruthie's response to this letter, predictably, was to reject my mother's
invitation. "I'm too worried about my own family to deal with your
mother's craziness," she told me. "You can go on visiting her without
me. Let her keep showing you off to her friends as her nice Jewish son.
I don't have time for this." I had produced no miracle of racial reconciliation, and had only locked Ruthie and my mother in mutual antag-
onism. But in pushing my relationship with my mother to a new level
of frankness, I achieved some peace of mind for myself.

When early September came, I could not wait to meet my students
and see what attitudes, experiences, and feelings they brought to the
study of black history. But when I arrived at the Institute of Afro-American Studies and asked for Professor Majors, the receptionist told me he
had left the Institute and introduced me to Bob Bennett, the new acting
director. Bob, who had graduated from Fordham College only two

months before, told me that the pressure of running the Institute, writing a dissertation, and dealing with a new baby had proved too much for Majors. Until a qualified replacement could be found, Bob, who was not even enrolled in graduate school, would have to run the Institute!

This news stunned me. Not only was I concerned for Majors but the intellectual vacuum created by his departure was enormous. More than anyone else, Stanley Majors had shaped the philosophy of the Institute and sustained its credibility with the two constituencies most critical to its survival: the Fordham administration and the university's black student population. Backed by a powerful student movement, Majors had won formal recognition for the Institute's academic programs. Further, he had helped persuade the administration to convert a small building near the university's main entrance into a black student cultural center and community school. Students called it "Spirit House," after the cultural center Imamu Amiri Baraka had opened in Newark. But Majors had also insisted that the Institute's academic program was open to the *entire* university community and that white students were welcome in its classes. Majors's capacity to adopt multiple rhetorical stances, to move between the language of black nationalism and the universalistic ideas of Jesuit education, had made him a singularly effective leader at Fordham. The skills and hard work of many people would be needed for the Institute to function in his absence.

After Bob Bennett gave me keys and assigned me a desk—which I was to share with two part-time instructors—I took the measure of my new work environment. The Institute's biggest enclosure was its reception area, which contained a receptionist's desk, a large table with chairs, and a padded bench. It was ideal for chatting, studying, reading, and holding meetings, and it seemed to serve as an informal black student social center. The cubicle that would serve as my office, immediately to the right of the reception area, contained three wooden desks in a ten-by-ten space. It also housed Quinton Wilkes, the other full-time faculty member, as well as four adjuncts. The director's cubicle, another ten-by-ten space, adjoined ours. Because the cubicles had no ceilings, none of us had any privacy. In addition, because the Institute served as a communication center for Society for African American Leadership (SAAL), the Fordham black student organization, almost every politically active black student at Fordham regularly dropped by Dealy 205. If past experience was a guide, at least some of these students were going to disapprove of my presence, and I could be in for some awkward encounters in a very small space.

My fear of hostile encounters in the office, however, was more than offset by excitement about teaching. I had twenty students in my History of Black Protest course and thirty-two in my History of American Racism—excellent enrollments for a professor no one knew. In preparing my courses, I had the benefit of a host of recently published materials in the field of race relations and African-American history. These ranged from two excellent new collections of documents, one titled *White Racism* the other *Black Protest*, to recently republished slave narratives by Frederick Douglass, Solomon Northrup, and Henry Bibb, to classics works of history like W.E.B Du Bois's *Black Reconstruction* and C.L.R. James's *The Black Jacobins*. I supplemented these with two collections of essays on African-American history: *Amistad 1*, which presented interpretive writings of nationalist and Marxist scholars; and *Key Issues in the African-American Experience*, which presented the latest research on African-American life during and after slavery. These materials gave me the opportunity to bring black history to life as an adventure in rethinking American and world civilization. With the help of pioneering black scholars and contemporary historians, I was going to ask students to imagine what America looked like to its subject and conquered peoples, and then reimagine what it might look like as a genuinely democratic society.

When I actually met with my classes, however, I realized that teaching black history to a multiracial group was far more difficult than teaching it to an all-black class. Nearly two-thirds of the students in my American Racism course, and half of those in the Black Protest course, were lower-middle-class Irish and Italian kids from the Bronx, Westchester, and Queens who commuted to their classes by car and subway. Products of Catholic high schools, often the first people in their families to attend college, they seemed torn between the conservative values of their parents, who felt physically and culturally threatened by black militancy, and the optimistic, tolerant spirit of the counterculture. Extremely curious about black culture, particularly black music, they were wary of probing too deeply into their own racial attitudes and provoking their African-American classmates. By contrast, the black students in my classes tended to view racial hostility as an inevitable by-product of America's oppressive history, something that needed to be aired and analyzed in classroom discussions. Although many came from upwardly mobile families and attended Catholic high schools, a large number lived in all-black neighborhoods and were skeptical that integration, at least outside the workplace, was really possible in the United States. Convinced that they would remain isolated and embattled even if they became professionally successful, they wanted to explore black history for contemporary political lessons, and draw inspiration from episodes of black solidarity and resistance.

Given that my black and white students lived in different neighborhoods, had radically different ways of perceiving American society, and, with rare exceptions, went their separate ways outside of the classroom, I faced a formidable challenge in creating a unified class atmosphere. The one problem I *did not* face—which confronted professors at colleges whose white students came from wealthy suburbs and whose black students were from the inner city—was a huge economic and educational gap between blacks and whites. Most Fordham students, of both races, were lower middle class, and had solid, occasionally excellent Catholic school educations. Even students in the Higher Education Opportunity Program, who constituted about a third of the black students at Fordham, had often been among the better students at their inner-city public high schools. Knowing that most of my students could read and absorb complex material, I was able to use group projects to foster an interracial dialogue that would not necessarily occur without my prodding. By the middle of the semester, I had divided my classes into groups of three and four, pairing black and white students when possible, and asked them to make oral presentations on assigned topics.

None of these pedagogical strategies might have worked, however, if I had not tried to win students' confidence outside the classroom. I was only three or four years older than most of my students, and I shared their anxieties about the war and the government, and had similar tastes in music. Hanging out with them was easy and fun. By the middle of my first semester, I was regularly going to demonstrations, meetings, and parties with my students, drinking with them at local bars, eating lunch with them on and off campus, and playing basketball with them in the Fordham gym. Confident that I could best convey my ideas and values if I was immersed in their lives, I threw out every model of professorial distance I had been exposed to in college and, like many other radical professors in my cohort, tried to become friends with my students.

Some powerful experiences resulted. Early in the semester, I began to have intense, far-ranging discussions with Vicki Simmons, an African-American woman in her mid-twenties who was one of the few black students in my American Racism class. Fascinated by the conflicting narratives I presented about how racism evolved, she would come to my office after class to discuss historical theories for which her younger classmates had little patience. Soon Vicki, who had two young children, also began to talk with me about her experiences living and growing up in the Bronx. She and her brother, the NBA point guard and school-yard legend Nate "Tiny" Archibald, had both grown up in the South Bronx but had followed completely different paths as they matured, Vicki choosing academics and Nate choosing basketball. Vicki's tales of streets and schoolyards struck a powerful chord, and soon I was telling her about my own Brooklyn upbringing and my relationship with Ruthie and her family. Vicki became my first real confidante at Fordham. Having her as a friend made me much more optimistic that I could establish rapport with black students if I worked hard and remained patient.

Although no single friendship with a white student matched my ties to Vicki, I probably spent more time outside of class with white students than black ones, particularly those involved in Fordham's antiwar movement and counterculture. Following the American invasion of Cambodia in the spring of 1970, Fordham had been the scene of a month-long student strike during which unknown persons had set fire to the Student Activities Building. Signs of anti-authoritarian behavior abounded on campus. On sunny days, a minimally observant person could see, and smell, groups of students openly smoking marijuana on Edwards Parade, the large square lawn in the center of campus, or outside Martyr's Court, the main residence halls. Students in those circles, some of whom were in my classes, viewed taking black studies courses as part of a generalized pattern of defiance against authority. They invited me to go with them to marches and rallies to end the war, which were still a monthly occurrence, eat lunch with them in the cafeteria, and join them at meetings and parties. They were warm, open, and generous and quickly made me feel at home on campus.

But the social and political circles they drew me into, like those of Columbia SDS and the Bronx Coalition, included few black students, and I found myself once again gravitating between a white sphere and a black sphere, with the classroom forming the only neutral ground. Even there, my efforts to stimulate discussion and create emotional investment in the material did not easily produce a strong sense of community. My black students easily situated themselves in history, imagining themselves as bitter fieldhands, wily house servants, ambitious mechanics, or revolutionary leaders like Nat Turner or Sojourner Truth. But my white students resisted identifying with the historic roles of plantation owners, overseers, and pro-slavery intellectuals; they wanted to distance themselves from the sins of past generations and imagine a new America free of racial hatred. These two dynamics were not easily reconciled. Six weeks after I began teaching, I wrote Paul Buhle that I was "rather pessimistic about the possibilities of whites and blacks relating to each other with anything more positive than reluctant coexistence. The cultural worlds of black youth and white youth are so alien to one another (even when they think of themselves as revolutionary!), that there is precious little room for relaxed contact and discussion: the best that one can expect is negotiation."

I also had to cope with tensions in the Institute office. During my first few weeks on the job, some black students noted my presence with looks, and sometimes comments, that revealed considerable skepticism about my hiring. Not everyone who came to the Institute office felt that way. Betty Noel and Sheila Stainback, two brilliant Thomas More* juniors who were members of the Institute's governing board, were always cordial and helpful, willing to answer any questions I had about Fordham and the Institute. Their quiet professionalism became a source of comfort. Another student leader, Alvin Leonard, played an even more important role in making me welcome, although not before testing me to see if I was fit for the job. A handsome, powerfully built young man who bore an uncanny physical resemblance to Marcus Garvey, Alvin was charming but extremely direct. "So you're the white man they just hired to teach in the Institute?" Alvin asked me with a big grin. "Are you some kind of trouble maker?" "I guess so," I replied. "Well, if we're going to hire a white man, he might as well be a radical," Alvin responded. "We need a revolution at Fordham to get more black students into the school. Will you be down when we need you?" "You

---

*Thomas More College was the women's college on Fordham's Bronx campus. It merged with Fordham College in the early 1970s.

know where to find me," I replied. So began a relationship that involved considerable verbal sparring, but also encompassed a shared love for ideas and a commitment to social justice. One of the first black students at Fordham ever to come from Theodore Roosevelt, the notoriously tough public high school across the street from the university, Alvin reminded me of the street-smart, passionately intelligent students I had taught at Double Discovery. My face lit up every time I saw him enter the office.

Not every interaction with black students was this positive, however. One of the most influential black student leaders on the campus, Gary Allston, fixed upon me a look of raw hatred every time he came to the office. Medium-sized and light-skinned, with a face that showed the effects of a tough childhood on the streets of the Bronx, Gary came to the Institute office regularly to solicit help for the community-outreach programs of the black student cultural center, particularly its children's school. Gary never threatened me directly, or indeed said anything to me at all, but his contemptuous stares, which were repeated by the tough-looking friends who often accompanied him, triggered my deeply rooted street paranoia, something neither education nor radical politics had managed to erase. I felt my muscles tighten every time he came into the office, and I consciously forced myself to maintain eye contact when he glared at me, adopting a cold, deadpan expression that suggested I would respond in kind to any assault, whether physical or political.

But my main response to hostility, real or imagined, was to seek reassurance in the one activity that had always bound me to men in the black community—basketball. During September and October, fierce full-court basketball games took place in the Fordham gym involving players from Fordham's nationally ranked basketball team and a few courageous outsiders. In the best shape of my life because of the running and the lifting I had done to prepare for a possible jail sentence, I started showing up on the sidelines, waiting for my "next," and I gradually earned acceptance as a regular participant. Although my skills were definitely in the lower ranks, the fact that I could jump and run well enough to compete at all gained me a measure of respect. Soon, players I had met in the gym were greeting me effusively when they saw me on campus and asking about my spring classes. One of the players I got most friendly with, Nat Fripp, who had quit the Fordham team but had great basketball skills, was an officer of SAAL and a leader of Spirit House. I hoped that his support, and that of key black players on the Fordham team, would deter my detractors from any open campaign to remove me.

In the long run, however, I suspected that my survival in black studies depended most on my relationship with my colleagues. I identified two areas where I thought I could help the Institute: recruiting students for courses and writing memorandums to the Fordham administration, and I let my colleagues know I was willing to do both these things. Bob Bennett, the Institute's genial acting director, gratefully accepted my help in these areas, and in the process we discovered a shared passion for jazz. By the end of the semester, we were regularly driving to lunch at McDonald's on Gun Hill Road, then the only one in the Bronx, while listening to Pharaoh Sanders on his tape deck.

I developed a more substantial relationship with Quinton Wilkes, the talented psychology graduate student who had helped Stanley Majors found the Institute and whose courses in black psychology were a bulwark of its curriculum. A large, solidly built man who had played high school football in North Carolina and attended Morgan State College in Baltimore, Quinton had the thoughtful, measured manner of a therapist (which he was) and an intellectual seriousness that instantly commanded respect. Working in an environment where indignation seemed part of the intellectual atmosphere, Quinton stood out for his calmness and objectivity. But Quinton was as passionate about his intellectual work as anyone in the department. Convinced that psychologists had underestimated the impact of racism on their patients and research subjects, Quinton was among the pioneers in developing a new "black psychology" and helping train a generation of black therapists to counteract the effects of racist socialization. Teacher, mentor, and spiritual leader to Fordham's African-American students, Quinton lived by the precepts of the Institute's founding statement: "We must see Black people as a people and each of us as parts of one whole. . . . When we say brother, sister, blood, we must feel it as well as mean it."

I found Quinton to be a thoughtful and considerate colleague who patiently answered my questions about Fordham and quietly extended himself to make me feel at home. When he greeted me, he clasped my hand and looked me in the eye as if I were a fellow congregant in his church, and we soon found ourselves sharing details of our private lives as well as our concerns about the Institute's future. Linked by a love of sports and a passion for teaching, we soon became good friends.

Through Quinton, I met another individual who would play a critical role in the Institute's history and become a friend for thirty years, Claude Mangum, director of Fordham's Upward Bound program. A doctoral student at Columbia Teachers College whose research area was the history of black education, Claude often dropped in on us from his office across the hall to socialize with our students and faculty. He had a particularly close relationship with Quinton, and I found myself listening to, and eventually joining, their conversations about the Institute's future. Claude fascinated me. The product of a middle-class Queens family of mixed West Indian and African-American heritage, extremely handsome and gracious, Claude viewed the creation of strong black institutions and the promotion of black history and culture as preconditions for African-American progress in American universities and in American society as a whole. Although he was regarded as a mainstream figure by people in the Fordham administration, Claude seemed irresistibly drawn to the intellectual ferment in the Institute. By the end of the semester, he was spending almost as much time in our office as he was at Upward Bound and was playing a key role in the Institute's personnel and curricular decisions. It was Claude who recruited its new director in the spring of 1971, a fellow graduate student at Columbia Teachers College named Matthew Mbote, and we found ourselves increasingly using his contacts, inside the university and out, to help us gain access to needed resources.

Matthew Mbote, sometimes called "the big M" by his students, completed the triad of full-time faculty in the Institute. Born in Kenya, educated in England, Mbote had the charm of a diplomat and the style of a British barrister. A man of impressive height and girth, well over six feet tall and two hundred pounds, he contributed to his flamboyant image by always coming to work in formal dress, whether in business suits or dashikis. Mbote had extraordinary confidence in his teaching ability. At Fordham and elsewhere, he volunteered to teach a staggering variety of courses, ranging from African politics and history to African-American sociology and the politics of black education. And students, especially black students, seemed to love him. His infectious enthusiasm, his sense of humor, and his uncompromising sense of personal dignity and honor made him a commanding presence on the Fordham campus.

As I became closer to my colleagues and students, the Institute became the focus of my political and intellectual life. When I accepted the job at Fordham, I viewed it as an extension of my organizing in the Bronx, and hoped that I could use it to recruit students for the various projects of the Bronx Coalition. But by the time the first semester ended, the Bronx Coalition had disintegrated, and my political work increasingly consisted of what I did on the Fordham campus. Some of that work included protesting the war, but my most significant mission was educating people about racism and helping to build a black institution on a campus where its very existence challenged traditional ways of thinking. From the outside, my position looked untenable—I was the only white person teaching black studies at any university in New York City—but as I developed friendships with the people I worked with, I increasingly felt part of a community of struggle as well as an academic enterprise.

The emotional sustenance I drew from my work, inside and outside the classroom, helped me cope with the problems I faced in my relationship with Ruthie, which were growing more confusing and frustrating daily. Although we finally resumed living together in the fall of 1970 (she had been away, on and off, for nearly a year with her family in Georgia), she seemed distant and emotionally constricted in our private encounters. I desperately tried to rekindle her feelings for me, and her zest for life, by taking her to movies, nightclubs, and restaurants, and helping her with family responsibilities, but none of this produced the desired thaw. The relationship that had once been the focal point of my scholarship and politics, the source of utopian dreams and deep resentments, had now become confusing and difficult in ways that could not be reduced to race.

Ironically, public disapproval of our relationship from blacks—once a major source of tension—seemed to have little to do with Ruthie's remoteness. During her mother's illness, she had drifted away from the Columbia friends who had urged her to break up with me; and in her family and her professional world, where she now spent most of her time, I was welcomed with open arms. When she first returned from Georgia, Ruthie took me everyplace she went. We spent literally hundreds of hours visiting with her sisters in the Bronx, going with her younger sister and her boyfriend to nightclubs and dances, and attending fund-raising dinners and parties for the Children's Community

Work Shop School, an experimental elementary school on the West Side where she worked as a teacher. Moreover, the Institute faculty and staff was as welcoming of Ruthie as her family and school were of me. When I took her to parties at the Bronx apartments of Quinton Wilkes or Claude Mangum, Ruthie quickly made friends with the people there, and she danced, ate, and conversed with great enthusiasm. Our social life was lively and rewarding, but there was no rekindling of our physical relationship. I still loved Ruthie but did not know how much longer I could live without warmth and intimacy.

As my private frustrations mounted, I put more and more energy into my teaching. My classes during the spring were even bigger than in the fall: over forty in my History of American Racism, twenty-five in my History of Black Protest, and twenty in a new seminar called Selected Topics in the African-American Experience. The students I drew were racially and culturally diverse, and they included players on the Fordham basketball team, former members of Fordham SDS, leaders of the Fordham student government, and a sizable group of black students who were musicians or political activists.

Excited by these large enrollments, I became more overtly political in my pedagogy. Keeping the discussion format that I used in the first semester, I interspersed readings on black history with contemporary writings by black revolutionaries, such as Eldridge Cleaver's *Soul On Ice*, George Jackson's *Soledad Brother*, and Frantz Fanon's *Wretched of the Earth*. I also included works on the "white backlash," such as Peter Binzen's *Whitetown USA* and Andrew Greeley's *Why Can't They Be Like Us* to show how working- and middle-class whites had reacted against black unrest. I asked my students to speculate how, if it all, these divisions could be overcome. As a community-building experience, I added music sessions to all my classes, illustrating how black musicians were the source of almost all creative innovation in rock and roll and how contemporary musicians were breaking free of old forms, creating transracial identities and trying to unite people politically and musically.

These music sessions became a powerful release for me, a chance to share my dreams, my frustrations, and my hopes for a better world and, for at least a moment, to commune with my students in a zone free of war and hatred. I played hard-driving soul classics like Ray Charles's "What I Say" and James Brown's "Super Bad." I played Janis Joplin and The Doors, to show how white children of the counterculture adopted blues themes as their own. I played the newly political music of The Temptations, moving from the somber "Papa Was a Rolling Stone" to angry and prophetic "Run Charlie Run, the Niggers are Coming," a song about white flight. I played cross-racial rock and jazz, starting with Sly and the Family Stone, moving to War and Santana, and then onto Mandrill, a New York group who fused Latin, soul, and rock. But above all I played Jimi Hendrix, the African-American guitarist and rock prophet who reinvented his instrument and deconstructed racial identities in a burst of creativity and excess that ultimately took his life. With shaking hands, I would put on *Band of Gypsies,* the live recording Hendrix made with Billy Cox and Buddy Miles at the Fillmore East on New Year's Eve 1969. I would began with "Machine Gun," Hendrix's twelve-minute evocation of the sounds and feelings of the Vietnam War. As Hendrix turned his guitar into a battery of weapons and chanted "evil man let me kill you, evil man let you kill me," the entire class, including me, withdrew into thoughts of friends who had died in the war or had destroyed their lives resisting it. I ended with the deeply spiritual "Power of Love," in which Hendrix dared to dream that blacks and whites could ultimately be united in a common celebration of life. As Hendrix chanted "with the power of soul, anything is possible," my classes and I entered the zone of utopian possibility that Martin Luther King had touched in his "I Have a Dream Speech," and we left the classroom uplifted and exhausted.

As I threw caution to the wind inside the classroom, my ties to students multiplied. My life on campus became an exhilarating round of basketball games, potluck dinners, demonstrations, political meetings, and passionate conversations. "Things are really going well now ..." I wrote Paul Buhle in late March 1971:

> I have made surprising headway in forming working relationships with black students and staff. There is very little hostility and suspicion of me now (always SOME) primarily because people are convinced I am so crazy that I just can't be fit in any stereotype of a white liberal or radical. This can change overnite if I step on the wrong toes. It's basically an unstable position. But when it goes well, it's a gas.

Despite these successes, I still felt some anxiety about the racial politics of my job. Some of this derived from purely local events. My old nemesis Gary Allston, undeterred by the growing popularity of my courses, continued to glower at me every time he visited the Institute, joined by a new partner, John Fulton, who helped him run the community pro-grams in Spirit House. I was rattled enough by their staring that for a few weeks I carried a butcher knife in my briefcase (which I conspicu-ously let drop out on a few occasions) and walked around campus with an informal bodyguard, a black student in my classes who had been a sergeant in the Special Forces in Vietnam. I ended this foolishness when I realized that they had no intention of physically harming me, but their hostility reminded me that some black students opposed what I did on principle and could not be won over.

Events off the campus also contributed to my sense of vulnerability. As an avid reader of the black and mainstream press, I was keenly aware that many blacks were skeptical that whites could interpret the black experience accurately. Historian Sterling Stuckey's observation that white scholars of black history "were about as popular among black people as white policemen" captured the polarized nature of scholar-ship on race relations. I carefully followed the controversies surround-ing Daniel Moynihan's report *The Negro Family: The Case for National Action*, and William Styron's novel *The Confessions of Nat Turner*, each of which had inspired angry attacks on their authors by black journalists and scholars. Closer to home was the fall 1970 suicide of Robert Starobin, a young radical scholar I knew who was teaching African-American history at the State University of New York at Binghamton. According to mutual friends, the hostility of black students at his school had con-tributed powerfully to his depression, although it was a shattered love affair that provoked his actual suicide. The loneliness of the white scholar of black history represented the dominant theme in the remark-able tribute to Bob written by Julius Lester in *Liberation* magazine. In this piece, Lester confessed deep regret for attacking Bob harshly at a con-ference on slave autobiography at Wayne State University the previous spring:

> It was one of those situations that are unavoidable when blacks and whites come together in post–Black Power America, a situation in which people are not individuals, but historical actors playing out a drama whose begin-nings are now so submerged that we will never find them. . . . At Wayne State, my heart ached for Bob. I didn't know him, but I knew what I had to do . . . and I did so, employing every forensic skill which two genera-tions of ministers in my family had bequeathed to me. I bowed to the demands of history that day and will loathe myself forever for having done so.

Lester's heartfelt apology moved me greatly, but also made me take a frank look at my own situation. When Lester wrote "these days, a white man who devotes himself to teaching and writing about black history must have the strength and fortitude of a bull elephant because blacks will let him know that his presence is unwanted and undesirable," he seemed to be talking about me. Rightly or wrongly, I was convinced that my imposing physical presence was as important as my scholarly commitments in assuring my survival in black studies. Would I have felt comfortable at Fordham if I was not able to "run with the brothers" on the basketball court and bond with my male colleagues through sports and music? Was the Brooklyn street macho that enabled me to stare down nationalist students the only thing that separated me from Bob Starobin?

Although my machismo had been critiqued and discredited in the Bronx Coalition, I clung to it as a weapon of last resort against anyone who made me a target for their anger. In the politically charged—and highly masculinist—atmosphere of early black studies programs, it seemed to be a useful affectation. From casual comments by black students about "white devils" and "yacus," to poems and plays that fantasized about killing whites and Jews, I periodically encountered a discourse, first popularized by Malcolm X in his Nation of Islam years, that extolled hatred of whites as a liberating emotion. It was impossible to work in black studies in the early 1970s and not encounter rhetoric that mocked or demonized whites, whether in the journals, newspapers, and texts that were circulating in program offices, or in the cultural events sponsored by black student organizations. One also encountered, at least in some programs, an aura of physical intimidation that was part of the nationalist mystique of the late 1960s and early 1970s.

But the feelings of isolation I experienced as a white person in a black domain were more than compensated for by the camaraderie and sense of mission I shared with my colleagues and students. The black studies culture at Fordham, although it reflected racial tensions in the larger society, encouraged hospitality and generosity as well as political and intellectual commitment. Handshakes and hugs, the sharing of music and food, loud laughter, and passionate discussion bound me to my colleagues in a community of feeling that incorporated powerful African-American traditions yet transcended racial boundaries. Contrary to what Lester suggested, not every politically aware black intellectual felt compelled to attack whites who studied the black experience. My colleagues at Fordham were all race-conscious individuals, but I never heard one of them attack a white student for wanting to take one of their courses or argue that research on the black community should be the exclusive preserve of blacks. Receptive to my work as a teacher and a scholar, they also extended me ties of friendship and welcomed me into their social circles.

Lester's provocative piece was one of the things that helped convince me that I was temperamentally suited to work in black studies. During the spring of 1971, I moved to strengthen my academic credentials by getting my dissertation proposal approved at Columbia and publishing a long article in *Radical America* entitled "Marxism and Black Radicalism in America: Notes on a Long (and Continuing) Journey." My plan for the summer was to conduct research for my dissertation at the Southern Historical Collection in Chapel Hill, where I expected to find more material on interracial sharecroppers' unions organized during the Depression. I would also teach an urban studies course in the Fordham Upward Bound program.

But most important, I became deeply involved in strategic planning for the Institute, which was under pressure from the Fordham administration to become more academically rigorous. The impetus for my involvement was an announcement by the administration that it was eliminating Bob Bennett's position as administrative assistant. When our governing board challenged Bob's removal, arguing that it would decimate the Institute's cultural and community programs, the administration countered that no other academic department had an administrative assistant and that the university could no longer afford to give us one.

However, the deans privately told our faculty that they would be willing to replace Bob, who had only a bachelor's degree, with another full-time faculty member if we could find a strong person with at least a master's degree. Immediately we thought of Claude Mangum. He was extremely well liked by the administration, had a master's degree from Columbia, and seemed to enjoy spending time in the Institute as much as he did in his own office. I was assigned the task of recruiting Claude, who initially hesitated to accept our offer because he had always dreamed of being a high school principal. I appealed to his intellectual curiosity and love of good conversation, warning that, as a school administrator, he would be so occupied with evaluating teachers and disciplining students that he would have little time to exchange ideas and talk about politics and history. "If you join the Institute faculty," I coaxed him, "you'll actually be getting paid for doing what you love best."

Claude, after some soul-searching, decided to join our faculty. The Institute now had four full-time faculty members for the 1971–72 academic year, three with master's degrees from Columbia and one from Fordham. Quinton Wilkes, perhaps the most universally respected of our faculty, agreed to become director, giving us much-needed stability at the helm. Our curriculum for the fall consisted of fourteen courses, eleven taught by full-time faculty, three by adjuncts. They approached the black experience from several different disciplines—history, sociology, psychology, political science, theology, economics, and theater. When the semester ended, I could not wait to start teaching again.

10   Riders on the Storm

FOR FACULTY members in Fordham's Institute of Afro-American Studies, the early 1970s were a heady time. Spurred by a final wave of sixties idealism, enrollments skyrocketed, reaching a peak of 345 students in the spring of 1972, over half of them white and Latino. On a campus where less than 6 percent of full-time undergraduates were black, Institute classes emerged as the most racially diverse in the university, places where students could study and discuss racial issues in a vibrant polyglot atmosphere. Inventing new courses each semester, our faculty created what amounted to a university within the university, a place where students could study history, politics, religion, and other disciplines from a black (and in some cases a radical) perspective and redefine their own identities in a society undergoing rapid social change.

Our ability to sustain this momentum in a time of intense racial polarization—when New York's black and white residents were bitterly divided over control of the schools and police, over the expansion of welfare benefits, and, more immediately, over Governor Nelson Rockefeller's violent suppression of an inmate revolt at Attica State Prison in September 1971—reflected the growing influence of the left in the city's institutions of higher learning. The implementation of an open-admissions policy in the City University system in 1970, itself a product of student protest, tripled the number of black and Latino students at CUNY institutions between 1969 and 1972 and led to the hiring of scores of black and Latino faculty, mostly in remedial education and ethnic studies, and an even greater number of white progressives. Although the world outside Fordham's gates was in turmoil, with rising crime rates, deteriorating housing, and Irish and Jewish residents departing by the thousands for Yonkers and Co-op City, the huge middle-income housing development recently opened in the Northeast Bronx, our faculty and students, buoyed by what was happening at other campuses, were determined to turn black studies at Fordham into a beachhead of democratic change.

The four faculty members who shaped this educational experiment, Quinton Wilkes, Claude Mangum, Matthew Mbote, and I, had no blueprint for what we were doing. Although we had friends in other programs, and read the periodical literature on the black studies movement, especially the *Black Scholar*, what we built at Fordham was unique, influenced by the university's demography and traditions as much as our own intellectual and political interests. Some universities in our area, especially the CUNY schools after open admissions, had enough black students to support a black studies department. But there were fewer than two hundred black students on Fordham's Bronx campus, so the success of the Institute depended on getting the virtually unanimous support of African-American students while aggressively attracting significant numbers of other students. Quinton Wilkes, our new director, encouraged multiple recruiting strategies, some emphasizing black solidarity, others appealing to a broad, campus-wide interest in black culture and history. In the summer of 1971, right before registration, Quinton sent a letter to every black student at Fordham urging them to support "*your* Institute of Afro-American Studies," and concluding, "Our very *survival* depends upon it!" He also asked our faculty to spread the message that "Black studies courses were for everyone."

Buoyed by these multiple recruiting strategies, our fall 1971 enrollments represented a major breakthrough for the Institute. Most of Fordham's African-American students, white hippies, and antiwar activists, the entire basketball team, much of the football team, and, most remarkably, a group of over thirty Italian-American students brought in by student body president Bob Vinci, signed up for our courses. In addition, Claude Mangum helped recruit a substantial number of Latino students, consolidating our character as a place where inner-city, working-class students of diverse races and nationalities could feel at home. For the Italian and Puerto Rican students, who encountered little representation of their cultural traditions on the Fordham campus (the administration and faculty were still heavily Irish), African-American studies courses created a discourse on race and culture that resonated with their own experience, both as ethnic outsiders in a changing Catholic university and as products of a black-influenced New York street culture. Claude Mangum and I, who had both grown up in the city and attended multiethnic public high schools, welcomed this discourse and incorporated it into our recruiting pitch and our classes.

This explosion in enrollments was helped by support from the dean's office, which allowed Institute courses to fulfill freshman and sophomore requirements in traditional departments, sometimes against the wishes of their chairs. The dean of Fordham College, Father George McMahon, viewed the Institute as a valuable asset in helping black and Latino students adjust to a predominantly Irish and Italian campus, and he was willing to bend the rules to help us succeed. A kindly, balding man in his late forties, who had the unaffected warmth of a parish priest in a working-class neighborhood, Father McMahon came to our registration table regularly to ask how we were doing and to greet black students personally and let them know they were welcome on the Fordham campus.

Support from the dean, however, was not echoed by the heads of major academic departments. When the high enrollments in Institute courses became public knowledge, they challenged the use of Institute courses to fulfill distribution requirements. Much of this was self-interest. If black history courses could substitute for world history or American history in meeting freshman history requirements, the lost enrollments might well lead to a loss of faculty, especially in a university experiencing fiscal austerity. Of deeper concern to us were accusations that our courses were too political, our standards too low, our grades too high, and our faculty too poorly prepared to play a role in the core curriculum. These perceptions of black studies, which were widely shared by mainstream faculty throughout the country, resonated with the academic vice president, Dr. John Rayburn. An extremely bright, deeply religious man who had once taught in the Department of Sociology, Rayburn still felt the effects of brutal encounters with the first director of the Institute, a black anthropologist who had been terminated before I arrived. She had told him, when her contract was not renewed, that "the history of black people in America has been one of four hundred years of social injustice at the hands of white racists such as you and white racist institutions such as you represent." Shaken by such attacks, which echoed what he read about black studies in the mainstream and academic press, Rayburn was determined to keep the Institute on a tight leash. Whereas Father McMahon was prepared to circumvent the major departments to assure a strong black cultural presence on campus, Rayburn was determined that minority students should assimilate to mainstream academic culture. Fearful that too much autonomy would encourage the

Institute faculty to act more like street organizers than scholars, Rayburn wanted us to meet the same professional standards as instructors in history, sociology, or political science.

At our faculty meetings that fall, we mapped a strategy to protect our educational mission from external attack. A militant black student movement, we agreed, could insulate the Institute from direct threats to its existence, but could not easily be mobilized for complex negotiations over the budgetary, hiring, and curriculum policies that would shape the Institute's future. We also could not depend on off-campus black organizations to defend us; the neighborhoods immediately surrounding Fordham, though changing rapidly, were still predominantly Irish, Jewish, and Italian. We had to keep nurturing our student base, but also had to become more skilled at cultivating allies within the faculty and administration. Here Claude Mangum would play a critical role. In his two years running Upward Bound, Claude had won the respect of many Fordham administrators. Gracious, skilled at small talk, able to control his temper under the most extreme provocation, Claude had none of the bristly machismo of black studies pioneers like UCLA's Ron Karenga, the founder of Kwanzaa, whose sunglasses, shaved head, and armed bodyguards represented the face of black studies to much of the American public. But Claude was as stubborn as he was polite, a tough and principled negotiator who could get concessions through sheer persistence. Claude also understood the value of social interaction for defusing stereotypes and cultivating political support. Through him, I became involved in weekly basketball games with Father McMahon and his two assistants, Jay McGowan and Jim Loughran, building relationships that would prove of great value to the survival of Afro-American studies at Fordham.

However, no amount of bonding with the deans could protect us from the growing hostility of Fordham's faculty, which had not been involved in the Institute's creation and had little stake in its success. During the Institute's first two years, the faculty had kept the Institute at arm's length, regarding it as a temporary expedient to keep militant black students from burning down the university. But now that its enrollments were skyrocketing, and white students were flocking to its courses, they feared the Institute was diminishing the quality of a Fordham education. Not convinced that there was real intellectual substance in Institute courses, or even in our professed mission of promoting scholarship on African peoples, they suspected we were attracting students by giving them easy A's.

The response we developed to the faculty's attacks, after intense internal discussion, shaped the development of black studies at Fordham for many years to come. Unlike black studies programs at some other campuses, we did not treat the very posing of the standards question as a form of academic colonialism. In fact, privately we shared some of the concerns of our critics about the atmosphere in Institute courses. We *did* have a small number of students who resisted being judged by the rules of standard English grammar. Others believed that we should give them A's irrespective of their performance, to compensate for the racist treatment they got from other professors. And a small number of our students had difficulty with expository writing, not because of ideological resistance but of poor academic training in inner-city high schools. Students in these categories, we all agreed, had to be brought up to the level of their better-prepared classmates. To reinforce a tone of academic seriousness in Institute classes, we adopted a tough new writing policy. All Institute faculty would assign term papers in their courses and count literary quality in computing final grades. To ease the transition to this new policy, the Institute created a writing clinic, where faculty on our own time taught students how to research and organize term papers, and followed their progress through multiple drafts.

To address the issue of faculty qualifications, which also made us vulnerable, we formed a doctoral study group within the Institute and developed a plan that would allow our four full-time faculty to earn doctoral degrees prior to their tenure reviews. We asked Fordham to create a new full-time faculty line in Afro-American literature, and offered to take staggered leaves of absence so we could upgrade our credentials without sacrificing our curriculum. If the administration agreed to this, we argued, Fordham would have "one of the best black studies programs in the entire country, one which combine[d] a reputation for original scholarship with a commitment to effective teaching."

The strategies we developed should have earned us some increased good will among the faculty. We were adding new subjects to the curriculum and exploring new areas of research, not demanding recognition of an alternative black worldview. But our efforts to tailor black studies to traditional academic standards won us little credibility with colleagues who viewed American civilization as exclusively derived from Europe. Because few Fordham professors had ever done research on African-American history and culture or had social or professional relationships with black scholars, they tended to regard black studies as intellectually suspect, something that—if it had to exist at all—should be forced into the narrowest possible channels of university life.

The Institute's performance during the spring of 1972 only intensified the campaign to limit our role in Fordham's curriculum. That semester we enrolled 345 students in eleven courses. Two of our courses had over 55 students, and every other course had more than 20. White and Latino students flocked to the Institute, becoming the majority in many of our classes. Without sacrificing our special mission to black students, we had created a multiethnic program where some of the most controversial and difficult issues in American society could be studied and debated.

During that spring semester, black studies at Fordham was infused with an energy and optimism that would not be matched till the mid-90s. At that historic moment, our faculty still believed that if black people could redefine their lives and rewrite their history, America would become a more democratic society. We saw uncovering the lost history of black people as an act of communal revitalization, and we displayed our commitments in the way we dressed as well as in what we taught. From the afros and dashikis worn by Institute faculty, to the jazz playing in its office, to the posters of black revolutionary heroes and advertisements for trips to Africa on the walls of its faculty cubicles, to the books by Frantz Fanon and George Jackson on our reading lists, the atmosphere of the Institute was insurgent and countercultural, if aggressively male. When Claude, Quinton, Matthew, and I walked together on campus, faculty and staff members usually looked down and walked faster while students often greeted us with smiles and raised fists. Culturally and politically, we had become a touchstone for powerful feelings, some positive and some negative, on a campus that only ten years before had an all-white, all-male student population.

Despite or perhaps because of our successes, we found ourselves in a defensive position in negotiations with the academic vice president. Citing a hiring freeze throughout the university occasioned by a growing budget deficit, he refused to increase our budget to support five full-time faculty. We had to choose between retaining our current staffing pattern, with four male faculty members, all in the social sciences, or agreeing to a complicated system of unpaid leaves of absence that would allow us to hire an instructor in African-American literature (whom we all agreed should be a woman). We decided that we had to diversify our faculty, but we paid a heavy price. To fund the new literature position, Claude had to move to the college dean's office for the 1972–73 academic year, and Quinton and I had to take one-semester unpaid research leaves during the next year. We could not guess how our students would respond to the temporary departure of popular teachers.

Our position in the curriculum was also undermined when the department chairs persuaded the college dean to give them exclusive control of introductory courses. Starting in the fall of 1972, our faculty would have to go to the history, sociology, political science, and English departments if we wanted our courses to get credit in the freshman core. We now faced the choice of teaching only electives, open largely to juniors and seniors, or persuading the traditional departments that black studies courses could be substituted for their survey courses. To protect the Institute's position, we would have to convince skeptical colleagues that the significant new work being done on race and culture should not be excluded from the curriculum and that the contributions of non-European peoples to world civilization, when documented by sound scholarship, should be a central component of a Fordham education. Given the Western background and training of the vast majority of the Fordham faculty, that was going to be a very hard sell.

The terms of this battle influenced both my course selection and the way I presented myself on the Fordham campus. To open lines of communication between the Institute and the history department, I set up a meeting with Dr. Ashton McMurray, the only Americanist in that department familiar with African-American history. My meeting with Dr. McMurray, a nattily dressed man whose specialty was congressional behavior, dramatized how much I would have to mute my activism to gain acceptance from the Fordham faculty. Outfitted for the occasion in a sports jacket and tie, I told him a little about my background, leaving out the arrests and the demonstrations, and handed him copies of several of my articles from *Radical America*. He told me that he was a cultural conservative who thought that the New Left and the counterculture were undermining academic standards. But he respected the work being done in African-American history by scholars like Kenneth Stampp and John Hope Franklin, and the new scholarship in social history by Eugene Genovese and Herbert Gutman. Since nobody in the history department specialized in these areas, he told me I had a real opportunity to make a contribution if I toned down my radicalism and accentuated my scholarship.

Shortly after this meeting, I designed a new course called Racial and Ethnic Conflict in the American City, which won acceptance as a history elective. Unlike my American Racism and Black Protest courses, which included incendiary contemporary works like *Soul On Ice* and *Die Nigger Die*, this course syllabus relied on the writings of professional historians and a few sociological works and government documents. Comparing Irish nativist conflicts of the mid nineteenth century and early twentieth-century race riots with the black urban uprisings of the 1960s, I designed the course to place contemporary racial issues in historical perspective and to show the history department that our teaching could meet its standards.

I also began to set aside more time for my own doctoral research, hoping that the arduous process of earning a Ph.D. would not cripple my political effectiveness. Fortunately, the subject that I had chosen for my dissertation, race and American communism, had a powerful connection to my teaching and my personal politics. Here my intellectual mission diverged from Claude's and Quinton's, whose teaching and research focused on recovering African-American traditions. While their quest for a usable past led them to examine black institutions that had endured the ravages of American racism, especially schools, churches, and fraternal organizations, mine led me to explore movements that promoted social, political, and economic cooperation across racial barriers. Before the civil rights movements of the 1950s and 1960s, the American Communist Party was the most influential organization in the United States to practice, as well as preach, interracial solidarity. In choosing the interracial organizing of the Communist Party as the subject of my dissertation, I examined a subject other scholars had neglected while I also sought to make sense of my own life.

My research strongly reaffirmed my conviction that race was central to the fate of radical movements in the United States. Not only did I uncover a pattern of radical interracial activity that had been virtually erased from historical memory, I met and befriended some fascinating individuals who had shattered racial barriers during the 1930s and 1940s and who had then been ostracized and silenced during the McCarthy era.

Of all the persons I interviewed, the one who had the greatest influence on me was Claude Williams, a white Presbyterian minister from the South who had shed his segregationist past and become a prophet of interracial trade unionism among southern workers, black and white. A legendary figure among southern radicals, Williams had at various times been beaten, shot at, exiled, denounced by congressional investigating committees, and put on trial for heresy by the Presbyterian Church. I was taken to meet him by H. L. Mitchell, former head of the Southern Tenants Farmers Union, while I was doing research at the University of North Carolina. Williams lived in Fungo Hollow, Alabama, a small town thirty miles south of Birmingham, and still preached his unique form of "liberation theology" to anyone who would listen.

On the long drive from North Carolina to Alabama, Mitchell told me how he and Williams had been on opposite sides of a 1939 socialist-communist split in the Southern Tenants Farmers Union. But the two had recently reconciled. "We decided to let bygones be bygones," he told me. "We're the last of a dying breed—southern white men who stood up against segregation." But Mitchell also warned me that Claude could be difficult with anyone who challenged his pro-Soviet views. When we arrived at Claude's home, a small wooden farmhouse a mile and a half off the Birmingham-Montgomery highway, my excitement contained a twinge of fear. Just three years before, Mitchell told me, Claude had been punched in the face at a local supermarket by a member of the Klan who objected to the interracial meetings taking place at Claude's house.

I was greeted by a tall, rawboned man with a shock of white hair and a ramrod-straight posture. Dressed in work clothes, he greeted me with a loud "howdy" and a bone-crushing handshake. Beside him was a small, gray-haired woman in a cotton dress whose voice quavered with nervousness. They were so stereotypically southern that I was momentarily taken aback. But as began to talk with them, I realized that the civil rights journey of Claude and Joyce Williams was different from any I was familiar with. They had grown up in small towns in Tennessee where separation of the races was unquestioned and biblical literalism prevailed. But Claude had become restless with this narrow worldview and decided to attended classes at Vanderbilt Theological Seminary to expose him to a critical, historical view of the bible and Christianity. At one of the seminary's conferences, Claude had been forced to share a room with a black student and had a "conversion experience" when he discovered how much the two had in common. Claude decided to share this insight with his congregation in Tennessee and was immediately expelled from his pulpit. This began a journey that took him to Paris, Arkansas, where he preached to impoverished miners; to the presidency of the Commonwealth Labor College in Arkansas, where he trained union organizers; and to the interracial organizing drives of the Southern Tenants Farmers Union and the Food and Tobacco Workers Union in Arkansas, Missouri, Tennessee, and North Carolina. Along the way, he developed a close tie to the Communist Party and created an organization called the People's Institute of Applied Religion to train fundamentalist ministers as labor organizers.

I was very interested in writing about Claude's activities, but Claude was initially suspicious of my motives. "How do I know I can trust you?" he asked. "What makes you different from all the other professors who have come here wanting to use my files? How do I know that you're not an anticommunist?"

To win the Williams's confidence, I launched into a brief, impassioned version of my life history. As I spoke of the difficulties I experienced for being involved in an interracial relationship and in searching for a context for interracial political organizing, I could see Joyce become openly sympathetic and Claude's harsh expression soften. As I concluded my story, I felt as though I were pouring my heart out to trusted grandparents. "Joyce, I think we've found our man," Claude told his wife. Turning to me he said, "For years, the University of Tennessee Library has wanted to put our personal papers in its special collections section. But we need someone who knows the history to organize them. I think you're the person we've been looking for. We'll give you unlimited access to our files for your research if you'll catalogue and file the papers and correspondence we've kept for the last forty years."

This offer was too good to pass up, even if it would take months, if not years, away from my dissertation. The Williams papers documented a hidden history of interracial action that my generation desperately needed to understand, and they afforded a rare window into movements that linked popular religion to organized labor. But my motives for taking on the project were also deeply personal. As a white person teaching in black studies and living in a black family, I craved the guidance and support of parental figures who approved what I was doing. Not only did the Williamses offer unconditional support for my interracial lifestyle but they provided an example of perseverance in the face of hardship that I found profoundly inspirational.

When I returned to New York, I applied for, and received, a grant for twenty-five hundred dollars from the Rabinowitz Foundation to finance my work with the Williamses. In late May 1972, as soon as my semester at Fordham ended, I flew down to Birmingham, rented a car, and drove out to Fungo Hollow, where I planned to spend a month conducting a preliminary analysis of the files, coupled with in-depth interviews with Claude and Joyce in order to place what I had found in context.

The month I spent at the Williams home had a profound effect on my life and career. My research there contributed to several papers and journal articles. But more importantly, the Williamses gave me confidence in the choices I had made in my political and personal life. Interracial solidarity, they insisted, was not an impossible dream; it was latent in cultural and biological connections between blacks and whites that had long been denied. White people who sought a relationship with the black community, they believed, were claiming a suppressed part of their own cultural identity, not crossing into an alien world. My work as a teacher and scholar in black studies, and the attraction to black culture that had begun in my teenage years, made perfect sense to them.

The perspective they put forward gave me a firmer theoretical grounding for what I was doing at Fordham, something that I would need in the trying times that lay ahead. In the fall of 1972, the Institute suffered a major decline in enrollment, prompted by the first serious enforcement of provisions excluding us from freshman and sophomore course requirements. Overall registration dropped by a third; my two most popular courses had only half their spring enrollments. In the classes themselves, the mood seemed more sober and pessimistic than in previous years. The popularity of Richard Nixon, on the verge of a decisive reelection victory, seemed to depress my more radical students. In white working-class and middle-class sections of Brooklyn, Queens, the Bronx, and the adjoining suburbs, formerly Democratic voters, some of them the parents of my students, were rallying to Nixon's candidacy as a bulwark against black insurgency and countercultural values. The country's decisive turn to the right seemed to mock and undermine revolutionary dreams. Students simply did not respond to the writings of Frantz Fanon, Eldridge Cleaver, or George Jackson, or the visionary music of Jimi Hendrix and the Jefferson Airplane, the way they had when I first started teaching.

Additionally, new and frightening developments in neighborhoods closer to Fordham weighed heavily on students' minds. Throughout the semester, more and more students recounted grim stories of South Bronx buildings being torched by landlords looking for insurance payments, welfare recipients looking for relocation payments, and teenagers looking for a thrill. Thousands of people had already lost their homes, and thousands more were trying to leave their neighborhoods. Students from the West and Central Bronx, most of them white, complained of a sudden influx of poor and desperate people and warned that virtually all of their white neighbors were talking about leaving for the white suburbs.

My students were talking about more than the incremental northward movement of black and Latino people that I had observed during my days with the Bronx Coalition. This was an ecological and human catastrophe that had no precedent in the city's history. In all my years of living in New York, I had never seen an abandoned building, not even in crowded tenement neighborhoods like East Harlem and the Lower East Side. Poverty in those areas had been defined by crowding, rat infestations, uncollected garbage, broken fixtures, and collapsing walls and ceilings. But now in a section of the Bronx bound by Webster Avenue on the West, the Sheridan Expressway on the East, the Cross Bronx Expressway to the North, and the East River to the South, the charred shells of tenements, row houses, and apartment buildings began to dot the landscape. Like most New Yorkers, and indeed most Bronx residents, I had not seen this coming. But when I took the Third Avenue El to work, as I now forced myself to do, taking the four-mile trip aboveground from 149th Street and Third Avenue to Fordham Road, I watched neighborhoods die before my eyes. Every week I looked out the windows and saw a different building go down. Occasionally, I actually saw firefighters grappling with the flames; but most of the time, I just saw blackened carcasses oozing smoke where houses once had stood. I also saw an increasing number of physically sound buildings abandoned by their owners, their windows broken or boarded up. Mutilated cars lined the streets. Rotting wood and twisted metal littered sidewalks.

I had no explanations for this terrifying vista, much less a political strategy to deal with it. The forces that I had hoped would organize black and Latino communities, the Black Panther Party and the Young Lords, had dissolved into warring factions, leaving the neighborhoods they had once worked in, including the South Bronx, without a disciplined radical voice. White leftists in New York City, had, with few exceptions, retreated into middle-class enclaves physically separated from the South Bronx and were reluctant to resume organizing in black and Latino neighborhoods, where they believed whites were no longer welcome. Although I felt enraged and depressed, like most of my former comrades I did not drop everything to try to stop the fires, or to force the city to build housing in the devastated areas. Absorbed in my doctoral research, my response was to affiliate with the Fordham urban studies program, whose director, a political scientist named Steven David, was an expert on New York City housing policy.

The movements and ideas that had shaped my development seemed to have lost their political influence. Not only was the New Left in disarray but even mainstream liberalism seemed to be in full-scale retreat. Richard Nixon's crushing defeat of George McGovern symbolized a growing popular reaction against liberalism as well as hostility to the antiwar movement, the counterculture, and black unrest. The destruction of the Bronx proceeded like a force of nature, ignored by political leaders in both parties, and the movement I was part of seemed powerless to resist. I did, however, have an institutional base from which to express discontent with what was happening. Hamstrung though it was by faculty contempt and administration pressure, the Institute offered a platform from which to bear witness to social injustice and disseminate visions of a more democratic America. As the nation, and the city, turned to the right, it was more important than ever to make sure the Institute survived.

In the midst of this turmoil and soul-searching, Ruthie and I decided to separate. The initiative was largely hers. For over a year, we had been lovers in name only, and she repeatedly rebuffed my attempts at intimacy by calling attention to her failing health and family pressures. But in truth, though she was loathe to admit it, she was falling out of love with me, and when a six-room apartment opened up across the hall, I decided to rent it with my Bronx Coalition friend Ray Reece. Although this arrangement theoretically allowed for the possibility of reconciliation, both of us seemed relieved to be living apart. The break was neither clean nor easy. Many people who knew us were deeply disturbed by our separation. Kids from Double Discovery and Ruthie's siblings seemed particularly upset. Reluctant to lose the interracial community that had surrounded our relationship for so many years, I became prone to bouts of melancholy, and sometimes told people, in moments of depression, that we might get back together.

Most of the time, however, I was happy to be living where I could see other women without complications or guilt. For at least a year, frustrated by Ruthie's remoteness, I had been surreptitiously seeing other people. Most of these encounters were one-night stands, although one long-term affair with a former student helped me realize how starved I was for physical affection. The liaison began in the summer of 1971, and it had a lighthearted quality that was a welcome antidote for my difficulties with Ruthie. The affair ended amicably a year after it began, but the experience only made me more determined to attend to my emotional needs, whether I stayed with Ruthie or not.

However, dating was rarely uncomplicated, even after I got my own apartment. I still carried an idealized image of Ruthie in my head, and I had difficulty being responsive and emotionally available to other women. I had a number of unsatisfying encounters with former students, women who lived in my building, and women I dated when I was in Alabama. Then my luck changed. A friend and fellow scholar in black history, Marty Dann, offered to introduce me to two attractive and intelligent single women who were taking his New School course on violence in America. His matchmaking method was highly unorthodox. He invited me to his class to give a lecture on slave resistance in the United States, and then brought me back to his apartment and gave me the phone numbers of the two women he had in mind. I was reluctant at first to make the calls. I thought there was something unprofessional, and slightly immoral, about using my position as a guest lecturer to solicit dates. But after three shots of bourbon, my resistance evaporated. Both women were extremely good looking, and I was extremely lonely. With Marty hovering over me like an anxious parent, I called one of them, an assistant editor at Random House named Liz Phillips, and asked her out. After taking a few seconds to figure out who I was (we had never actually spoken during the class), she said, "Sure, why not," and agreed to meet me for dinner.

Insecure about what was essentially a blind date, I pulled out all the stops to make a first impression. I put on my new cowboy boots, my brown and white stretch bell-bottoms, and my $180 suede jacket and took Liz for dinner to Umberto's Clam House in the West Village, where the mobster Joey Gallo had been gunned down the week before. The product of an affluent, politically liberal family from the Westchester town of Hartsdale, Liz looked like the popular girls I had been afraid to ask out in high school. She had a beautiful face with classic, even features, long silken brown hair, and the hint of a voluptuous body hidden under tasteful, loose-fitting clothing. But it was not just her beauty that rattled me; it was the fact that, as she made clear in our conversation, she loved her parents, loved her job, and generally loved her life! Surprised to find myself with someone so secure and comfortable, I resorted to melodrama, describing myself as a tragic figure, focusing on my parents' rejection of Ruthie, my arrests, my near-expulsion from Columbia, my encounters with Weatherman, and my loss of friends to the underground.

When the dinner ended, I felt sure that our date was going nowhere. But when we went back to Liz's apartment, a duplex on West 24th Street that she shared with two college friends, instead of thanking me and sending me on my way, Liz invited me in, and we ended up spending the night together. On our next date, a steak dinner at my apartment, I discovered aspects of Liz that helped to explain our mutual attraction. Although her appearance was not countercultural, she had been a rebel and an activist most of her life. Brought up in the only school district in Westchester that voluntarily used busing to achieve integration, Liz had grown up with black friends and classmates and a family that encouraged her to work for civil rights. At Denison College in Ohio, Liz became a leader of the local antiwar movement and a strong supporter of black student protests. Liz also had experiences, in college and after, that stirred her feminist consciousness. At Denison, Liz had been given an award as the outstanding student of history in her graduating class, but none of her professors had encouraged her to go on to graduate school, as they did with talented male students. Instead, she moved to New York City to work in publishing, where she started, as all women did, in a secretarial position, gradually working her way up to assistant editor.

The more time I spent with Liz, the more I felt our attraction deepening. By the end of November, we were seeing one another three or four times a week. In February of the next year, Liz joined me in the apartment on 99th Street, and I began to introduce her to everyone I knew as my girlfriend. Because Ruthie and I had been such a high-profile couple, reactions to Liz varied. My colleagues at Fordham were friendly and supportive. Friends from the defunct Bronx Coalition, who were now scattered around the city, quickly welcomed Liz into their communal social life. But the reaction of Ruthie's family and some of the young people Ruthie and I had mentored was more ambivalent. Paul, who still lived across the hall, was always polite, but Ruthie's younger brother and sister tended to barge in to talk with me as though Liz did not exist. Ruthie also dropped by regularly to borrow sugar or coffee or detergent, looking Liz over with a frank curiosity that must have been disconcerting.

Liz handled the scrutiny calmly, becoming a partner with whom I could share everything in my life—my friendships, my teaching, my dissertation research, my political activities. In turn, I benefited from the warmth and encouragement I received from Liz's parents and extended family, who accepted me unreservedly from the moment we met. Liz's father, Harry, was a high-powered insurance executive, and her mother, Marge, divided her time between community work and raising three children. Both were lifetime liberals who were deeply committed to the cause of racial integration. And even though they lived in a big house with a swimming pool on two acres of land, they actually seemed excited by the prospect of having a radical historian in the family.

As Liz and I moved toward marriage, my life began to assume a different texture. Ruthie and I, still living across the hall from one another, were now only good friends, sharing information about family and friends with an exaggerated kindness that bespoke both caution and mutual respect. Engaged to an African-American man who was living with her, she had little contact with me on a day-to-day basis, though what we once symbolized as a couple still had a powerful influence on my values and ideals. My movement out of a black working-class family and into a white middle-class one, even one so liberal as the Phillipses, posed challenges to the identity that I had carved out in the late 60s. I found the comfort and security the Phillips family offered attractive, but I also knew that if I did not work hard at sustaining my ties to the black community, I could easily fall into the racially isolated lifestyle that many white liberals and radicals had stumbled into in the early 1970s. More than ever, the Institute became the focal point of the hopes and dreams I had nurtured during my years with Ruthie, a place where I could be centrally involved with race issues on a social as well as intellectual level.

The Institute, however, faced difficult adjustments when Claude Mangum took over as Institute director. In the fall of 1973, Quinton Wilkes and I had both been confident enough about the Institute's future to take one-semester leaves to work on our dissertations. But Claude quickly discovered that Fordham was in full-scale retreat from the intellectual and cultural experimentation that had flourished there in the late 1960s and early 1970s. As New York City's economy started to falter in the early 1970s, particularly its weak manufacturing sector, resulting in rising unemployment and steady inflation, the university felt compelled to take strong measures to shore up its deteriorating economic position. On the initiative of Fordham's board of trustees, reformers in key academic positions were replaced by traditionalists, armed with a mandate to restore fiscal discipline and raise academic standards. One change was in the president's office; another was in the college dean's office, where our good friend George McMahon was no longer present. The replacements were fair, decent individuals; but they did not have the history of involvement in civil rights, or commitment to expanding minority enrollments, that had distinguished their predecessors. During their tenure, Fordham's demographic profile began to diverge sharply from that of the CUNY schools, which were bringing in thousands of black and Latino students through their open-admissions program. In an effort to reduce the university's deficit, Fordham froze scholarship funds for minority students at 1972 levels, leading to a slow decline in black student enrollments at a time when the neighborhoods surrounding the Bronx campus were becoming increasingly black and Latino.

During the fall of 1973, total Institute enrollment dropped to 169—from 268 the semester before—much of it due to a decline in white student interest. The white activists who had joined protests on behalf of the Institute in the spring of 1969 and had led a student strike against the American invasion of Cambodia a year later had by now all graduated. A new group of white kids on campus, a post-sixties generation, came from families who had recently moved to the suburbs to escape urban blight and who saw blacks as a threat to their livelihoods, homes, and safety. Their sense of personal vulnerability, fueled by crime and urban decay, had a visible impact on the atmosphere of the campus.

Even under the best of circumstances, Claude would have had his hands full confronting these powerful forces, but serious problems developed in regard to the two full-time faculty members left to work with him while Quinton and I were on leave: Matthew Mbote, our long-time Africanist, and Vivian Robertson, our new literature teacher. Mbote, the sole support of several young children, had compensated for his low Fordham salary by taking a full-time teaching position at another institution without Claude's knowledge or permission. The academic vice president found out about it and placed Mbote on a terminal contract and eliminated his faculty position. Claude vigorously protested that the Institute, and the university, could not function effectively without a full-time Africanist, but he succeeded only in extending Mbote's contract until the spring of 1975.

At about the same time, some students disrupted the classes of our literature specialist and only woman faculty member, Vivian Robertson. Born in Sierra Leone to African parents and educated in England, Professor Robertson used a highly formal teaching style that seemed to infuriate a few of her African-American male students. They came late to class, interrupted her lectures, fought with her over grades, and eventually organized an informal boycott of her classes. Whether her methods, British accent, or her gender was the key issue was never resolved, but the implications for the Institute were disturbing. One year after she began teaching, her three literature electives had a total of nine students, jeopardizing both the renewal of her own contract and our ability to offer literature courses. Claude's attempts to mediate the dispute found neither side willing to bend. Professor Robertson, outraged by the students' rudeness, decided to return to England, leaving us with a gap in our literature offerings.

When I returned to Fordham after my sabbatical, the Institute was in a weakened state and the campus atmosphere was dramatically different from when I first started teaching. Rising crime rates, the weak local economy, the financial crisis in the university, the OPEC oil boycott, and the relentless northward movement of the arson-and-abandonment cycle in the Bronx had created a bunker mentality among many in the university. "Students were panicked about getting into graduate school," I wrote in a student publication. "Faculty members were worried about losing jobs. . . . And virtually everyone seemed afraid of getting robbed, mugged, or ripped off by someone who had less than they did." The fraying of the city's social fabric gave substance to these insecurities. Between 1965 and 1972, reported crimes in New York had doubled, and reported murders had *tripled*. In some sections of the Bronx, the multiples were far greater.

Fortunately, Claude refused to be paralyzed by the atmosphere of pessimism on campus. To offset the decline in white interest in our courses, he arranged for Institute faculty to teach in Fordham's adult education division, the School of General Studies, which had a 30 percent black enrollment. His first course there, Social Problems of the Black Community, attracted twenty-two students, most of them African-Americans who lived and worked in the Bronx. He also joined the faculty of Fordham's Puerto Rican studies program, hoping to expand the Institute's appeal to Latino students, whose presence in Fordham College was growing faster than that of blacks.

To supplement Claude's efforts, I developed two courses designed to create a niche for the Institute in important subject areas that other departments had not engaged. The first of these, a fieldwork course called Action Research in the Urban Community, placed students in community organizations that were dealing with the economic and political issues facing beleaguered Bronx residents. Designed to train Fordham students as tenant organizers, youth leaders, and community developers, Action Research represented my personal act of resistance to the arson-and-abandonment cycle, which had begun to move into formerly middle-class neighborhoods in the West and Central Bronx. Whereas the first wave of abandonment had hit the borough's poorest communities, whose housing stock consisted largely of tenements and frame houses, now the blight had begun to claim row houses and elevator apartment buildings on the Grand Concourse and University Avenue, which were once symbols of prosperity and achievement for the Bronx's Irish and Jewish population. As the devastation headed northward, many individuals and institutions panicked; businesses shut their doors, tenants fled, and New York University decided to close down its flagship Bronx campus. The students in my course, most of them Bronx residents, were determined to resist. Small in number, high in courage and ingenuity, they fanned out into the neighborhoods threatened by the fires and became a valued resource to the churches, tenant organizations, and youth groups seeking to contain the destruction and rebuild devastated areas.

My second course, the Black Athlete and the Crisis in American Sports, was designed to draw apolitical students into a dialogue about race. Many whites, and more than a few blacks, were convinced that black athletes excelled because of biological advantages in strength, speed, and agility, a perspective that was openly espoused by numerous coaches and sports writers. The black sociologist Harry Edwards challenged this viewpoint in a series of brilliant articles, and his writings formed the basis for a course that raised questions about the history of race in the United States and the cultural forces that shaped athletic excellence, including gender attitudes. From its inception, the class proved popular, attracting athletes, fans, and journalism majors. The discussion was frank, vivid, and deeply personal, focusing particular attention on the experience of black and female athletes at Fordham.

My growing concern with gender issues, a tribute to Liz's influence, paralleled a similar evolution in my colleagues' thinking, prompted in part by the tensions surrounding Vivian Robertson's departure. Although the term "sexual harassment" had not yet entered our vocabulary, Claude, Quinton, and I were concerned that students had singled out our only female faculty member for insulting treatment. To make sure that male-female tensions were discussed in the Institute curriculum, we created two new courses: one on the contemporary African-American woman offered by a brilliant, street-smart graduate student in psychology, Beverly Lockett, and one on the black family offered by Quinton Wilkes. We also tried, with varying degrees of success, to modify our teaching styles and ways of interacting with one another to avoid reinforcing the machismo of our male students. Having an outspoken feminist like Beverly Lockett in our inner circle subtly modified the atmosphere of the Institute office, making our male faculty think twice before using chest bumps and high-fives to show their solidarity with their male students and one another.

During this difficult transition period, Claude Mangum's graceful, low-voltage leadership style served the Institute well. A skilled administrator who solicited the opinions of his colleagues on important issues, Claude was a genius at networking. He made it his business to know every black and Latino administrator on the Fordham campus, and he developed allies of all races in the dean's office, the HEOP and

Upward Bound programs, the newly established affirmative-action office and the School of General Studies. He also established ties with the two most important professional organizations in the field of black studies, the Association for the Study of Negro Life and History, founded by Carter Woodson fifty years earlier, and the newly formed African Heritage Studies Association, founded in 1972 by the black studies faculty in the CUNY system. Through the latter organization, Claude developed contacts with faculty and administrators in the rapidly growing black studies programs at Queens, Brooklyn, Hunter, City, and Lehman Colleges, most of which had much larger enrollments than we did at Fordham.

By the time I took a second leave of absence to complete my dissertation, I felt more confident about the Institute's future. We had survived losses in enrollments, exclusion from the core curriculum, changes in the political climate, and internal gender problems and still managed to retain an important place in the university. My own research had also taken a favorable turn. I had narrowed my dissertation topic to a case study of communism in Harlem during the 1930s and had uncovered an extraordinary experiment in interracialism in one New York neighborhood. In Harlem in the 1930s, black and white communists stopped evictions together, marched against lynching, integrated theaters, parks, and restaurants, challenged discrimination by stores and utilities, joined study groups and sang in choruses, demonstrated against the rise of fascism, and danced together, socialized, and married. After poring over collections of documents, reading through black and communist newspapers, and interviewing some of the leading black organizers, I had pieced together the story of an organization whose unabashed defiance of racial barriers, especially taboos on interracial dating and marriage, sharply distinguished it from every other religious, labor, and civil rights organization of its era. I had drawn on this research for several conference papers and was confident that my dissertation, which I nearly finished during my leave, would turn into a book.

However, my optimism proved to be short-lived. In late December 1974, I received an anguished call from Claude Mangum telling me that the academic vice president, John Rayburn, had decided to dissolve the Institute and replace it with an interdisciplinary black studies program with faculty housed in traditional departments. Shaking with rage, Claude read me Rayburn's letter, which contained a litany of complaints against the Institute including low enrollments, isolation from the mainstream faculty, exclusion from the core curriculum, and inability to attract talented faculty. The decision was made, said Rayburn, not only because of the Institute's enrollment problems but because he had become convinced, from his own reading of higher education journals, that you could not persuade the most talented black scholars to accept appointments in black studies departments. "Accomplished blacks prefer established disciplines," he insisted.

Over the next few days, Claude, Quinton, and I tried to make sense of the academic vice president's actions. Never a strong supporter of the Institute, he had refrained from moving for the Institute's dissolution until he was sure student militancy had declined enough so he would not provoke a strike or a building occupation. But while his assessment of student attitudes may have been correct, his analysis of the Institute and its faculty, and the reasons he cited for moving black studies to the departments, were filled with inaccuracies and half-truths.

First among these was the belief that serious black scholars shunned appointments in black studies departments. For an older generation of black scholars, who had gotten their doctorates prior to the 1960s, this may have been true. John Hope Franklin, Nathan Huggins, Benjamin Quarles, and John Blassingame, the most important black scholars in African-American history at the time, all held appointments in history departments. But many younger black scholars, whose intellectual development had been shaped by the civil rights and black power movements, consciously chose to work in black studies in order to place their knowledge at the service of the black struggle and to challenge the academic community's neglect of the black experience. Some of the best young black historians I knew, people doing ground-breaking work in black urban history and the history of black protest movements, had appointments in black studies departments.

Second, giving control of black studies to the established departments, at a school with Fordham's history, could quickly erase everything the Institute had accomplished. For a major university, Fordham had a weak record in race-relations scholarship. The departments Rayburn had in mind as homes for Institute faculty—English, history, sociology, political science, theology, and philosophy—had no black faculty and no courses on the black experience! In fact, they had fought tooth and nail to keep black studies courses out of the core curriculum. It was hard to imagine these departments providing a supportive climate for research on black history and culture; it was even harder to imagine them sponsoring cultural programs and support services for African-American students. More importantly, none of these departments had ever asked to be given responsibility for administering black studies. What the academic vice president was suggesting was a forced marriage that would save the university money but would leave the Institute faculty, none of them tenured, at a huge disadvantage.

In early January, Claude called together our faculty to map out a battle plan. We began by mobilizing students. We contacted heads of the black and Latino student organizations, captains of teams, reporters for the student press, and individual students who were black studies majors or minors and told them to get everyone they knew to sign up for Institute courses. When registration ended, we had signed up 283 students, the most the Institute had registered since the spring of 1972. Claude also launched a ferocious counterattack against the academic vice president in the student press. If the Institute had enrollment problems, Claude insisted, it was because the major departments, none of whom had black faculty, had frozen it out of the required section of the curriculum. "He has left us with no alternative," Claude told the major student newspaper, "but to acquire broadcast and print media support in our efforts to maintain the Institute's current status."

The tough but civil language that Claude employed in this campaign helped the Institute seize the moral high ground from the academic vice president. In defending his plan, Rayburn invoked the image of the black studies department as an outlaw entity, a place where race baiting, character assassination, and physical intimidation were acceptable forms of behavior. Claude's discipline and restraint shattered that image. Whether he was addressing a public rally or being interviewed for the student newspaper, Claude never resorted to race baiting or personal insults. His cerebral style of leadership spilled over to our student supporters. With rare exceptions, the multiracial group of students circulating petitions, writing articles in the student newspaper, and picketing the administration building used irony and sarcasm, rather than blanket accusations of racism, to discredit the administration's proposals. The timing of the academic vice president's plan, one student journalist wrote, "raises the loathsome possibility that the programs were originally created during the late Sixties as a stopgap measure to defuse Black and Puerto Rican students' criticism of the traditional curriculum's orientation. Now six years later, the Administration may feel campus activism is at a low enough ebb to allow the 'tactful' phasing out of minority studies."

In addition to mobilizing students, Claude proposed that Fordham College set up a blue-ribbon committee, composed of faculty, administration, and students, to examine black studies at Fordham and determine if dissolution of the Institute made sense. The college dean, a former theology professor, quickly agreed to this proposal. Anxious to avoid a racial confrontation on campus, he appointed Jay McGowan, the member of his staff most familiar with the Institute, as chair of the committee. Even John Rayburn, who had severely underestimated our support among students, came to endorse this plan. By the time the committee was officially created in April 1975, Rayburn was so rattled by student protests and attacks in the campus press that he agreed to abide by the committee's recommendations.

The creation of the committee proved to be a milestone in the Institute's history. We now had an opportunity to challenge the stereotypes and misconceptions that influenced the faculty's perception of the Institute, and let people know who we were and what we did. That the committee had as a member Father Joseph Fitzpatrick, one of the nation's leading authorities on Puerto Rican migration to the United States, and the most respected person on the Fordham faculty, gave its deliberations added weight. A theological and political liberal, Father Fitzpatrick was deeply committed to expanding the minority presence at Fordham, but he was also a brilliant sociologist who spent considerable time as an activist and scholar in working-class and immigrant communities. To get him on our side, we would have to provide solid empirical evidence that the interdisciplinary program Rayburn proposed would not work as well at Fordham as the autonomous Institute we already had.

Claude appointed me the Institute's liaison to the dean's investigating committee, giving me primary responsibility for presenting the Institute's case to the Fordham faculty. The choice had powerful symbolic significance. Some faculty members I met during the investigation were shocked to discover that a white person was teaching Afro-American studies. With the exception of Father Fitzpatrick, many seemed wary of black studies and were reassured to discover that we were an academically credible operation. Showing them our syllabi and curriculum vitae, and introducing them to our students, gave me an opportunity to address their private fears. We did not promote black separatism. Our classes were multiracial and approached subjects from a variety of perspectives. We were not trying to isolate ourselves from the rest of the faculty. We participated in interdisciplinary programs and were willing to cross-list any course in our area that was offered by other departments. We did not devalue scholarship. Look at the articles we had written, the convention papers we had delivered, and the dissertations we were completing.

I reinforced this portrait of the Institute with a history of the black studies movement, reinforced by articles from the *Chronicle of Higher Education* and the *New York Times,* showing that it had helped spark a revolution in scholarship and forced universities to come to terms with the experience of many groups once deemed marginal—workers, racial minorities, women, and people in colonial societies. Although black studies departments had begun as protest organizations, I argued, many now engaged in innovative research and teaching that had the potential to change the way scholars in all disciplines approached the subject of race.

I concluded by claiming that housing black faculty in established departments, given the departments' lack of familiarity with subjects we explored, would increase racial tensions on campus. Was it really in the university's interest to dismantle one of the few social spaces on campus where black students felt at home and where all students had an opportunity to discuss racial issues? Would an interdisciplinary program be as effective as the Institute in counseling black students, sponsoring black student clubs, organizing lectures and concerts, and offering fieldwork courses that promoted community involvement? The Institute, I argued, was a cultural and intellectual resource for the university, helping Fordham adjust to a multiracial student population and an increasingly multiracial surrounding neighborhood.

The last of these arguments struck a powerful chord with Father Fitzpatrick. From his decades-long experience in the Puerto Rican community, Father Fitzpatrick knew how hard it was for blacks and Latinos to feel comfortable in white institutions, especially those with a history of racial exclusiveness. Because institutional cultures, whether of religious denominations or universities, tended to change at a glacial pace, Fitzpatrick believed that racial minorities needed identifiable spaces where their traditions would be treated with respect and their problems of cultural adjustment would be carefully analyzed.

By the fall of 1975, Father Fitzpatrick was not only forcefully defending the Institute in committee meetings, he was calling me into his office for long discussions about minority students at Fordham and Fordham's role in a rapidly changing Bronx community. More than anyone I had met at Fordham, Father Fitzpatrick understood why I had immersed myself in the black community and dedicated myself to learning about the impact of race on American culture. Most of his adult life had been devoted to understanding the lives of Puerto Rican immigrants, and he had reinforced this commitment with forty years of pastoral service in New York's Puerto Rican neighborhoods. Community involvement had been as much a part of his life as scholarship, and he was active in youth programs in Hunts Point and Tremont, neighborhoods that were being savaged by fires and disinvestment. Although his activism flowed from religion and mine came from secular politics, we both hoped our scholarship would heal social divisions. The Institute had found an advocate; I had found a mentor and friend.

Father Fitzpatrick's friendship helped ease the burden of leadership that fell upon me in the fall of 1975, when both Claude and Quinton took leaves of absence to complete their dissertations, Claude for a semester and Quinton for a year. For a short but critical period, I would have to serve as the major spokesperson for Afro-American studies at Fordham, the person the investigating committee, the administration, and even the students looked to to represent the Institute's philosophy. Aware that I felt uneasy about this responsibility, Claude called me every day to offer advice and reassurance, but I still worried that students, and the administration, might interpret the emergence of a white faculty member as the Institute's public spokesperson as a sign of weakness.

However, because of several adjustments we had made in the Institute's programs and curriculum, my position proved to be far less burdensome than I had feared. Foremost among these was the decision to hire Melvin Dixon, a brilliant young poet and literary critic from the American studies program at Brown, as a one-year replacement for Quinton. A protégé of Richard Wright biographer Michel Fabré and a gay man, Dixon accepted the position in the Institute because he wanted to move to New York and because he sensed, correctly, that we would be able to take his sexual orientation in stride. Dixon lit up the Institute with his energy and creativity. Giving poetry readings on campus, taking students to plays, discussing black literature with the dean's investigating committee, holding court at Institute parties with stories of life in Paris, Dixon added style to the Institute's ranks. Stunned that the Institute could recruit a black scholar of such obvious promise, the administration began to look at us with newfound respect.

Our decision to assume leadership of the Fordham urban studies program, which had been without a full-time director for nearly a year, also strengthened the Institute's position. The urban studies majors were some of Fordham's most impressive students—tough, gutsy kids willing to do battle with banks, landlords, and insurance companies to save the Bronx's embattled neighborhoods; but it was hard to find faculty members in other departments who had the time and grassroots organizing experience to give them effective guidance. With Claude and Quinton's encouragement, I became director of urban studies and relocated the program in the Institute offices. The absorption of urban studies into the Institute solidified our commitment to a Bronx-based neighborhood activism. We were now explicitly defined as black *and* interracial, academic *and* community minded.

The diversity of the Institute's programs and culture allowed me to speak for it, not just as a white man in black studies but as the advocate of a multiracial institution energized by a strong relationship to black culture. The distinction was crucial. Some black studies programs had limited interest in addressing nonblack constituencies or nurturing modes of thought that fell outside a pan-African framework. "Black Studies should be linked directly to the overall black struggle," *Black Scholar* publisher Nathan Hare told the *New York Times* (March 16, 1975). "Scholars holding that view . . . would naturally question white participation in the development and implementation of the program." Black studies at Fordham had evolved in a different direction, embracing a racially diverse constituency, encouraging a variety of cultural philosophies, being open to feminist influences. The Institute claimed the entire university community as its audience, and I could draw upon my own experience as a metaphor for its potential. An engagement with black history and culture, I argued passionately, could help students make sense of America's tangled racial past and understand the rapidly changing communities outside the university's gates.

How many people at Fordham agreed with this position remains unclear, but the most important audience, the dean's investigating committee, responded positively. In December 1975, it formally recommended that the Institute be elevated to department status rather than reorganized as an interdisciplinary program. Written by Father Fitzpatrick, the committee's report was a stunning endorsement of the Institute's faculty and curriculum. When it was presented to the Fordham College Council, it was approved by a near-unanimous margin and quickly implemented by the vice presidents and deans. In the spring of 1976, we officially became the Department of Afro-American Studies, making us the only independent black studies department at any private university in New York City area.

The creation of the department was extremely gratifying personally. For most of my adult life, I had struggled to understand, and to challenge, the forces that had made Americans prisoners of their racial identities. Driven by love and friendship more than a coherent political vision, I had immersed myself in the black community and then tried to apply what I had learned to the political struggles of the time, often with disappointing results. SDS and the Bronx Coalition, the groups I had joined, had been effective antiwar organizations, but were unable to build stable interracial coalitions that spoke to the needs of working-class people. The Institute was the only organization I had ever been associated with that could foster serious discussion of race without falling apart or splitting into hostile factions. It had carved out a space where both black solidarity and cross-racial dialogue were encouraged, and where scholarly inquiry and political action each had an honored place. Now it was a permanent institution, able to fight for its vision inside and outside the university. As part of its faculty, I could be both an urban community activist and a scholar of African-American history.

My colleagues and I had no illusions about our future. New York City's fiscal crisis, which had come to a head the previous spring, had been an unmitigated disaster for the city's poorest neighborhoods. Under pressure from fiscal monitors, the city had shrunk its police force, cut sanitation services, closed schools and fire houses, sharply curtailed its budgets for parks and libraries, and imposed tuition in the City University. These sudden cuts in vital services frayed the social contract and intensified racial tensions. You could feel the rage and despair on the streets of the Bronx, especially among its black and Hispanic residents, and you could detect fear in the voices of whites on the Fordham campus. In subsequent years, we would have to steer the department though a racial and cultural minefield, characterized by a deep pessimism about the state of the city, the Bronx, and American society. Our own ideals, and the goodwill we had earned from administration and faculty, would be put to a severe test.

11   Close to the Edge

A LINE from Grandmaster Flash's "The Message"—"don't push me, 'cause I'm close to the edge"—does a good job of capturing my political outlook from the late seventies to the early nineties. I had a secure job and a happy family, but my ideas about race and politics seemed to have gone out of fashion. In a time of factory closings and government bankruptcies, bitter racial conflicts, and attacks on affirmative action, the prospects of uniting blacks, whites, and Latinos to fight for racial justice and a more equitable distribution of wealth appeared dim. Increasingly, my position at Fordham seemed more like a bunker than a pulpit, a place where a visionary racial discourse was tightly confined by the nation's conservative mood, escalating white rage, fear of crime, and rising nationalist sentiment in the black community.

Contradictory memories flash into my mind when I think of the late seventies and early eighties. Some of them bring a smile to my face: The radical historians' forums Liz and I attended on the Upper West Side, where young scholars unveiled their work on women's, black, and working-class history and then discussed their findings over dinner at Cuban-Chinese restaurants. The sounds of Joni Mitchell, Linda Ronstadt, Joan Baez, and Emmylou Harris floating through our apartment on 99th Street, providing a harmonic escape from the turbulence of city streets. The excitement of purchasing half a brownstone in the Park Slope section of Brooklyn, a working-class neighborhood that had just caught the attention of teachers, artists, and activists. The birth of our daughter Sara, named for a haunting Bob Dylan song on his Desire album, and the birth of our son Eric four years later. The joy of watching my mother let go of her anger and become a devoted, generous grandparent, showering my children with love, attention and extraordinary food. The annual Kwanzaa celebrations at Fordham, observed with solemn rituals and stirring poetry, where I was always welcomed in a spirit of friendship. The community meetings at churches in the Northwest Bronx, where black and Latino families joined with elderly

Irish and Jewish residents to try to keep the tragedy that had befallen the South Bronx from destroying their area.

But other memories are grimmer: The huge stretches of vacant land in the South Bronx and Brownsville, filled with weeds and piles of rubble, where homeless men warmed themselves with fires set in trash barrels. The packs of angry teenagers who wandered the streets of poorer neighborhoods, set adrift by the closing of youth centers and after-school programs during the city's fiscal crisis. The homeless Vietnam veterans who congregated in the vest-pocket park near the Fordham train station, or who stood outside Park Slope's methadone clinic, a block from my house. The sometimes breathtaking, often indecipherable graffiti that covered the subway trains, inside and out, and marked almost every building in inner-city neighborhoods. The violence that erupted in many communities during the blackout of 1977, which I experienced first-hand when I had to dodge flying bullets as I left a meeting on West 106th. The bitterness that erupted between black and Jewish leaders following Andrew Young's forced resignation as UN ambassador during Jimmy Carter's presidency. Mayor Ed Koch's promises to "hold the line against racial quotas" and his abrasive posture toward the city's black leaders, which stoked a sense of grievance among the city's white ethnics.

In some respects, Fordham provided a refuge from violence and racial bitterness. The favorable outcome of the Institute investigation inspired an outpouring of goodwill toward individual members of our faculty. We now often got smiles and waves, instead of blank stares, from other faculty members when we walked on campus. After years of isolation, we suddenly began to receive invitations to serve on key university committees, to teach graduate courses in our fields, to mentor dissertations, to go on retreats with other faculty and students, even to join our colleagues for lunch at the faculty cafeteria or the Jesuit residence. Claude and I, who had done the bulk of the work in presenting the Institute's case, became Fordham insiders, the recipients of numerous small acts of hospitality from people who had previously kept us at arm's length.

But these individual acts of kindness, while gratifying, were undermined by a shift in Fordham's institutional strategy that had disturbing racial implications. In the late 1970s, Fordham decided to move from being a commuter school that attracted the children of upwardly mobile immigrants to a residential college that recruited throughout the North-east. After carefully evaluating demographic trends in New York City, which was simultaneously experiencing economic stagnation and massive white flight, the university concluded that it would have to change its recruiting strategy—and its entire institutional profile—to find enough college-age students interested in Fordham and able to afford its tuition. Focusing on suburban Catholic families who wanted a Jesuit education for their children, along with the professional opportunities New York City could provide, the university turned three classroom buildings into residence halls and sent its admissions officers to Jesuit high schools in Cleveland, Buffalo, Philadelphia, Baltimore, and Washington to spread the word that Fordham was "going national."

Although the motive for this policy was to protect the university's economic viability, it had a powerful impact on the campus racial atmosphere. Whether by accident or design, Fordham began to build dormitories at precisely the time that the racial composition of the surrounding neighborhoods was changing at a breakneck speed. Between 1970 and 1980, the neighborhood immediately west of the university, Fordham Bedford, went from being 92 percent white to 80 percent black and Latino, while the neighborhood immediately to its south, Arthur Avenue, lost over half its white residents. This remarkable demographic shift was readily visible on Fordham Road, which turned from being the shopping district of choice for the Bronx's white residents into an inner-city thoroughfare filled with discount stores, Medicaid clinics, and gypsy cabs. As Fordham brought more and more white suburbanites into what was becoming a poor minority area, the easy symbiosis between university and community began to erode. The race and class division between Fordham students and neighborhood residents turned into a chasm, defined by the gates and guard booths that surrounded the campus and the bitterness and suspicion that emerged on both sides of the divide. By the early 1980s, many local residents had come to view Fordham as "a rich white kids' school," while many Fordham students thought of the Bronx as a haven for "welfare cheats and muggers."

Not everyone at Fordham turned their backs on the university's new neighbors. In 1974 a group of Jesuit scholastics (Jesuits in training) and graduate students helped form a remarkable interracial community organization, the Northwest Bronx Community and Clergy Coalition, which used innovative tactics to prevent disinvestment from savaging still-intact Bronx neighborhoods. Threatening to withdraw deposits from banks that refused to make loans in Bronx neighborhoods, picketing the suburban homes of landlords who neglected their properties, holding sit-ins at the offices of city officials who refused to meet with local residents, the Coalition created a vibrant interracial protest culture by focusing on simple goals that residents held in common—safe, well-maintained apartment buildings, clean streets, good schools, efficient police and fire protection—and mercilessly harassing officials who denied them these services.

But many students and faculty members never knew this organization existed. Although Jesuits had been among the founders of the Coalition, and Fordham students played a key role in it as volunteers and paid organizers, the grassroots populism it fostered, and its remarkable success in building interracial solidarity, seemed to have little impact on the university's academic culture. By the late 1970s, few people on the faculty, or in academic administration, were willing to give more than lip service to the ideals of fostering cultural diversity or affirming the university's urban identity. In Afro-American studies, we experienced this as a period of retreat from racial idealism, a time when personnel and curriculum decisions were made that virtually assured our intellectual marginality right after the moment of our greatest triumph.

The first sign of the changed intellectual climate came in the spring of 1977, when the university denied tenure to Quinton Wilkes, the brilliant teacher who had done so much to give the Institute stability and definition during its early years. Protected by rules of confidentiality, no members of the tenure committee, or the university's tenure-review board, would tell Claude Mangum and me why they had voted against Quinton. But when we approached the academic deans to protest the decision, they implied that the committee had voted against Quinton because they believed he was more of a clinical practitioner than a scholar. Tenure quotas, they also insisted, had a great influence on the faculty's deliberations. Because our department operated under a two-thirds quota for tenured faculty, members of the tenure-review committee had been forced to make some hard decisions, and had selected Claude and me to fill the two slots allotted for Afro-American studies because we had shown a greater commitment to teaching and university life.

The decision took away much of the joy Claude and I felt upon gaining tenure. Quinton's departure left a huge gap in wisdom and intellectual leadership. Quinton was not only a great teacher and a special friend, he was a counselor and mentor to the university's black students, who turned to him for help in coping with feelings of racial isolation as well as academic and personal problems. His forced departure from academia—leading him to pursue a successful career as a therapist, lecturer, and public health official—not only seemed like a stunning display of cultural insensitivity, it cast doubts on Fordham's commitment to affirmative action. During the year Quinton came up for tenure, 1977, Fordham had precisely *one* black tenured faculty member on its Bronx campus, a professor in its chemistry department. What did rejecting Quinton's tenure application say to black students about where *they* fit, and how important their presence was, within the residential college that Fordham was becoming?

The implementation of a new college curriculum in the fall of 1979, which excluded non-Western subjects from its core, further reinforced our feelings of marginality. Throughout the middle and late 1970s, Fordham regularly held meetings and workshops to discuss educational philosophy, hoping to develop a curriculum that would highlight its distinctive traditions and distinguish it from other schools with whom it was competed for students. Claude and I were invited to these meetings and presented our own vision of a Fordham education. We called for a curriculum that would teach students to appreciate different cultures, that would let minority students know their traditions were respected, and that would help bridge the gap between the university and its surrounding neighborhoods. Although we were treated with great deference, our viewpoint was completely excluded from the final product. Ignoring new scholarship on the multicultural origins of American civilization, the curriculum gave extraordinary weight to the legacy of medieval and Renaissance Europe, and it pushed Africa, Asia, and Latin America to the margins. Every Fordham freshman had to read Chaucer, Milton, and Shakespeare. Students could substitute medieval history for the American and world history surveys, but could not take black or Latino history until their junior and senior years. Out of the nearly fifty courses that could fill the philosophy and theology requirements, only two or three dealt with non-Western religions and traditions. What kind of curriculum was this for a school located squarely in the middle of the Bronx? What kind of message did it send to students about which cultural traditions were important and which were marginal?

In the three years that had passed between the creation of the Afro-American studies department and the implementation of Fordham's new curriculum, our institutional influence had diminished markedly. Matthew Mbote and Quinton Wilkes were gone. Melvin Dixon had taken a position at Williams College, and his line had been moved to the English Department. Our department now consisted of two full-time faculty and four adjunct instructors, working in a school where black student enrollment was declining and where it was difficult to take black studies courses until the junior and senior years. The era of sixties idealism at Fordham had ended. The school was rapidly becoming a "white island in a black and brown sea," rendered complacent by a curriculum that presumed that all wisdom came from the West.

Enrollments in my courses plummeted. Between 1977 and 1983, I rarely had more than fifteen students in my Afro-American studies electives and was forced to teach introductory American history in order to pull my weight. With rare exceptions, the white students in my American history classes looked at me as a comic, almost pathetic figure, a relic of an era when people wasted precious time and energy on social experiments that were doomed to fail. Some students snickered when I lectured on what blacks had contributed to American society or analyzed how the nation's democratic heritage had been corrupted by white supremacy.

The indifference of white students to black history and culture and their equally conspicuous lack of empathy with the people of the Bronx led me to rein in the spontaneity that had been a hallmark of my teaching style. Fearing ridicule and rejection, I stopped embellishing my lectures with stories of my movement experiences or utopian visions of a just society. I stopped playing music in class. Retaining group projects as a concession to classroom democracy, I hid my disappointments behind a mask of scholarly distance, interspersing carefully written lectures with ironic asides about those who were displaced or suppressed, at home and abroad, to achieve the triumph of American democracy.

The only place I could let my hair down was with my African-American students, who shared my disappointment with the political climate in the nation and the racial atmosphere at Fordham. As the white enrollment in our department plummeted, I found myself drawn more deeply into the increasingly embattled African-American community on campus, of which Claude had emerged as undisputed leader following Quinton's departure. In awe and admiration, I watched as, almost single-handedly, Claude built a powerful support system for black students and faculty, consisting of an academic club and a student cultural organization, a chapter of a national black fraternity, a black faculty and staff organization, and a black and Latino alumni association. With Claude's encouragement, I was incorporated into this community, first as a mentor and advisor to African-American students, and then as a faculty participant in black students' cultural events.

My position on campus had changed dramatically. I was no longer perceived by black students, as I had been in the early seventies, as the representative of a generation of white radicals who had immersed themselves in black culture and identified with black aspirations. I had no white following, on or off campus, and no movement to point to as a sign of hope. I had nothing to contribute but my knowledge, empathy, and a need to share my anger about where America had gone in the preceding ten years. And yet, in the absence of strong black leadership figures on the campus, I found black students gravitating to me as they never had when the Institute was thriving. Whether or not they were in my classes, black students, men and women, athletes and intellectuals, suburbanites and city kids, came to my office regularly to talk about their lives, their careers, and the racial climate on campus, or to discuss politics, sports, and music. No one looked at me strangely or showed me the slightest sign of hostility. I was treated as a full member of the black extended family Claude had created, someone whose reliability compensated for his slightly eccentric appearance.

While being trusted by our black students was deeply gratifying, I was frustrated by my inability to promote institutional changes that would make their position less burdensome. Claude and I, whose friendship deepened with each passing year, lost battle after battle to change Fordham's curriculum and hiring policies, not because of administration recalcitrance but because of the university's fiscal problems and the conservative attitudes of the faculty.

Nowhere was the faculty's traditionalism more tellingly displayed than in its response to our efforts to recruit the nation's premier scholar in African-American women's literature, Dr. Mary Helen Washington, for a position in the Fordham English department. Washington had come to the attention of Claude and me when she was working with my wife, Liz, who had become an editor at the Feminist Press, on the first edited collection of Zora Neale Hurston's writings. A professor at the University of Detroit, Washington wanted to move to New York, and asked me if there were any openings at Fordham. When I found out there were four openings in the English department, I set up an appointment for her with the new academic vice president, Robert O'Brien, who offered to exempt her from existing tenure quotas to encourage the English department to hire her. This was a rare opportunity for the university. Not only was Washington a national figure in her field but she was a practicing Catholic who had gotten her doctorate from a Jesuit university. She seemed a perfect fit for Fordham.

The English Department disagreed. After we brought Washington to campus for a lecture that explored subjects and images distinctive to black women's writing, both formal and vernacular, the department voted not to nominate her for any of their vacant posts. Not only did she not fit the English department's needs, its chair told the academic vice president, but most of its faculty did not regard black women's literature as a legitimate field of study. Claude and I hit the ceiling. The English department had just failed to renew the contract of its only black faculty member because of a weak publication record and now refused to hire one of the most extensively published young black scholars in the country because its members did not understand her field. If affirmative action did not apply in this case, we told Dr. O'Brien, then the university's affirmative action policies were not worth the paper they were written on. O'Brien agreed with us but insisted that he lacked the authority to order the department to hire someone it did not want.

Coming only one year after the implementation of the new curriculum, the Washington affair nearly drove Claude and me out of Fordham. We both uncovered some interesting job possibilities at other universities, but we hadn't the heart to abandon our students or watch the dismantling of the department we had struggled so hard to build. Our of sheer stubbornness, we decided to stay, hoping that conditions might eventually be more propitious for studying black culture and for prodding the university to become more receptive to the multiracial community outside its gates.

But for many years to come, this incident would cast a pall over our work at Fordham. We were able to keep the department alive, but the passion and optimism that once characterized our work diminished markedly. I taught my classes, advised my students, did my research; but for a long while, the things that mattered most to me were parenting, coaching, community organizing, and competing in sports.

Although my retreat from academe had a political rationale, I would be lying if I said it wasn't also driven by personal demons. The frustration I felt about my failures at Fordham, and the collapse of radical activism in the city and the nation, drove me back into sports with renewed ferocity. Filled with pent-up aggression, I craved the physical release I got on the athletic field. The less effective I felt as a teacher, the more fanatically I lifted, ran, and competed. Unable to budge my faculty colleagues on curriculum and hiring issues, I found satisfaction in beating them in games of tennis, racquetball, and squash. Marginalized by my status as the faculty's resident oddball—the white Jewish radical in Afro-American studies—I looked to athletic success to shore up my lagging self-confidence and give me a sense of efficacy that I no longer found in the classroom.

This passion for sports spilled over into my parenting. When Liz and I married, we decided to raise our children according to feminist principles. When our daughter Sara was born, we gave her a hyphenated last name (Naison-Phillips) and split our child-care responsibilities evenly; I did half the feedings, the diaper changes, the playtime, and the trips to the park. As soon as Sara could walk, I began introducing her to sports. I taught her to hit, catch, and throw, and encouraged her to take pride in her strength and aggressiveness. When she reached the age of five, I enrolled her in St. Saviour's community baseball league in Park Slope, where I also became a coach.

Thus began an odyssey that quickly assumed political overtones. With Liz's support, and the encouragement of other coaches and parents (including many Park Slope radicals who also got involved in the league), I took great pride in helping Sara, who learned to throw and hit as well as any boy, turn into a top-flight competitor in baseball, basketball, and tennis. But by the time Sara was eight and good enough to play on boys' traveling teams, doors began to shut. We had to threaten lawsuits and media exposure to allow her to compete in top Brooklyn sports leagues, culminating in a successful campaign against the Brooklyn Catholic Youth Organization, which tried to ban Sara from boys' basketball after her team won the Brooklyn championship in the ten-year-old division. This battle, extensively covered by the local media and made the subject of a film by Sesame Street, brought a great deal of favorable attention to the cause of girls' sports, and helped open opportunities for other girls in our community. This involvement in training and coaching children's sports only intensified when Eric, my equally athletic son, came of age. Then for four years, from 1980 to 1984, I spent nearly twenty hours a week in the South Bronx as an organizer and board chair for Sports for the People, a multiracial advocacy group that fought to protect public recreation from political attacks, expand sports opportunities for women, and defend the rights of college athletes. Begun as a discussion group of radical athletes on the Upper West Side of Manhattan, Sports for the People evolved into a multimillion-dollar agency that owned a six-story building in the South Bronx and, at various times, locked horns with South Bronx boss Ramon Velez, the Bronx Democratic Party machine, the Koch and Reagan administrations, and the leadership of the National Collegiate Athletic Association (NCAA).

When Sports for the People was founded in 1976, we never expected to own a building in the South Bronx. Our first big projects were a senior citizens' sports festival in Riverside Park and a "People's Opening Day" at Yankee Stadium, where we joined with several other groups in protesting the city's failure to invest in the neighborhoods surrounding the ballpark. However, during the People's Opening Day campaign, our best organizer, a former Colgate football player named Cary Goodman, caught the attention of Gilberto Gerena-Valentin, a radical South Bronx attorney who was running for city council. A veteran left wing activist, Valentin put Cary on his campaign staff. After his victory, he offered to give Sports for the People an abandoned apartment building on 156th Street and Prospect Avenue if it would incorporate as a nonprofit organization and solicit grants to turn the facility into an all-purpose community center.

Asked by Cary and Genera to chair the new organization, I watched in astonishment as they turned their dream into reality. Within two years of its incorporation, Sports for the People had won a state grant to run a senior citizens' fitness program and city and state grants to run youth programs. It had turned the first three floors of the building, which it renamed the Clemente-Robeson Center, into office space and a recreation area with mats, free weights, and a universal weight machine. Preoccupied with turning my dissertation into a book and trying to influence curriculum and hiring decisions at Fordham, I initially spent little time at the center. But in the spring of 1980, with my book nearly finished and with my anger at a fever pitch due to the Mary Helen Washington affair, I decided to plunge into the day-to-day operations of Sports for the People as a volunteer fund-raiser and program developer.

This activity drew me into a community whose hospitality was as striking as the adversity that had befallen it. The Clemente-Robeson Center was located on a block on which at least half of the original structures had been burned or torn down. There was a bodega on one corner and a tire store on the other, each a congregating point for Puerto Rican men. Teenagers and children roamed the streets in groups, seeking security in numbers. The Clemente-Robeson Center was a hub of activity. We sponsored exercise classes for senior citizens; boxing, gymnastics, dance, and martial arts for local youth; a women's fitness program featuring weight training and aerobics; and lectures, poetry, and political-action classes. Hundreds of people participated in these programs, most of them from the immediate neighborhood, and hundreds more worked in the home-health-care agency that operated within our building and helped pay our bills. Contributing to this activity, even in my limited role as a fund-raiser, was a powerful antidote to my frustrations with Fordham. I started going to the Center three or four days a week, sometimes for meetings, sometimes just to socialize, and began bringing my daughter Sara there for special events.

However, I helped shape one Sports for the People project more directly—the Center for Athletes Rights and Education (given the acronym CARE). Jointly sponsored by Sports for the People, the National Football Players Association, and the National Conference of Black Lawyers, CARE sought to protect college athletes from economic and educational exploitation by demanding that their educations be paid for through graduation, that they be guaranteed medical care, and that they be entitled to worker's compensation in the event of injury. Appalled by the abysmally low graduation rates of black athletes in revenue-producing collegiate sports, CARE took the revolutionary position that college athletes were employees who deserved a fair return for their labor, and it implied that unionization might be necessary if universities failed to protect their players' interests. Under a proposal that I helped write, CARE received a three-year grant from the Fund for the Improvement of Post-Secondary Education, a federal agency, in the last years of the Carter administration, and began operating as a funded agency in the fall of 1980.

From its office in the heart of the South Bronx, CARE sent a tremor through the college sports industry. Our new executive director, Alan Sack, had an unsurpassed knowledge of the economic and educational dimensions of college sports, both as an trained sociologist and as a player on Notre Dame's 1966 national championship football team. Sack was able to get major national publications to debate CARE's program, especially its controversial proposal that college athletes be unionized. He put teeth in this proposal by offering free legal representation to athletes who had been injured or who had lost their scholarships. Sack also shook up the athletic establishment by appealing to college presidents to clamp down on sports programs whose athletes failed to graduate. After CARE held a press conference at the 1981 NCAA convention, the NCAA leadership began lobbying the Reagan administration to cut off CARE's funding. Their appeal struck a chord with conservative intellectuals in the new administration. In the beginning of 1982, the Department of Education informed CARE that its grant had been terminated because it had engaged in "advocacy" in behalf of college athletes.

The suspension of this contract proved to be only the first in a series of disasters that struck the organization. In the next six months, Sports for the People lost its dance and gymnastics program for South Bronx youth as well as its multimillion-dollar home-health-care grant, which paid most of the expenses of running our building. These multiple setbacks left the organization virtually bankrupt. Caught up in the excitement of exposing injustices and creating new programs, Sports for the People's leaders had failed to develop an accounting system appropriate to the organization's size and complexity. Seemingly unaware that taking controversial positions would invite careful scrutiny of Sports for the People's finances, they accumulated large debts to utilities and contractors, transferred funds between programs without keeping accurate records, and were so erratic in their tax payments that the organization's bank accounts were regularly seized by the IRS and the State of New York.

By the summer of 1982, my role as board chair had turned from one of cheerleader, fund-raiser, and sometime spokesperson to the leader expected to guide the organization out of a legal and administrative nightmare. For the next two years, I spent thirty hours a week working with our board and staff to untangle the organization's finances, retain our remaining grants, and raise enough money to get us out of debt. My time was swallowed up by meetings with lawyers, accountants, and tax officials, in tennis and squash games with potential contributors, and by meetings with politicians, foundation executives, and community leaders from the South Bronx. Terrified that our creditors would garnish our bank accounts, or seize our building for unpaid taxes, I took solace in every day the Clemente-Robeson Center and CARE remained open for business. But despite the heroic efforts of our paid staff, many of whom lived in the South Bronx, and the hard work of our board of directors, we never could raise enough money to liquidate our debts, avoid crippling tax liens, and fight the lawsuits filed by creditors and former employees. In March 1984, Sports for the People closed operations and gave its building to United Bronx Parents, a South Bronx organization that had the resources to maintain it.

The collapse of Sports for the People taught me valuable lessons about institution building and community activism. Frustrated with my work at Fordham, I had leaped blindly at the opportunity to bring new programs to the South Bronx, ignoring accounting and tax matters until after our organization had entered a terminal crisis. I would not make this mistake again. In my subsequent ventures into community economic development, I would make sure the organizations I worked with had a sound fiscal and legal foundation before we started offering services.

I also began to look more closely at groups who were able to organize effectively in low-income neighborhoods, especially the church-based, community-development corporations that were rebuilding devastated sections of Brooklyn and the Bronx. Avoiding broad-based attacks on racism or critiques of capitalism, these organizations mobilized people across racial and religious lines to take control of their neighborhoods, building by building and block by block, and to demand that the government, banks, and insurance companies reinvest in their areas. Basing political action within religious organizations proved to be a brilliant strategy in a conservative time. Not only were churches the major (and in some cases, the only) place in poor neighborhoods where large numbers of people felt safe in gathering, but their leaders were experienced in managing buildings and administering large sums of money honestly and efficiently. By the early 1980s, two organizations engaged in church-based organizing, East Brooklyn Churches and the Northwest Bronx Community and Clergy Coalition, had begun to transform the physical landscape of their areas dramatically, the former by building inexpensive single-family homes, the latter by using government and private funding to rehabilitate abandoned apartment buildings and create nonprofit management corporations to run them.

Using my position at Fordham to help these organizations was one way I could still participate in community activism. During the last, depressing days of Sports for the People, I began to aggressively recruit students for the Northwest Bronx Community and Clergy Coalition, as well as for schools, youth centers, and homeless shelters in the South and Central Bronx. To my surprise and relief, I got a good response. After years of apathy, more and more students seemed willing to immerse themselves in the struggling communities outside the university's gates. The Reagan presidency had much to do with this. His cuts in housing assistance, Medicaid, and welfare benefits, coupled with the near-elimination of community legal services, not only made life harder for the city's poor but pushed tens of thousands of people into homelessness, creating personal calamities to an extent not seen since the Depression. The crowds of people sleeping in subway cars and public buildings, the appearance of makeshift shantytowns under bridges and highways, and the squeegee men congregating at major highway intersections seemed to tug at the conscience of some Fordham students. By 1982 and 1983, the internships and Bronx tours that I sponsored through the urban studies program, which had languished for several years, started growing in popularity, and students began coming to my office to talk about politics and community organizing. These encounters did wonders for my morale. For the first time since the mid-1970s, I started to feel connected to white as well as black and Latino students. In the spring of 1983, when I decided to test the new climate on campus by offering a course on "The Sixties," forty-five students enrolled.

The popularity of this course gave me an opening to prompt discussion of the deep, and sometimes explosive, racial tensions on the Fordham campus. In the mid-1980s, many white students brought deep resentments and stereotypes to their encounters with Bronx residents and with the black and Latino students they met on campus. In a time of declining real income for most American workers, conservatives had been able to stigmatize racial minorities as hustlers and social parasites, draining tax dollars through welfare, stealing opportunities through affirmative action, and intimidating whites, individually and collectively, through crime and threats of violence. An undercurrent of racial anger existed on the overwhelmingly white Fordham campus, and it occasionally surfaced in the drunken racial epithets shouted at black students walking through the campus at night, the snide comments made to students in the Higher Education Opportunity Program when they used their scholarships for free books, and the negative comments about local residents made to students doing community service. But some white students were in active rebellion against this mentality, and it was those students I wanted to encourage and support.

Two black students in my Sixties class, Sybil McPherson and Lois Pilgrim, came to me with a brilliant strategy for promoting more enlightened racial attitudes on campus. Convinced that white students actually become *more* racist the longer they lived on the Fordham campus, they wanted to encourage modes of contact with the Bronx other than trips to the local bars, where students got in fights with local teenagers and shouting matches with neighbors irate about their late-night rowdiness, and where they were sometimes mugged in their inebriated state. As organizers for the Northwest Bronx Community and Clergy Coalition, Sybil and Lois had been moved by the quiet heroism of families in neighborhoods adjoining the campus, and they believed that promoting community service might be the most effective way to uproot racial stereotypes. With my encouragement, they formed a Community Action Council, which began holding forums and dinners to promote community activism, and they began lobbying the Fordham administration to hire a paid community-service coordinator, who would recruit and train students to serve as tutors, recreation leaders, tenant organizers, and workers in local soup kitchens and homeless shelters.

Their initiative came at a time when Fordham was steadily increasing its institutional commitment to neighborhood redevelopment. The university had hired two former executive staff members of the Northwest Bronx Community and Clergy Coalition, Brian Byrne and Joe Muriana, as high-level administrators handling community outreach, capital projects, and government relations. Under their leadership, the university made a major financial commitment to the health of neighborhoods surrounding the university. These administrators endorsed the work of the Community Action Council, as did the new Fordham president, Father Joseph O'Hare. A tough, urbane scholar-journalist who had spent time in the Far East, O'Hare confirmed his commitment to the Bronx by hiring a full-time community service coordinator and publicly declaring that community service was an important part of Fordham's mission. Within three years of his appointment as Fordham's president, several hundred students were working as volunteers in Bronx organizations and bringing these experiences into the intellectual and cultural life of the campus.

As I encountered more students with a commitment to social justice, the joy and passion returned to my teaching. By the late 1980s, my Sixties course was attracting nearly a hundred students, and my action-research course, which had enrolled no more seven in the lean years, was drawing between twenty and thirty-five students. I was marching with my students in anti-apartheid protests and demonstrations against American intervention in Central America, and joining them in potluck dinners, where we listened to singers Gil Scott Heron, Jackson Browne, and Joni Mitchell dissect the casual cruelty and materialism of 1980s American culture.

Although Fordham became a more activist campus in the mid-1980s, it was still not an easy place for black students to go to school. With a curriculum that postponed examination of non-Western cultures to the junior and senior years, a faculty with only four African-Americans in tenure-track positions, and a campus that offered few social spaces where students of color could congregate, Fordham found itself losing black students to universities with more diverse curricula and more supportive social environments. By 1986 black enrollment on the Bronx campus had dipped to fewer than 140 students, about 3 percent of the total student population. In such small numbers, black students had precious little insulation from the periodic explosions of racial anger that still occurred on campus.

I experienced this first-hand when I brought a guest speaker to my Sixties class to talk about the Howard Beach incident of December 1986, when three young black men were chased and beaten, and one was killed, after their car broke down in an all-white, largely Italian section of Queens. The minute the speaker mentioned the word "racism," white students in the class erupted in anger: "How come it's only racism when a black person gets jumped?" a 240-pound football player from Queens shouted. "White people are beaten and robbed by black people all the time. Why don't you organize demonstrations for them?" Another student argued, "We're the real victims on this country. There are ten white people beaten up by blacks for every black person beaten up by whites. Why doesn't that get covered on the evening news?" As these expressions of anger escalated, the seven or eight black and Latino students in the class sank into their seats. They were outnumbered ten to one, and were too intimidated (or too cynical) to tell their white classmates how ordinary, daily racism pervaded their lives—when they went shopping, hailed a cab, looked for jobs, or passed the guards at the entrance to the Fordham campus. I said these things in their behalf, but the angry white students seemed unable to hear me.

Because of incidents like this, the African-American studies faculty was spending growing portions of its time counseling black students on how to deal with racial tensions. Powerful relationships occasionally developed from these encounters. The incident in my Sixties class triggered regular office visits from a brilliant black student named Craig Stephen Wilder, who, after engaging me in long discussions about politics and history, decided to pursue graduate work in American history and subsequently became a distinguished urban historian. But many of our meetings with black students were far less positive. Our newest faculty member, Sister Francesca Thompson, a black theater scholar who had become especially close to black women students, was so shaken by their stories of racial divisions on campus that she found it difficult to sleep. We repeatedly warned the administration that Fordham was headed for a racial explosion, but our comments were greeted skeptically until February 1987, when reports of a shocking incident in a nearby restaurant started to circulate on campus. On Martin Luther King's birthday, a white Fordham student and several of his friends had gone to Beefsteak Charlie's on Fordham Road, gotten drunk, and started chanting, "Hip hip hooray for James Earl Ray." When black and Latino patrons threatened them and one man pulled a gun, the restaurant manager quickly ushered the white kids into the street. As he got them out of harm's way, they showed their gratitude by calling him a "dirty spic."

This frightening incident forced our administration, for the first time since the Institute investigation, to focus full attention on racial issues on the Fordham campus. Father O'Hare wrote a letter to the university community expressing his personal outrage at the Beefsteak Charlie incident, and he appointed a President's Commission on Minority Problems with a mandate to recommend changes in curriculum, hiring, admissions, student advisement, and cultural programming on the Fordham campus.

Father O'Hare's intervention came at a dangerous moment, not only in the history of Fordham but in the racial politics of New York City. In the coming years, the city would suffer four traumatic events that evoked deep-rooted racial feelings in black and white New Yorkers: the rape allegations Tawana Brawley directed against a group of unidentified white men and Al Sharpton amplified with charges of a government coverup; the brutal rape and beating of a white jogger in Central Park by black and Latino teenagers; the murder of sixteen-year-old Yusuf Hawkins by white youths as he was shopping for a car in Bensonhurst; and the community boycott of a Korean-owned grocery in Flatbush led by longtime black activist Sonny Carson. In all of these cases, with the possible exception of the Central Park jogger, the rage and frustration of black New Yorkers became a story in itself. The Reverend Al Sharpton's talent for expressing those frustrations, through nonviolent protest marches following the Howard Beach and Bensonhurst murders, and through demagogic accusations against state officials during the Tawana Brawley episode, turned him into the city's most visible African-American leader. At a time when much of the white public, as well as the national and city governments, seemed to have retreated from racial liberalism, Sharpton's charges of a "white conspiracy" to keep blacks powerless touched a powerful chord among his African-American listeners while making him a hated man among the city's whites.

The tone of desperation in African-American public discourse was intensified by a terrifying new drug epidemic that struck the working-class black and Latino communities in the middle and late 1980s. Battered by the arson-and-abandonment cycle of the 1970s, strained to the limit by the withdrawal of public services, struggling neighborhoods, some of which had begun to rebuild their housing stock, were flooded with an inexpensive cocaine derivative, known on the street as "crack," which instantly created tens of thousands of new addicts and lured a generation of urban adolescents into a violent, competitive drug business that turned street corners, stoops, and schoolyards into zones of fear. By the end of the 1980s, teenage drug crews were conducting brutal struggles for supremacy in the streets and housing projects of East New York, Harlem, Washington Heights, the South and Central Bronx, and even in sections of Queens and Central Harlem, placing shoppers, schoolchildren, churchgoers, and community organizers at risk in their own neighborhoods. The casualties were marked not only in shooting deaths, some of them of uninvolved bystanders hit by stray bullets, but also in addicted babies abandoned in city hospitals, children raised by grandmothers, and schools filled with youngsters too traumatized to concentrate.

The tragic events of the late 1980s and early 1990s pushed me to devote more time to coaching and youth work, and they forced me to confront, and defend, the racial politics of my job more directly than I had in years. Being the parent of two highly successful athletes brought me into recesses of Brooklyn where professors were rarely seen and made me an object of intense curiosity among the other parents and coaches. By the time she was fourteen, Sara was a nationally ranked tennis player, requiring nearly fifteen hours per week of practice, while ten-year-old Eric had become a top-flight competitor in sandlot baseball and Catholic Youth Organization basketball. I now spent far more time in gyms and ballfields than in archives and libraries, and I was doing as much journalism as historical writing. The more visibility I acquired as an op-ed writer on urban problems for *Newsday* and the *Daily News* (and as Sara and Eric's coach, parent, and chauffeur), the more questions I fielded about racial problems in New York and my experiences teaching black studies. I had to patiently explain, more times than I could count, that I was able to teach in a black studies department without exposing myself to physical danger and that most black students were not separatists or anti-Semites and most black professors were scholars, not demagogues.

That teachers, lawyers, and firefighters, people I met at ballfields and basketball courts, had such strong feelings about what went on in black studies was not only a sign of the overheated state of the city's race relations; it was also a commentary on the celebrity status attained by Leonard Jeffries, the head of black studies at City College and the first, and perhaps the only, black professor ever to become a household name in New York City. Jeffries achieved this dubious honor in 1991, by making anti-Semitic and antiwhite remarks at a statewide conference of black educators in Albany. This led to calls for his removal by the mayor, the governor, and leaders of Jewish organizations. Jeffries, who seemed to love his moment in the limelight, fueled a media frenzy by continuing to expound his theories in press conferences and lectures. Once a widely respected advocate for the teaching of African history and the reform of school curricula, Jeffries had become increasingly eccentric in the late 1980s, creating a difficult dilemma for the black studies movement. Millions of people who knew nothing about black studies were getting their impressions of the discipline from someone who, as reporters quickly discovered, walked around campus with bodyguards, came late to classes, discouraged white students from taking his courses, and attributed the cognitive and cultural traits of European and African peoples to the amount of melanin in their skins.

Although I defended Jeffries' right to teach, I emphatically denied that his theories or professional conduct represented black studies. Why wasn't my colleague Claude Mangum on the front page of the *Daily News*? He had chaired a black studies program as long as Jeffries, and had fought just as hard for curricular reform. Or what about young historians like Henry Louis Taylor, Nell Irvin Painter, Darlene Clark Hine, and Robin Kelley, who had done ground-breaking work in black history and were generous to fellow scholars irrespective of race? Yes, some black intellectuals believed that there was a distinctively African way of seeing the world and that black Americans should immerse themselves in African values and traditions as a way to insulate themselves from the effects of American racism. But the most respected of the afrocentrists, John Henrik Clarke, Ivan Von Sertima, and Molefi Asante, never made the headlines Jeffries did, leaving the public representation of their ideas to a man who had never published a single article and who littered his speeches with ethnocentric statements.

The Jeffries controversy, which stayed in the news for several years, forced me to take a hard look at my own life and experiences. For twenty-odd years, I had taught in a black studies department, experiencing friendship and solidarity with black students and colleagues, and introducing hundreds of white and Latino students to African-American history and culture. I loved my job, yet in the eyes of 90 percent of the white people I met, I wasn't supposed to exist! What kind of black studies department kept a white Jewish historian on its faculty and welcomed white students into its classes? Didn't black students want to separate from whites? Weren't they anti-Semitic?

My experiences had been rendered invisible by a media-constructed portrait of black extremism that exerted enormous influence upon public racial discourse. After ten years of conservative domination of politics and the airwaves, many whites believed that blacks were so filled with hatred and rage that they were incapable of living and working with other groups. Not only did this perception discourage whites from examining their own prejudices, it made it seem as though ending segregation, and confronting discrimination, crime, and poverty, were exclusively black responsibilities. This worldview was not just politically dangerous, it was plain wrong. The most successful community redevelopment organizations in the city—the Northwest Bronx Community and Clergy Coalition, and Industrial Areas Foundation Church Coalitions in East Brooklyn and the South Bronx—had been interracial and multiethnic, bringing together blacks, whites, and Latinos to rebuild neighborhoods that had been given up for lost. Community baseball, soccer, and basketball leagues, especially in Brooklyn and Queens, brought together youngsters from Howard Beach, Gravesend, and Bensonhurst with those of Red Hook, Bedford-Stuyvesant, and Park Slope, quietly crossing racial and neighborhood boundaries often regarded as unbridgeable. Add to this the dance halls, clubs, and studios where blacks, Latinos, whites, and Asians partied and made music together, and the university classrooms where dialogue was fostered across racial lines, and you had a powerful culture of interracial interchange and sociability that was rarely acknowledged in public debate.

It was time for the people who had this information, and who were familiar with these interracial subcultures, to publicize this dimension of urban society. Strategies emphasizing racial solidarity had their place, but they also had limits. New York remained segregated by race and class, but it was no longer a black-white city. Almost every problem that affected the black community—from crack, to youth violence, to AIDS—also affected the Puerto Rican, Dominican, and Central American populations, which were growing at a rapid rate. Promoting Africa-centered schools, and an Africa-centered worldview, might save the lives of some black youth, but it would not draw other vulnerable peoples, many of whom lived and went to school with blacks, into struggles for political power and economic revitalization. If neighborhoods were to be rebuilt, schools improved, jobs created, workers' incomes raised, and young people rescued from drug-related violence, then cross-racial alliances, some based on class and some on common visions of a just society, required serious consideration. But advocates of multiracial solidarity had to go beyond rhetoric; they had to show that constituencies existed, with real power and influence, willing to confront racism openly, reach out to the black community, and confront the isolation and neglect it suffered during the Reagan-Bush years.

As the 1990s unfolded, more intellectuals began articulating transracial strategies for dealing with urban poverty and decay. Important contributors to this development were a group of strategically placed black intellectuals who challenged the very categories that Americans used to describe their racial identities. Henry Louis Gates, bell hooks, Hazel Carby, and Michael Eric Dyson argued that blacks and whites in America were racially and culturally hybrid peoples, whose identities were intertwined and constantly shifting. Challenging the idea of fixed racial differences, they explored ways in which gender, class, and exposure to the mass media were as important as race in determining how Americans saw themselves. Key journals of opinion like the *New York Times* and the *Atlantic Monthly* seized on their writings as a counter-narrative to afrocentrism and dubbed them "the black public intellectuals." Along with the philosopher Cornel West, the historian Manning Marable, and many others, they helped create a new discourse about race that invited Americans of all ethnic identities to affirm their connection to black culture while challenging the racially constructed power disparities that continued to deform American life. Although their ideas were not all new—Ralph Ellison and Albert Murray had presented similar views of American culture twenty years earlier—their individual brilliance and the cumulative weight of their scholarship emboldened thousands of "closet multiracialists," many of them young academics, to look more critically at racial identities in their teaching and writing.

Ultimately, however, the power of these ideas lay in their ability to help people understand how America was being transformed and stretched, racially and culturally, by immigration, intermarriage, and new forces in popular culture. I saw this firsthand in my work at Fordham. In the early and mid-1990s, African-American studies courses began to attract higher enrollments than they had since the 1970s. Some of this was due to greater administration support and the addition of new faculty. In 1992 Father O'Hare had personally intervened to create a new line in our department for Mark Chapman, a highly regarded expert on African-American religious thought whom the theology department had rejected after a joint search. The president's action—which came after Claude Mangum and I threatened to resign our jobs, fearing a repeat of the Mary Helen Washington affair!—gave us a dedicated teacher-activist with a passionate commitment to social justice. His classes became enormously popular, especially his new course on Martin Luther King, Jr., and Malcolm X, and he became a model for student activists through his prison ministry and his outreach to urban youth.

Although administration support played a big role in our revival, cultural and demographic shifts among the Fordham students were even more important. Our comparative, cross-cultural approach to race attracted Asian and mixed-race students, who had just began to appear in the Fordham community, along with students from Africa, the Caribbean, and South and Central America. Our white students also became more diverse. We continued to enroll athletes and political activists, but we also, for the first time since the 1970s, began to attract white students who defined their own identities through African-American music and cultural styles. The tensions that had divided the campus in the 1980s slowly began to recede. Music played a large part in this. The popularity of reggae, especially the music of Bob Marley, helped spread a transracial, international consciousness among students of many backgrounds, stirring their interest in Africa and the Caribbean. Hip hop was even more significant. The rap music and videos of the 1990s had many problematic features, among them a predatory attitude about sex and a stoicism about violence, but they brought a discourse about race and poverty into the homes of white Americans and in some cases prompted empathy for the inner-city poor.

Teaching in this setting was full of wonderful surprises. To many of my students my whiteness was no big deal. The boundary-crossing experiences that I had grappled with in my life were nothing new to many of them. Between the students of biracial ancestry, students who had been adopted by parents of a different race, students who were dating someone of a different race, and students who had immersed themselves in reggae or hip-hop culture despite parental disapproval,

I was surrounded by people in active rebellion against received racial categories. My students also provided me with a valuable window into the way immigration was reshaping New York's economy and social order. The papers and theses I received on Mexican restaurant workers, Dominican bodega owners, Irish construction workers, and intergenerational conflict among Nigerian and Haitian immigrants brought to life powerful experiences that I lacked the time and contacts to observe firsthand.

My students also helped give me a greater understanding of the culture and worldview of young people in the city's poorest neighborhoods. Challenging my moral objections to "gangsta rap," they forced me to sit down and listen to brutal, pessimistic songs like Cypress Hill's "If I Could Just Kill a Man" and Naughty By Nature's "Ghetto Bastard," and related them to the real-life experiences of kids growing up in the Bronx, who memorized their lyrics and repeated them obsessively. They brought the kids they were working with to my office, leaving me with haunting stories of neglect, abuse, betrayal, and the cruelty of Bronx streets. Frightened and moved by what my students had shown me, I began attending community antiviolence meetings in the Crotona community south of Fordham and working with educators and religious leaders to develop a jobs and mentoring program for the local teenagers who were killing one another at an alarming rate. Under the leadership of Father John Flynn, a visionary parish priest who had officiated at twenty-five funerals of young people in a single year, we formulated plans for a Bronx Conservation Corps, funded by the federal government, which would give young people an economic and moral alternative to the drug business. After two years of lobbying, we got funding from Americorps for a thirty-five-person program, which we called "Save a Generation." None of my work for this program, as a fundraiser, researcher, and proposal writer, would have happened if my students had not cared about me enough to challenge my generational prejudices and musical tastes.

In my late forties and early fifties, something odd and wonderful was happening to me. After a long and checkered teaching career, I was once again surrounded by students who were risk-takers and adventurers, who were willing to open their lives to me if I would share my knowledge and experience with them. Representing a wide range of colors and cultures, they were determined to reinvent an America that reflected their experience. A phrase they drew from hip hop, "keeping it real," was their credo and their badge of honor, and it was as useful an admonition for coaching and parenting as it was in teaching. As my own children became teenagers, streetwise student-athletes whose friends, teammates, and dating partners were racially and culturally mixed, what I learned from my students about rap music and the strategies city kids used to gain protection and respect proved invaluable in making their friends feel welcome in our home. My immersion in the urban vernacular also helped me gain the trust of the tough working-class kids I supervised in basketball leagues and baseball practices. African-American and Dominican kids from Gowanus and Red Hook, like the Puerto Rican and Mexican kids from Arthur Avenue my students brought to my office, responded to me in part because I was willing to listen to their music and hear their voices.

As the various components of my life came together in the 1990s, I thought about the path that had brought me to this place. I had made some questionable decisions in my life, but the one I never regretted was teaching African-American studies. The approach to black studies that our department developed, combining an intensive examination of black history and culture, community outreach and social activism, and a cross-cultural, ideologically diverse approach to the study of race, gave us the resilience to survive difficult times. Being part of this community infused my life with a sense of mission while alerting me to demographic and economic trends that were transforming American life. Because we had an intellectual and moral commitment to marginalized and forgotten people, our students and faculty marked their achievements by community organizing as well as academic inquiry. We were there, as observers and activists, when arson and abandonment swept through the Bronx, when neighborhoods were rebuilt, when the crack epidemic struck, and when people organized to save their youth from drugs and violence.

The intellectual richness of this experience, which I shared with extraordinary colleagues, cannot be underestimated. Because we were willing to listen to many voices, and to see race from multiple vantage points, our department provided an intellectual outlet for students of many backgrounds grappling with their racial and cultural identities. Without fanfare or outside support, we created an environment where fighting racism, and exploring the meaning of racial differences, became a moral and political imperative and the center of a vibrant intellectual community.

EPILOGUE

Sometimes the culture of an organization is best conveyed visually. In the hallways outside our department's offices, a series of clippings and photographs portray its history. The earliest go back to 1969, depicting the student sit-ins that led to the creation of the Afro-American Institute. The next set of clippings and photos come from 1975, when students and faculty fought the dissolution of the Institute and led a campaign to turn it into a department. The most recent pictures are of demonstrations. The first shows a march on New York's City Hall to protest the police killing of Haitian immigrant Amadou Diallo in February of 2000. The second shows a protest in Washington against George W. Bush's inauguration. In both sets of pictures, students and faculty from our department are seen marching together. These pictures are mounted next to the display case containing our faculty publications, showing that the tradition of engaged scholarship that motivated our program's founders is still alive and well. I can think of no place in a university community where I would rather be.